D0436633

The Tumbleweed Society

The Tumbleweed Society

Working and Caring in an Age of Insecurity

Allison J. Pugh

OXFORD
UNIVERSITY PRESS

OXFORD
UNIVERSITY PRESS

Oxford University Press is a department of the University of Oxford.
It furthers the University's objective of excellence in research, scholarship,
and education by publishing worldwide.

Oxford New York

Auckland Cape Town Dar es Salaam Hong Kong Karachi
Kuala Lumpur Madrid Melbourne Mexico City Nairobi
New Delhi Shanghai Taipei Toronto

With offices in

Argentina Austria Brazil Chile Czech Republic France Greece
Guatemala Hungary Italy Japan Poland Portugal Singapore
South Korea Switzerland Thailand Turkey Ukraine Vietnam

Oxford is a registered trade mark of Oxford University Press
in the UK and certain other countries.

Published in the United States of America by
Oxford University Press
198 Madison Avenue, New York, NY 10016

© Oxford University Press 2015

All rights reserved. No part of this publication may be reproduced,
stored in a retrieval system, or transmitted, in any form or by any means,
without the prior permission in writing of Oxford University Press,
or as expressly permitted by law, by license, or under terms agreed with the
appropriate reproduction rights organization. Inquiries concerning reproduction
outside the scope of the above should be sent to the Rights Department,
Oxford University Press, at the address above.

You must not circulate this work in any other form
and you must impose this same condition on any acquirer.

Library of Congress Cataloging-in-Publication Data
Pugh, Allison J.
The tumbleweed society : working and caring in an age of insecurity / Allison J. Pugh.
p. cm.
Includes bibliographical references and index.
ISBN 978-0-19-995771-2 (hardback)
1. Job security. 2. Marriage. 3. Families. 4. Work environment. 5. Parenting. I. Title.
HD5708.4.P84 2015
331.25'96—dc23
2014013277

1 3 5 7 9 8 6 4 2

Printed in the United States of America on acid-free paper

For Steve

CONTENTS

PREFACE

When I started on this book project, I thought I was interested in job insecurity simply because it is the challenge of our times, the source of much freedom and great sorrow. Work looms large in the United States, casting a long shadow far beyond the confines of the workplace, as people labor long hours to make enough to live on, or think about work long after they've left it, laying down the smartphone just in time to have dinner with the kids before picking it up to answer a few emails. People judge each other and themselves by how much they work or how much they seem to want to. Work is a secular religion in a land that does not suffer atheists gladly.

Given dramatic changes in work over the past quarter century—both in who does it and how it gets done—I wanted to think about how those changes reverberated beyond the cubicle, in intimate life, with romantic partners and friends and children. I tend to linger in the borderlands between work and love—where economic and intimate lives intertwine. My first book looked at the commercialization of childhood, partly because parents say spending for their children motivates them to work such long hours. I explored how children invested the artifacts of childhood—the electronic toys, the furry collectibles—with great significance for their social worlds, significance that made their yearnings difficult for parents to resist. For this book, I wanted to know: If work is so important, how might the new ways of working affect us in our nonwork lives, where there has been plenty of upheaval to match?[1]

I set out to talk to people with different vantage points on insecurity—relocators who moved for the job, people who had been laid off, others who were stably employed—to hear how they felt about working and caring in an insecure age. I wanted to be able to tell people's stories, to bring to life the chasm between the "winners" and "losers" of insecurity culture. I just thought they would be other people's stories.

But a funny thing happened on the way to finishing this book: I started feeling as if I was living bits and pieces of the stories that I had been told, from the perspective of each of my chosen groups. Soon after I completed the interviews, my family packed up and moved for the year to Australia, where I joined the United States Study Centre at the University of Sydney. The words of the relocators rang in my head as we steeled ourselves against the pangs of missing friends and family, as we relished the warmth and marvel of Australian life, as I watched my children learn lessons of flexibility and adaptability in dealing with the challenges of new schools—uniforms, commuting by train, "sport" and "maths"—and new friends. Where you sit at lunch, a conundrum that relocators told me mattered enormously, came to resonate in our house too.

Then we moved back home, and my spouse's job ended in a generally mutual parting, and the phrases of the laid-off—about what to expect from employers and how to move on from a job dislocation—started to sound more and more relevant. What *did* we owe each other at work? What *are* the betrayals that we can see and name? What kind of insecurity do we chalk up to the way things are today, and against what kind do we bar the door?

A short time later, I received tenure, a strange and marvelous gift that after all these tumbleweed conversations seemed like an anachronistic in-heritance from the bewigged Cambridge dons of the sixteenth century. I found myself sitting in faculty meetings, realizing I was in essence married-for-life to my colleagues as they were to me, while the words of the stably employed came to me, in all their pragmatic resignation, talking about family ties and forever. Like a visitor from a far-off land, then, I had carefully planned the different kinds of people I would talk to for the book, yet somehow—without underestimating the very great distances that can yawn between a retail clerk and a university professor—I came to take on some of the same perspectives, and to find some of the same answers to my questions.

Work and family life have changed dramatically in the last thirty to forty years. At work, arrangements vary widely, including part-time positions, flextime, and job sharing, as well as in the use of temporary and contract workers. Layoffs have spread as an industrial tactic in good times as well as bad. In the realm of intimacy, the married, heterosexual, nuclear-family household has been supplanted by a wide array of households including single-parent, same-sex, cohabiting, and extended families, and there are more transitions as families go from one to another of these different con-figurations. It is perhaps more appropriate to think less of work and family types, frozen in time, than it is to think of work and family phases, particu-lar shapes that we occupy as we move through life.[2]

We seem to have two approaches to thinking about the changes that have jostled workplaces and homes. One approach is via a path laden with nostalgia, yearning for olden days—when workers enjoyed job security and equity norms that shared profits and benefits more than is customary today, and when more people got married and more marriages lasted. This approach affords us a sharply critical stance on current trends, and allows us to acknowledge the full measure of people's anxiety about insecurity. As Studs Terkel observed in his treatise *Working*: "Perhaps it is this specter that haunts working men and women: the planned obsolescence of people that is a piece of the planned obsolescence of the things they make. Or sell." The "olden days," of course, have their own problems; despite the laudable endurance of their jobs and relationships, they were nonetheless saturated with inequalities, for white women unable to access those benefits except through marriage, for people of color locked out of opportunities, for gay men and lesbians and others not well served by rigid definitions of family.[3]

Another approach to these changes is a more celebratory tack, one that takes note of the new flexibility in both work and intimate life, which sets more people free of the strictures of the old system, which trapped some in unhappy marriages and dead-end jobs, with no hope but for more of the same. The new diversity of what work and intimacy look like, the shape of both jobs and relationships, has the potential for better matches for more adults. From this perspective, the contemporary era seems to offer everything—more freedom, more choice, more happiness—everything *but* endurance. This approach has less to say about the costs of all that flexibility, however: the uneven distribution of who can take advantage of it and the power that gives employers, the doubt it casts on mundane pleasures, the inconvenience it makes of sickness, old age, infancy, and other moments of need.

The two approaches to thinking about insecurity seem to force us to favor lasting connections or happy ones, endurance or desire, stability or diversity. Yet surely we can reject these false dichotomies; surely these changes call for neither nostalgia nor celebration. A more critical view allows us to evaluate the varied effects of job insecurity. How do we interpret, manage, and meet the challenges of flexibility and commitment? How do we know when to stay and when to go, at home and at work? What accommodations to an insecure age are people making in their inner landscapes? By listening to people with different vantage points on the new ways of organizing work, we can take the measure, on the job and at home, of both freedom and sorrow.

The Tumbleweed Society

CHAPTER 1

ↂ

Introduction

Fiona Parker is an independent soul. A white technical worker with some college in her background, she has had at last count something like eleven jobs since her now-teenaged child, Jimmy, was born, and she knows better than to expect any loyalty on the part of her employers. While she values working and considers herself a hard worker, when it comes to constancy she gives back as good as she gets, leaving jobs and taking new ones as other priorities come and go. Some people might be afraid of the new world of insecure work, of fleeting relationships and uncertain obligation, but not Fiona.[1]

Over the same period, she has had at least four serious, long-term relationships, Jimmy has attended five different schools, and they have moved multiple times, at times doubling up with family to save money, then setting up new households alone or with new romantic partners. Now in her thirties with a new husband and baby, Fiona is a reflective woman with a relaxed demeanor, and she walked with me in her jeans and construction boots through a forested city park, describing how she and Jimmy had always moved on together when a situation went sour.

> [Jimmy's grandmother] has always said it's me and Jimmy against the world. Like, that's how it's always been. It didn't, you know, I didn't care who you were. If you were a crappy boyfriend or whatever, nobody was going to stop me or get in my way. Like, and if something was—if something was bad, we just moved on. If it was a bad job, I got a new job. If it was a bad boy— . . . relationship, I moved or got out of it or whatever. I don't believe in sticking with something that's not working.

For Fiona, commitment is like the tether lines that keep a hot-air balloon from soaring. Attachment risks vulnerability to others who prove unworthy, while flexibility—the capacity to move on to something new, to change jobs or locations or relationships—brings the independence that she prizes. This logic extends across work and much of her intimate life in a remarkably coherent whole ("If it was a bad job, I got a new job. If it was a bad boy . . ."). Fiona Parker fully embraces her autonomy.[2]

What counts as commitment, when its terms are newly contested at work? When news of layoffs permeates the airwaves regardless of the economic climate, when synonyms for downsizing proliferate, when management gurus gain laurels for annual cuts of the "bottom tenth," how do we understand our responsibilities to others at the workplace, or in intimate life? I set out to study the broader effects of job insecurity—of what happens when we perceive that employers owe nothing to their employees other than, as one woman who had been laid off suggested, "their paycheck and a certain amount of respect, I would say." Talking to women and men who had been laid off or relocated by their employers, as well as those who were stably employed, gives us a broad view on how job insecurity—and flexibility—affects the measure people take of their own obligations, at work and in love.[3]

For Fiona, those obligations are minimal. While she is a thoughtful person—and one who has also sacrificed a lot for her son Jimmy throughout this tumultuous history—Fiona represents the dystopian vision that some writers see as they look down the barrel of the future. Shorn of commitments to each other at work and at home, so this story goes, we act in our own self-interest, leaving when situations get difficult, rarely carrying the load of other people's burdens, rarely vulnerable to other people's needs. We live, in this view, in a *tumbleweed society*. People are buffeted by broad social trends—the erosion of employer commitment, the withdrawal of the state—that encourage their uprooting from established jobs and existing relationships, that generate itinerant lives and transient selves, like the famous dried plants that roll across the plains.[4]

When some analysts look at the tumbleweed society, they seem to see only Fiona, perhaps because her unfettered independence is surely the only rational response to the unencumbered employer. As a longtime single mother shouldering the burden of caring for her child without much help, Fiona prioritizes her autonomy, from disappointing men, an unhelpful state, and relatives who fail you. To be sure, she values work, as her cherished self-sufficiency rests upon her continued employment; but even though she sees the job as offering a sweet clarity missing from the more tortuous negotiations of family and friends, she views her primary obligation there to be performance rather than loyalty. Yet, to some degree, Fiona's independence makes the best of a bad situation, and her paean to flexibility masks some dire economic straits she has endured in the past. Furthermore, her story—while surely true for some—does not capture the whole of the tumbleweed society. It does not represent those who celebrate the new flexibility at work, but who manage to create enduring relationships at home. It does not explain Holly Moore.[5]

Holly Moore is undisturbed by job insecurity, even though her husband, Luke, has changed companies multiple times, sometimes getting laid off, sometimes leaping for a better opportunity, moving the family across state lines several times as his career soared. A high-level sales executive and a hard worker, he has never been between jobs long enough for their three children to worry about it, and she has only ever worked exactly as much, and in whatever capacity, as she wanted, currently as a part-time interior designer in Virginia.

"In his industry, it seems like the phone's always ringing with the head-hunter, you know, waving money," she said. At this elite professional level, switching jobs does not cause much hardship; it is just what you do to get ahead or to further tailor your job to your interests. Job insecurity is less relevant, in her view, than job flexibility, the freedom to take advantage of external labor markets and jump. She recalls the offer that led to their most recent move from Boston. "A head-hunter came and waved money; . . . this offer came in and they really coerced. I mean, they took me out to lunch, trying to tell me how great this opportunity was."

At home, however, a different calculus applies. There, it is about staying the course, even when things are not perfect. Her tone here is resigned, pragmatic, matter of fact. "Well, we've been married almost twenty-five years and there are no big issues," she maintains. "But it's kind of gotten—we went through an 'empty nest' sort of situation and so we needed to figure out what we could do to reconnect." The two of them brought this moment on themselves, she says, by focusing so much on their children, who were not-quite-full-fledged adults. "I don't think we're heading for divorce," Holly said. "It's just a little rough patch we're going through." They were taking steps to change that now, going on trips together, electing to revitalize their union instead of drifting apart. Said another affluent professional, similarly: "It's not choosing the person as much as it is choosing to be committed."

Holly and Fiona share a blithe unconcern about insecure work, even though no one is calling Fiona up to wave money at her. What makes Fiona different from Holly and Luke, however, is that she has the same approach to intimate partners that she does to employers: expect little constancy and harbor little room for compromise. In contrast, advantaged couples represent a bit of a mystery: while people like Holly and Luke exhibit few regrets about moving from company to company in a quest for the best match of self to job, many of them are in long-term intimate relationships lasting twenty years or more. Like many advantaged couples, for whom divorce rates have been declining for decades to levels not seen since the 1960s, the ceaseless quest for "something better" that animates their behavior in the marketplace of jobs appears to be absent in their intimate lives. Advantaged workers seem to build what we might call a *moral wall*, a symbolic barrier keeping the insecurity—with which they are very comfortable at work—from infiltrating their home lives.[6]

Fiona may be hiding—from us and from herself—the trauma of insecurity at the bottom, given the financial troubles she has endured as a result of layoffs and company closures. But Holly and others like her mask something different: the compromises inherent in the longevity of their intimate relationships, and, to some degree, the surrender of the notion that there's a better option out there—paradoxically, the very same notion that lures them from job to job. Just as the "flexibility" language reworks job insecurity into something Fiona controls, Holly's "choosing" language transforms relationship compromise into a celebration of individualism. Both proffer visions of a decisive, autonomous self that fits in well with what we might call "insecurity culture," a culture of personal responsibility and risk, linked to the spread of precariousness at work, the neoliberal receding of the state, and the dominance of the market.[7]

As we consider Fiona and Holly, what is new here is not job insecurity—defined as the sense that one may lose one's job involuntarily. Precariousness at work is a powerful cultural theme, the topic of popular books, songs, and movies with titles like *The Disposable American* or *The Big Squeeze*, or articles such as "Job Insecurity: It's the Disease of the 21st Century" and "The Fear Economy." Analysts and pundits might disagree about whether and how much job insecurity has grown over the past thirty years—noting that the US economy has long been characterized by its dynamism, the combination of both losses and gains—but most Americans believe that it has. They look back to a time when some fathers, if not necessarily their own, worked for the same firms for twenty years or more, anchored by a social contract in which, in return for employee loyalty and adequate performance, employers owed security, opportunities for training and advancement, and benefits to a wide swath of both management and production workers. That this contract was limited to larger firms and mostly white, male workers does not dislodge the power of this iconic image, even for some women.[8]

Nor is it necessarily new that stark inequality such as that between Fiona and Holly can shape how such insecurity is felt, although the growing distance between the billionaires who have doubled their income in the last five years and those who cling to desperation wages can be shocking. Indeed, such inequality may in part generate the insecurity that prevails. Many of the factors that contribute to Holly and Luke's joyful take on the new ways of organizing work are those that contribute to Fiona's unmooring; among them are the rise in external labor markets and the shrinking of benefits, including security, to an increasingly rarefied core labor force.

What we do not yet know, however, and what I set out to discover, is how insecurity and inequality combine to generate consequences not just at work but in intimate life as well. When people believe that employers do not owe them much of anything, how do they interpret what they themselves owe to others? In an insecure age, how do we make sense of our own obligations?[9]

THE TUMBLEWEED SOCIETY AT WORK AND AT HOME

Job insecurity is conventional wisdom, conveyed in part by the constant drumbeat of job turnover news. Every month brings a new string of layoff announcements: in 2014, for example, Hewlett-Packard was expected to eliminate 34,000 jobs over the course of the year, while JC Penney, Sprint, and JP Morgan Chase also announced cuts, with the latter's workforce down by 20,000 since 2011. Workers' concerns for their own jobs have steadily increased since the mid-1970s, even taking into account those peaks in anxiety during recessionary periods. In most dual-earner families, one or both partners report having an insecure job; in almost half of these households, both partners think their employment is insecure.[10]

These perceptions are not entirely unfounded. Beyond the celebrated dynamism of the American economy, work in the United States has grown increasingly precarious since the 1970s, particularly for men employed in the private sector, who were the main beneficiaries of the twenty-year career and the gold watch—a model, of course, that lasted for a very finite period in US history, only forty years by some counts. The greater use of temporary workers, the pursuit of layoffs even in growth years, the weakening of labor unions, and the rise of external labor markets are some of the major factors contributing to this trend. A group of large US firms employing 1.2 million people told researchers that in 2011 they filled one-half to two-thirds of their vacancies with external hires, for example, rather than promoting from within; that figure used to be just 10 percent. There are now more than one and a half times as many "contingent workers"—meaning temporary or on-call workers, the self-employed, and contractors—as there are union members in the United States. These trends are most powerful in certain regions and in certain industries, such as information technology: every two years, analysts report, half of the workforce in a typical Silicon Valley firm is replaced.[11]

Part of what is new here is that employers are undertaking some of these restructuring moves not just in recessions but when times are flush, making job loss a bit less predictable, and thus likely contributing to a sense of insecurity. To be sure, over the past thirty years, the US economy has been a powerful job-creation machine, adding some 60 million net new jobs and contributing to the sanguinity of many economists. But as Princeton economist Henry Farber concludes, "There is ample evidence that long-term employment is on the decline in the United States."[12]

The sense of rapid turnover at work is matched by seemingly parallel changes in intimacy. Romantic partnerships dissolve and re-form much more quickly than they did a half century ago, leading sociologist Andrew Cherlin to dub this phenomenon the "marriage-go-round." While marriage rates remain high overall (about 90 percent of people have been married by the time they are 55), they have decreased dramatically for African-Americans (only 39 percent of African-American women aged fifteen to forty-four report ever having been married, compared to 63 percent of white women, while the former used to be *more* likely to marry) and for couples without a college degree, who are more likely to cohabit. In 2010, 8.1 million American couples cohabited together, and almost 60 percent of women report having done so, more than double the rate thirty years before; these trends have implications for stability, as half of American cohabiters break up within five years.[13]

While it is possible that the higher rates of cohabitation relieve some of the pressure from marriages, siphoning off those who might have broken up anyway, it is also true that even those who marry in the United States are not immune to dissolution trends. Divorce rates have plateaued since jumping to their peak in 1981, but men who married in the early 1960s had a greater chance of reaching their fortieth anniversary than those who married in the early 1980s had of reaching their twentieth anniversary. Today, 20 percent of American marriages break up by the time they hit the five-year mark, and 15 percent of children see their mother marry three different men by the time they are fifteen years old. American married couples even have a higher chance of breaking up than Swedish cohabiters, according to Cherlin. It is these kinds of unique family patterns that lead informed observers of both work and of family to use the word "churn" to describe these trends in the United States.[14]

TWO WHIRLWINDS

We are accustomed to drawing a distinct line between these domains, as if the whirlwind in one has no relationship to the whirlwind in the other. It seems we are willing to contemplate what precariousness at work does at work—to profits, productivity, wages, worker engagement, even health. While we know that job insecurity strains marriages, analysts have been more interested in explaining family churn with poverty or unemployment, the deinstitutionalization of marriage or the rise in expressive individualism. There has generally been less inquiry about the impact of job insecurity beyond the cubicle.[15]

To be sure, the seeming simultaneity of the trends—the rise in divorce and the rise in job insecurity—does not necessarily imply their linkage. The differences in the stories of Holly and Fiona should help us see that it is hardly that simple, as does a breakdown of these trends. Job insecurity is generally believed to have hit blue-collar workers in the 1970s and '80s, at the onset of massive contractions in American manufacturing, and white-collar workers not until the 1980s and '90s, when the increasing influence of shareholder-driven management led to widespread outsourcing, downsizing, and subcontracting. But divorce trends, which we might consider a rough proxy for instability on the home front, diverge markedly by class over this period. The divorce rate for people without college education rose sharply in the 1970s and has remained high. In contrast, however, the rate for college-educated couples peaked in 1980 and has descended ever since, now back down to 1960s levels; their job insecurity trends show no such climb and fall. At the very least, a closer look at these patterns suggests that if there is a relationship between trends in work and intimacy, it is a complex one, not given to easy one-for-one conclusions about linked destabilization.[16]

Yet we know that the old ways of organizing work—the social compact, the lifetime careers—had their own broader impacts, on the workplace and beyond. We know, for example, that stable Fordist work relied upon and produced certain visions of honorable behavior at work; a standardized model of mass education; particular identities of gender, race, and class; and notions of a "normal" adulthood as a fixed identity one achieved and, by extension, what it meant to grow up. In particular, stable work, buttressed by state policies, encouraged particular kinds of intimacy, and particular kinds of families, with pronounced homogeneity and fixedness, families that excluded some forms of intimacy while enshrining one model—that of the heterosexual, childbearing, male breadwinner/female caregiver marriage—for all.[17]

Work and employment are a powerful force in the United States, and the way we organize work shapes much more than simply how work gets done. Indeed, the organization of work bears implications for the expectations we hold at work and in our intimate lives, for the kind of families we can sustain, and even for the kind of selves we strive to be. What, then, are the broader implications of precarious work, particularly for the conduct of intimate life?

FENDING OFF INSECURITY

Gary Gilbert offers another perspective on the impact of job insecurity on intimate life, demonstrating the power of our expectations either to cushion or to amplify the blow. A thoughtful tradesman with tattoos up and down his arms, like Plato with a pack of cigarettes rolled in his sleeve, Gary cares about job insecurity more than Fiona—he said he was "crushed" when he lost his job as a contracting manager—but he too does not expect any loyalty from his employer. Though he worked hard and consistently, he blames himself for the layoff, calling it "the biggest mistake I ever made." His mistake? Getting hired in the first place, putting himself and his livelihood in their hands, when he had been doing fine as a tradesman on his own.

But if all we can do is expect insecurity at work, he thinks, surely at home it should be different; Gary builds a moral wall like the elite professionals, but instead of their matter-of-fact pragmatism, he clings to the notion of duty in the home as if it will fend off the insecurity that prevails in the workplace. Duty's rigidity seems to flip easily to righteous indignation, however, and the guilt and self-blame he feels at work transform themselves into something closer to anger and outrage at home, where he feels the loss of other people's obligations—particularly, the personal and dedicated care of women—acutely.

Gary has a longtime girlfriend, but he stopped marrying after his second try collapsed like the first. While he says "I am a very committed person," not everyone else is, he maintains. "The hurt that's been caused to me by a lack of commitment on the part of other people, I know how devastating that can be . . ." Gary's keen sense of duty makes him see and name betrayal at home but not at work, displacing his feelings from one place to the other.

The notion of duty has a certain strength to it, and its power can propel people to great sacrifice—we shall hear later of people whose sense of duty inspires feats of heroic commitment. Gary shows us, however, that duty is also a brittle master, one that leaves him, and other angry white men, with little option but outrage when it is forsaken. "Marriage is—it's not—it's not what it used to be. People don't have the commitment that they used to," Gary said. "Marriage can be tossed out like a Pepsi can."

What do Holly and Luke, Gary and Fiona have in common? They have all experienced layoffs at work, directly feeling the impact of employer indifference. Despite their dissimilarities, all of them view that indifference as if it is as inevitable as a weather event, something to endure or exploit but certainly beyond their control or steering. None expects much of anything from employers, but they all attest to their own strong work ethic, suggesting a *one-way honor system* that dictates strict rules for themselves but not their employers. The inevitability stems from the conventional wisdom of job insecurity, a "common sense" that contributes to the fatalistic acquiescence of those who are immersed in precarious work, but that does not absolve them from work's moral measure. What was once a social contract has become instead an "employee covenant."[18]

Each of them also shares another crucial similarity: their dedication to children. While some men view their care for children as optional, for many people immersed in insecure work, particularly women, children are commitment's final frontier. What do we owe them? "Everything," Gary says. "My life. Everything." Even Fiona, who qualifies her pledge with a cautionary tale about the dangers of enabling troubled teenagers, encircles Jimmy within her moral wall; recall her words "It's me and Jimmy against the world. Like, that's how it's always been." Ironically, given their differences about how they view insecurity, they also agree upon the sort of world they are preparing their children for, one that requires flexibility, resilience, and a certain independence.

When it comes to their romantic partnerships however, they truly diverge. From the grim triumph of Fiona's independence, to the calm matter-of-factness of Holly's pragmatism, to the outrage of Gary's fealty to duty, they each adopt a particular stance toward intimate obligation, one that shapes the way they make sense of commitment at home.

While Fiona, Holly, and Gary help us to see some of the effects of job insecurity—the way it can make the less advantaged commit too much or hardly at all, how it seems to offer the advantaged the choice of when and where they might pledge themselves—we can also get a sense of the impact of job precariousness by looking at those who do not feel much of it, at people such as Ed Case.

Ed, a firefighter, knows he is lucky. Sharing a coffee with me in the spare room off the main firehouse bay, Ed said he had been a telecom technician for fifteen years already before he got hired onto the local fire rescue crew. While he is quite familiar with the sacrifices required in firefighting, he considers himself fortunate, as he never finished his associate's degree in machinist technology, which he views as a dying field. Instead, he now enjoys a secure job with a livable wage and a marriage of more than two decades, with three kids and a house nestled in a small town with good schools.

"We're making it. I guess where everybody is afraid of losing a job, we don't have that fear," he says. "It was a lot of luck, I made the leap [from his former job] not knowing the economy was going to turn the way it was. We are probably behind from what we were two or three years ago because of the economy, inflation and things like that, but hey, at least we're—but it's steady. We don't have a whole lot in the end, but then again I do not have the repo man ready to come and get the house next week." Ed is aware of how it could have turned out for him, even as he is straightforward about the compromises of firefighting: of being constantly on-call, of the unpredictable hours, of the bodily risks, and, finally, of living and working in the same place for such a long time. But Ed does not talk like Gary, his words rife with the fervor of duty. Instead, his talk features a resignation that bespeaks pragmatism at both work and home. "[Work] is kind of like a marriage," he said; "you kind of give a little and take a little."

About his twenty-three-year marriage, he is the same. "Some good years, some bad, I guess like everybody else," Ed said. "I mean there are some times where I'm sure she would like to trade me for a new model. And sometimes it's probably the same for me. So it's tough, but we keep trudging on." Ed's metaphor—"It's tough, but we keep trudging on"—draws a picture of endurance, of compromise and constancy, that exemplifies the pragmatism of settling down. Unlike Fiona or Gary, Ed neither defies nor avows his commitment to other people; unlike Holly, his pragmatic approach applies to work as well.

To some degree, in the United States, and in other advanced industrialized nations, we are all immersed in the tumbleweed society, where many employers seem to owe little but "respect and a paycheck." The common sense of job insecurity suggests it surely transcends the boundaries of our particular workplaces and whether or not we ourselves have experienced it personally. One does not need to get laid off to know that layoffs are possible, even expected, to feel the cultural shift of the new ways of organizing work. Like flyaway balls of tinder, in this vision, people roll hither and yon.

Yet Fiona, Holly, Gary, and Ed should help us see the very specificity of its impact. Some people roll, some people are pushed, and some people are staying put, at work and at home. The story of Ed, a stably employed worker, is important because it tells us that the actual experience of job insecurity surely matters in shaping how we approach our obligations, but Fiona, Holly, and Gary tell us that its impact is a complex one, one that varies depending on one's relative advantage, one's gender, and the expectations and resources that accompany these factors—a combination that helps to produce the lenses through which we view our responsibilities.

As an image of the impact of job insecurity, then, the tumbleweed society is partial truth, and partial dystopic possibility. It renders starkly what people fear about contemporary trends and captures the widespread sense of inevitability, the notion that we are all buffeted by winds beyond our control. But while Fiona—that rational, independent soul—is one important outgrowth, we must also see beyond her, to those who demand or strive for commitment, as well as to those who maintain expectations of mutual accountability at work and at home. Only then can we grasp how far people are willing to bend to accommodate themselves and their family lives to the demands of the market; only then can we understand the limits of what is hardly inevitable. Only then can we see our way to the alternatives.

GENDER, CARE, AND THE TUMBLEWEED SOCIETY

In examining the tumbleweed society, there are good reasons to focus on women. Much existing writing on job insecurity tells a story of decline, with some arguing that in the new economy our own character has weakened, because we suffer an increasing distance from those institutions like work that would shore up our ability to commit to others. The work lives these writers mourn, however, are mostly those of white men, whose lifelong careers of the mid-twentieth century provide the "before" to the "after" of the broken social contract and the loss of loyalty at work and at home.[19]

In contrast, women's lives have featured *more* work commitment than their mothers or grandmothers had, with rising job tenure and an increasing attachment to paid labor. To be sure, this trend reflects women's increasing labor force engagement more than their uniquely secure positions in the job market—as researcher Peter Cappelli notes, it's still a down escalator for work stability, even if women are up a few steps higher on it. Women's perspectives generate far more ambivalence about the "flexible turn," however, in that women, even low-income women, have gained independence, autonomy, and improved wages from some of the very trends that these writers lament.[20]

Women's perspectives are also crucial in our reckoning of the tumbleweed society, however, in that its most significant challenge is not one of the negotiability of what commitment looks like nor of the individual's loss of character, but rather a collective one: the problem that insecurity makes of dependency. How does a society predicated on mobility handle the bothersome needs of the young, the sick, and the elderly, which can drag caregivers down from the stratosphere of choice and flexibility?

Perceived mobility is valuable in the tumbleweed society, translating into more influence and stature personally and professionally, as expressed in enhanced resources and decreased obligations. Who can leave; who is stuck; who is being coveted, recruited, lured and who is not: the answers are the currency of power, and the questions are evidence of market thinking at work and at home. In the new ways of working, anything that acts as ballast, anchoring workers against their mobility across jobs, companies, or geographic locations, serves to depress their wages and signal their impaired "commitment" to the job.

No group suffers the consequences of this "autonomy myth" more obviously than mothers, but scholars have found that caregivers of any kind endure a wage and promotion penalty, for taking on responsibilities to someone else outside of work that mean they might have other priorities. Women continue to have primary responsibility for caregiving, despite the movement of some men toward more care involvement, and thus they are a fulcrum where dependency and mobility meet, crucial for evaluating how the tumbleweed society affects our perceived obligations.[21]

Responsibilities for children, the sick, and the elderly limit women's capacity to be mobile, to be independent, to be able to take advantage of all the promise the new freedoms can offer. This conflict likely encourages the deprecation of care and dependency; as women, particularly those who are white and middle-class, gain further access to the intensive work of the upper echelons, care work is further denigrated, sloughed off where possible to poor, underpaid immigrant women of color. In an insecure age, those who can be are wayward, itinerant souls. Those who cannot be, then, are a newly visible problem.[22]

The trouble is that for those who are left behind, as opposed to the leavers, the new freedoms can feel a lot like the old abandonment. As social theorist Zygmunt Bauman puts it: "Some of the world's residents are on the move; for the rest it is the world itself that refuses to stand still." By primarily focusing on women's lives and work, the gendered provision of care, and meanings of dependence, we can absorb exactly what we have lost, what we have gained, and why.[23]

TALKING TO PEOPLE ABOUT HOW THEY COMMIT

This book helps to untangle these knots of gender, class, and precariousness at work and at home, in a study of how eighty people—most of them women—talk about commitment, obligation, and change. I talked to people in three groups: those who had been let go at work or who had been so desperate they moved in search of a job (the "laid-off"); high-skilled, highly paid people whose employers moved them for their jobs or their spouses ("relocators"); and those employed in "lifetime" jobs like firefighters, teachers, or health paraprofessionals (the "stably employed"). We thus hear from two groups immersed in insecurity culture—those whom we might consider the "losers" and "winners" of job precariousness—and we can compare their experiences to the stably employed, who work at some distance from the churn.

At the same time, the groups comprise one of privilege and two that are comparatively disadvantaged. Relocators were generally elites with graduate degrees and ample six-figure household incomes. In contrast, many of the stably employed and the laid-off had some college and lower incomes; they best fit the label "moderately educated," which actually constitutes the majority of women of reproductive age in the United States. While there was some range in their education—most of the teachers had college degrees and a few had master's degrees, but other stably employed had just a few years of college or high school degrees—their responses coalesced in important ways. The stably employed also had an average income in the mid-five figures, with the laid-off having a lower mean figure in part due to the fact that some of them were not working. The different groups allow us, then, to think in different ways about the interplay of insecurity and inequality in shaping views on what we owe each other at work and at home.[24]

Most interviews took place in Washington, DC, and environs, as well as two large cities and a smaller city in Virginia. Most interviewees— sixty-three—were women, in order to center the project on women's work and caregiving experience. All of them were parents of teenagers, because I wanted to hear how they discussed commitment with their progeny. I include more information about my research in Appendix A.[25]

Talking to eighty people cannot tell us how widespread a trend is, but instead offers us a window into how people make sense of particular situations or relationships. In-depth interviews let us focus on people's own expectations and emotions, by listening not just to what people say but how they say it—the jokes, metaphors, and other means of expressing what they think is meaningful, ideal, or virtuous. Thus we attend not just to their claims to honor but also to what they think is honorable, not just to how they might rationalize behavior but also to what counts as a valid justification, not just how they feel about a situation but to how they feel about their feelings—a glimpse of how they see themselves, in relation to the people around them.

STANCES OF OBLIGATION

As Fiona, Holly, Gary, and Ed demonstrate, people seem to adopt different stances of obligation, which then act like lenses or frames, shaping what sort of responsibilities they can even see, let alone which ones they might expect or fulfill. These stances vary in two particular dimensions: the expectation of constancy and the predilection for compromise—in other words, how much we prioritize endurance, and how many of our other principles are we willing to bend in service to it.

Thus some people adopt an independent stance, in which they are principally focused on remaining invulnerable to fallible others, with little expectation of constancy and little inclination to compromise. Others adopt a stance of duty, dedicated to an expansive view of obligation that leads them to great heights of sacrifice or great lows of outrage; they generally have high expectations of constancy—which, when dashed, lead to a keen sense of betrayal—and a low capacity for compromise, since they are purists about righteous obligation. Finally a third stance is one of pragmatism, wherein people prefer a "get real" stance opposed to a naïve indulgence, and have both high expectations of constancy and also high predilections for compromise. While not exhaustive, these stances, in different configurations aimed at work and at home, comprise the bulk of how people construe their obligations and those of others.[26]

Each group of people poses its own puzzles, I found. How do so many attest to a powerful work ethic, for example, while minimizing their expectations of their employer? How do advantaged people seem to embrace independence, insecurity, and self-actualization at work, always on the lookout for something better, but at home tamp down their search for the perfect match, resigned to their enduring marriages? How do less advantaged men with precarious employment, like Gary, hold back their anger at work, only to give it free rein in the very place where they seem to yearn for stability?

These puzzles and others, as well as the clues to decode them, can be found in the intersections of precariousness and inequality. The primacy of work, and its cultural dominance over care in intimate life, does not give American workers much to fight back with against the influx of insecurity. Instead, as jobs become more precarious, they present isolated workers with individual predicaments of how to manage their family needs when employers, the state, and gender configure that responsibility in particular ways. These predicaments can sometimes feel like traps, laid for individual workers to solve individually, one family at a time, and are particularly difficult for less advantaged women and men. Workers' negotiations of commitment and obligation, then, reflect the challenges these predicaments put to them.

WHAT LIES AHEAD

This book's organization mirrors its argument, tracing how our experiences at work and our relative advantage shape our cultural framings of what we face at home. We start off with a chapter in the realm of work, looking at how people talk about job insecurity and what employers and employees owe each other. Under the one-way honor system, workers let employers off the hook as the soldiers of a social revolution beyond their control, while maintaining high standards for their own dedication as a sign of honorable personal character, an uneasy mismatch of expectations that generates emotional contradictions.

The next five chapters delve into different configurations of insecurity and inequality, and consider their impact on obligation at work and at home. We hear from the advantaged relocators, who, like Holly, adopt a wholly different stance for work as they do for intimacy, building a moral wall to cordon off their family life from the insecurity that they embrace at work. Chapter 4 looks at more disadvantaged insecure workers like Fiona, mostly women, who share the independent stance toward work, but who also apply it to their intimate lives. Chapters 5 and 6 look at those disadvantaged workers who use the stance of duty to make moral sense of their obligation: first off those men like Gary for whom duty brings with it a sense of being betrayed by others who fail to fulfill theirs, and then women who find in duty the mandate for rescuing, or taking on the overwhelming needs with which they are confronted.

Chapter 7 allows us to compare the stably employed to those who came before, highlighting the expectations of constancy and compromise at work and at home that make their pragmatic perspective distinct. Despite these differences, however, in chapter 8 we see how people converge in how they talk about childrearing: parents owe their progeny nothing less than their duty, even as they are trying to raise "flexible" children for an insecure world.

Chapter 9 offers an in-depth look at an unusual three-parent family that manages nonetheless to endure. Drawing upon their story, I sketch out an alternative vision I term the "coral society," wherein stable employment is part of the constellation of factors enabling both diversity and endurance in people's intimate lives. Finally, the epilogue summarizes the core themes of the book and explores some of its broader implications.

BEYOND THE CUBICLE

This book explores how job insecurity shapes our understanding of what we owe each other at work and at home, of when we stay and when we go, of what kind of promises we expect from our employers, our romantic partners, our children, and ourselves. We hear how people view their dilemmas, explain their choices, and corral their feelings to adapt to the kind of selves they think they must be. We bear witness to the tensions that arise between how they feel about their obligations and how they sense they are supposed to feel, and to the struggles that ensue as they try to reconcile those contradictions. We see how the stances they adopt to make sense of their responsibilities shape the very problems they can see, and the solutions they are obliged to try, in both work and in love.

Widespread insecurity, inflected by social inequality, has a profound impact, both the insecurity we choose and that which we are dealt, whether we are the leaver or the left behind. It magnifies dependency into a problem; it hides the way society organizes access to care as an individual solution; and it creates the sort of choices we face in charting our paths through care and connection. As long as the debate about job insecurity focuses on its effects at work and is largely silent about its impact on intimate life, we will misunderstand the challenges of commitment at home, where gendered traps of dependency and disadvantage offer few good options. Our silence about these effects allows employers—and the increasingly hands-off state—to get off scot-free, and mutes the criticism of those economic practices that amplify the effects of global trends.

How do people interpret and navigate the meanings of the new insecurities in their daily lives, and how does that vary by gender and class? This book shows how people make sense of precariousness at work and what it means for the rest of their lives. The full reckoning of the impact of job insecurity requires considering its influence beyond the cubicle.

CHAPTER 2

⌘

Managing the Unrequited Contract

Beth Mendel had had a successful career in design before she quit her job when her husband was relocated to Virginia from New York City, thinking that she would finally have a little time to be a stay-at-home mom with her four children. A tall woman with eyes crinkling in good humor behind horn-rimmed glasses, she sat across from me in a café, pulling her sweater more tightly around her as she narrated the move. They sold their apartment in the city, bought a house down south, and moved all four children into their new schools, with her parents joining them in the move, she recalled. But a few months later, the company called her husband back up north for an ominous meeting at headquarters; they fired him that day.

He had been assigned to Virginia to downsize the operations there, she remembered, but when that job was done, he was too. Her eyes widening in a can-you-believe-it sort of gentle parody of their shock, Beth invited me to picture the scene. "It was like, 'We think you're valuable enough to move you down to Virginia,' and then, 'Sorry, we got rid of the plant, and now you're not valuable anymore.' It was horrible," she said, recalling that fluctuations in the housing market meant there was no way they could easily return to their old life in New York. "So imagine him, he was definitely the hatchet man," she told me. "And then he was hatcheted."

Beth quickly went back to work, and has not stopped in the eight years since, switching careers to become a human resources manager for several different firms over the next decade. Her husband initially succumbed to a depression, and she would come home to find the kitchen dirty and the kids telling her that another day had gone by with Daddy not getting up from the sofa. Slowly, painfully, he regained his equilibrium enough to work, eventually finding his niche again but at much lower pay, as do a quarter of those displaced workers who find new jobs.[1]

In talking about work, it is not that Beth embraces the new insecurity, exactly. She calls what happened to their family "horrible," and remembers the trauma: "Oh my gosh, it was awful." But she also tries hard to move on, with little phrases of acceptance dotting her narrative like mental shrugs. "Yeah, but, you know, hindsight's 20/20," she said. "There's always bumps in the road," and "What are you going to do?" These little phrases serve to keep her expectations about work low, and contain the emotions she allows herself to feel, since job insecurity is just what we can all predict, simply part of the new economy.

On the other hand, Beth maintains high expectations of herself at work, as a core part of her identity. "Well, I'm a—myself, I'm a very loyal employee. I—when I accept a job, I'm—there's, you know, it's in my heart, it's in my gut," she said, describing situations in which she thought she probably should have left a company earlier than she did. "Yeah, I don't just go to a job nine to five, and at five o'clock, oh, it's time, goodbye. No, that's not me." Beth identifies with the employer's needs, even in an environment in which she knows, through bitter personal experience, that this sort of sentiment is unlikely to be reciprocated.[2]

What do employers owe us, and what do we owe our employers? The question goes to the heart of what we think counts as honorable behavior, of our sense of what we can control, and of what we perceive as the place of ethics in paid labor. Contemporary transformations of work have included the erosion of the old social contract, in which employers promised some sort of job security in return for workers' loyalty and effort. While that bargain was limited in time and its beneficiaries, increases in actual and perceived job insecurity suggest that for many employers, this set of obligations no longer applies. Yet, at the same time, full-time work continues to be a central component of identity for many, and for some populations—women, young adults—its importance has even increased. These opposing trends—the increases in actual and perceived job insecurity, which we might predict would promote less work attachment—and the increased intensity and cultural importance of full-time employment, which we might predict would promote more work attachment—generate a cultural and emotional collision in people's lives.[3]

With her opposing stances toward work—where she shrugs her shoulders about job insecurity but fervently avows her own dedication as a worker—Beth typifies a central paradox of our times. I call this lopsided calculus of obligation the "one-way honor system." Of course, some employed in precarious work sounded a different note, in which they were careful to distinguish between their dedication to peak performance, which is one dimension of work commitment, and their intent to remain in a particular job over time; I discuss these high-performance, low-loyalty workers in greater detail in the next chapter. Furthermore, stably employed workers—those public school teachers, firefighters, people employed in small, longstanding family firms, and the like—maintained high expectations for their employers' constancy, as well as their own.

Most of the rest, however, seemed to accept that insecurity prevails at work and, like Beth, excuse employers for "hatcheting," even as they maintained high expectations for their own duty and dedication. Ultimately, the one-way honor system generates a set of very real enigmas: Why do people hold themselves to a different standard of loyalty than they expect of their employers? Given the widespread sense that employers have left the terms of the old social contract behind, why are employees still affirming their own dedication? Furthermore, how do people reconcile themselves emotionally to the uneven balance of obligation at work?

WHAT WE EXPECT FROM EMPLOYERS

Most people in insecure work did not think employers owed their workforce very much at all, if anything. "I guess just respect and appreciation," said Vicky, a white woman with a master's degree and a household income of more than $500,000. "It would be nice to have job security, but I don't know if that's realistic."[4]

"I just think the employer is the superior, and they're in control, they're in charge. And if they decide to fire you, they can," said Claudia, a married white saleswoman who recently had to declare bankruptcy. "Of course I could leave, but, I mean, I believe that . . . what's the word, to be submissive to your employer, to obey their rules, I think we owe them—an employee owes their employer that. You know, when you're working, you should be working."

"I think they [employers] should definitely be *grateful* when they have a good employee," said Lola, a Latina public school teacher who—unusually—survived a recent bout of layoffs, and talked like a precarious worker. Her tone implying that their responsibilities do not extend much further, Lola was the one whose phrase "And [their employees] are owed their paycheck and a certain amount of respect, I would say" we heard in the last chapter.

Here we are not talking about whether or not people are worried about losing their jobs, the standard measure of perceived job insecurity, but instead whether or not they should have to worry about losing their jobs. In essence, we are taking a measure of the good, of what counts as honorable in the definition of our obligations. Obligations can be tricky to decipher, because to some degree they only matter when they are tested, when circumstances are less than ideal. On some level, commitment and loyalty only become salient under stress: What does an employer owe to a highly valued employee who experiences some sort of home calamity? What about when the company is under stress or changes hands?[5]

Phyllis, an African-American single mother recently laid off from a string of low-paying jobs, maintained that even good employees should not get special consideration from employers if they have a family situation or other emergency arise. "I think that employee needs to get a good, strong support system . . . outside of work. Keep it outside. Once you walk in that door, you're in a different mode," Phyllis said. "The employer owes absolutely nothing. And then once you get that into the relationship where you're bringing it to the employer's attention, it's going to be all throughout your business. So no, no, leave it out."

We might predict that those who are not particularly advantaged by the insecure economy—those at the bottom of the skill hierarchy, who would benefit from a system offering protection from the capricious forces of the job market—would be more likely to argue that employers owed some sort of loyalty, security, or dedication to their employees if those workers were experiencing a momentary emergency. Surely this more vulnerable population would feel more sympathy for the employee's need for accommodation, than for the employer's need for performance? Yet even most of those with low-skilled or lower-paying jobs seemed to put themselves in the employer's shoes.

Fiona, the white technical worker we heard from in the last chapter, who spent more than a decade as a single mother, had held the most jobs of those to whom I spoke (she stopped listing at eleven); several of those job changes had been involuntary. Even valuable employees need to keep up their productivity, she said. "I don't think an employer owes an employee [who's] not doing their job well anything."

WHAT WE EXPECT FROM EMPLOYEES

If employers owe little beyond respect, dignity, and pay, what do employees owe? According to most—even the stably employed—workers must give their all. Three-quarters of the people I spoke to talked about themselves as "workaholics," "passionate," with a "really overdrive work ethic." Sometimes it felt like there was an ongoing arms race in the percentages people assigned to their own effort, with tales of giving "100 percent," "110 percent," "150 percent," or even "200 percent" on the job. "When I work at a job, I work it as if it's my own company," said Nicki, an African-American woman with extensive caregiving obligations who had been laid off. "Their best interest is my best interest. Doing the best that I can to make sure that that company survives." "My father, you know, 'Work first, play second' is how I was raised," said Marin, who works for her husband's company. "And [if] you're due at work at eight, you'd better be there by 7:45, because if you're not there by 7:45, you may as well not show up. So work has always been very important to me." Marin's words capture an aspect that is widely shared here—her relationship to work is personal, as a reflection of her character, of her identity, much as Beth attested.

Like many Americans, most people laid claim to intense work commitment as a core part of being an honorable person. This was true even though the bulk of those with whom I spoke were women with children, some of whom had secondary jobs that provided a fraction of their household income, and a few had been stay-at-home mothers with more intermittent work experience. Women's paid work commitment has always been suspect, because their presumed dual commitment to childrearing meant they struggled with "competing devotions." Nonetheless, researchers have not found significant gender differences in measures of job involvement. Survey researchers report, for example, that about the same percentage of women as men—70 percent of full-time working women (both white-collar and blue-collar workers)—say they would continue to work if they suddenly had enough money to live comfortably for the rest of their lives, known as the "lottery question" (and used by researchers as a rough proxy for a work ethic). A strong work ethic was part of good character, part of being fully human, no matter your gender, people maintained.[6]

Becca, a single mother who pulled her family out of abject poverty by working as a rescue-squad dispatcher, said that it didn't matter to her what her kids chose to do, as long as they pursued it avidly.

> I'm a workaholic. I give 150 percent. And I expect my kids to too. My kids know you don't call in sick unless you are in the hospital or throwing up. That job is your livelihood. That's the line between having a home and not having a home. And they know what it was like to be right there where we didn't have a home. And I think because of that my kids are stronger, they have a stronger work ethic. I have a stronger work ethic. I told my kids and I'll tell anybody, I don't care what you do with your life as far as what you choose to be. If you want to muck out stables for the rest of your life, fine. As long as you do your best, I'll be proud.

Becca implies that only the work ethic is the source of human dignity, not the job.

Those who did not demonstrate an overweening commitment to work were moral transgressors who deserved some contempt, as we hear from Juliet, a teacher whose son had joined a band and dashed her hopes that he would go to college. She debated whether or not to continue supporting him, because she did not want to subsidize a lifestyle she did not value. "I *would* [support him]. I would if I saw a really strong work ethic towards it," Juliet asserted. Instead, "All I see is, 'We're playing a gig' or '[We're] playing video games.' I just don't see a strong work ethic, and I cannot stand individuals who don't have a strong work ethic. That just really gets in my craw."

THE GLUE OF WORK ATTACHMENT

One might think that the pervasive sense of increasing job insecurity— and its resigned acceptance by precarious workers—would give rise to increased detachment from work, as people adjust to a new employment bargain. When one party in an exchange is seen as withdrawing its commitment, surely it is a rational response for the other party to pull back as well. Furthermore, concerns about losing worker dedication might then in turn act as a counterweight to these trends, discouraging employers from retreating from commitments to their workforce. Employers, as well as scholars, are scrutinizing this drama closely, their interest animated by the question: When will workers perceive that the vaunted social contract has changed, and employers no longer feel obligated to them? It is as if both sides are on a see-saw, watching to see if the other one is going to get up and leave. In this vein, the business press has an annual ritual bemoaning workers' decreasing loyalty, reporting how many workers plan on looking for a job in the next year, for example (one widely distributed report claimed 84 percent of those who took an online survey had such plans; a more carefully conducted national survey concluded that 21 percent did).[7]

Yet a fuller picture actually belies this account, and instead of a predictable economic tango, one of the partners in this dance has made some perhaps unanticipated moves: workers have responded to perceived job insecurity by working harder and longer. American workers of every racialized group, gender, and wage level have increased their work hours since the late 1970s. Even with a postrecession dip, the United States logs higher average annual hours worked than the OECD average, with Americans working four more weeks than the British, nine more weeks than the French, and eleven more weeks than the Germans, although as recently as the late 1970s, American and European work hours were about the same. As Arlie Hochschild documented, people face a "time bind" in which they acquiesce to ever-increasing demands of work and find themselves squeezing their nonwork lives into ever-smaller increments.[8]

These trends are particularly true for more advantaged workers. One 2009 study found that 70 percent of US employees work beyond scheduled time and on weekends; more than half of these, along with 62 percent of middle-management employees, cited "self-imposed pressure" as the reason. Contrary to overly confident predictions such as "the four-hour workweek," work hours have increased so dramatically for college-educated men in the United States that a longstanding relationship between wages and hours has reversed, so that by 2002, the richer you were, the more likely you were to work long hours, instead of the opposite: the best-paid 20 percent are twice as likely to work long hours as the lowest-paid 20 percent, economists report. Furthermore, these trends go hand in hand with perceptions of insecurity, since the more advantaged you are, the more likely you are to consider that employer commitment has eroded, surveys suggest.[9]

To be sure, some of this behavior is driven by fear—if you perceive you are more likely to lose your job, you may work harder to make the employer want to keep you. At the same time, however, Americans do not just work hard: like Beth, Marin, and Nicki, many also profess great attachment to their work, identifying with employers' needs and perspectives and reserving admiration for busy people who work hard. American veneration of work is a longstanding cultural theme, remarked upon by such disparate observers as Thomas Jefferson, Alexis de Tocqueville, and Max Weber. In essence, given two possible responses to increased job insecurity—less work attachment, as they mirror what they get from employers, or more work attachment, as they strive to be among the chosen few who get to stay—American cultural heritage made choosing one of those paths much more likely.

In this vein, almost three-quarters of American workers say they are "willing to go beyond the requirements of my job to help my organization succeed," and 64 percent say they have a "strong sense of commitment" to their organizations. A 2011 study found that 83 percent of US employees are satisfied with their job, with 41 percent reporting they are very satisfied. American workers are more committed to their work and their organizations than their counterparts in Japan, Korea, the United Kingdom, and other countries, researchers have found. In the United States, what Mary Blair-Loy has called the cultural logic of "work devotion" is a principled stance, one that maps onto political discourse and acts as a form of "moral capital." The moral valence of work identification is so strong that it under-girds the polling patterns of some low-income people, who vote against policies that might help them survive their own bouts of unemployment, because they do not want to support a mythical population that "does not want to work."[10]

Furthermore, there are some indications that the symbolic importance of full-time work is rising, at least for some populations, as other markers of identity lose their widespread consensus as meaningful signs. Young adults face a changing set of milestones for what constitutes adulthood, for example; while marriage and childbearing has receded in importance as ev-idence of maturity, the full-time job has expanded as a crucial identity maker, a moment when people know they are adults. The presence and im-portance of paid work has also expanded in women's lives, not only in their increased labor force participation but also in the decline of marriage rates and thus men's support for their unpaid caring labor. The fervent avowals of Nicki, Marin, and Becca thus mimic a larger trend in the United States, one that constrains workers' available responses to job insecurity, inhibit-ing their capacity to walk away from the insecure workplace: the cultural dominance of work as moral proof.[11]

THE INEVITABILITY OF INSECURITY

Thus we come upon a crucial paradox. How do people hold both of these beliefs simultaneously, combining a high work ethic for themselves with low expectations for their employers, generating the one-way honor system? It is as if employee obligation is a private reflection of self, an iden-tity issue, with these pronouncements of work ethic serving as claims of honor as fundamental as "I strive to be a good parent" or "I don't lie, cheat, or steal." Any employer obligation, on the other hand, is dependent on the changing terms of a social contract, a social contract "we all know" has dis-appeared, and therefore no longer part of reasonable expectations.[12]

Employer obligations are not part of an individual's identity even when the employer is the head of the company. Mary Jordan, a white physical therapist and mother of three, related a story of when a company president had been grooming her husband, Peter, for top management, only to leave the company without a backward glance after it was bought out. The fact that the president didn't "take care" of Peter as promised, but instead walked away with a great windfall from the sale, did not besmirch his character, Mary assured me. "The president did very, very well and I don't blame him," she maintained. "He's not a bad guy. I think he just didn't know how to do it.

You know he had this company but yet he probably felt—did feel responsible for these guys that had really helped him build the company." Mary gives the president the benefit of the doubt, so that he was credited with having the feelings of responsibility without actually fulfilling those responsibilities; she maintains a distinct moral calculus for business, in part because such behavior is inevitable, as she saw it—"just what you would expect."

Inevitability works here as a sort of ideology, shoring up insecurity culture. The assumed inevitability of insecurity reflects the dominance of particular narratives about how the economy works, and is promulgated by institutional forces that benefit from it. As the anthropologist Karen Ho wrote in her ethnography of Wall Street, claims to "maximize shareholder value" are part of the ruling ideology of a particular time and place, "the central explanation and rationale for corporate restructuring, changing concepts of wealth and inequality, and the state of the American economy." Inevitability, of course, does not dictate how we feel about these changes; people might mourn them, or they might celebrate them, as do the Wall Street financiers in Ho's book who successfully peddle these ideas. Yet this "soft" social phenomenon—of what we think about the economy—has serious impact, I argue, in that if job insecurity is inevitable, then we all must simply adapt to it. Thus these ideas have important effects on the way people think, feel, and act, on what feels possible to change, and what feels important simply to manage.[13]

Collective notions of what we owe each other at work gain certain traction when they are institutionalized in state policies, workplace practices, and court decisions. In order to give employers as much flexibility as possible, for example, the American government is unusually hands-off when it comes to leaving workers at the mercy of employer tactics such as layoffs, outsourcing, downsizing, or the use of flexible time and place practices. Such a laissez-faire approach dovetails with the retreat of the state, with the decline of American unions, and with the widespread adoption of insecurity as corporate policy to push workers back on their heels.

These policies continue despite research suggesting that, generally, layoffs do not actually improve productivity or the stock price of the firm, but they do improve profits by depressing wages, essentially transferring money from workers to owners. As Northwestern sociologist Leslie McCall has argued, "Dominant, market-oriented responses to the economic crises of the 1970s and later were neither established 'best practices' at the time of adoption nor immune to significant economic inefficiencies. . . . Their diffusion and acceptance far exceeded what could be justified by existing theory, the downturn and, perhaps most importantly, the vast amount of wealth and inequality that was created over the very same period."[14]

Other nations do not necessarily throw up their hands in the face of increasing insecurity, however. Some European nations, for example, have sought to protect workers from what they call "precarity" ushered in by globalization by maintaining income security while loosening up hiring and firing regulations. While it is well known that most European nations offer more extensive public provisioning than the United States, some of these countries have also adopted explicit means of balancing the security needs of employees with the flexibility needs of employers. Denmark and the Netherlands have pursued a set of policies dubbed "flexicurity," combining, in part, the loosening of rules that oversee hiring and firing for employers with income security for employees. Of course, Europe and the United States have markedly different histories and institutions—80 percent of the Danish working population belongs to a trade union, for example—but the explicit European campaign to address, and also to temper, the needs of globalized business offers an alternative to the American juggernaut. According to Beth, Nicki, and other precarious workers, however, rampant insecurity is all we can expect from this new world order.[15]

The perceived inevitability of insecurity generates a mismatch between what workers expect of employers and what they expect of themselves, a mismatch even more acute among the laid-off. What kind of processes do workers undergo to gin up their own commitment to employers who very likely will not reciprocate? How do people reconcile themselves to these uneven obligations? To illustrate these processes, we turn to Gary Gilbert, whom we first met in the last chapter.

"THE BIGGEST MISTAKE I EVER MADE"

A philosophical man in his early forties, Gary professes a profound sense of personal responsibility at work, an abiding moral vision that, when insecurity rolled in like thunderheads, led him to absolve his employer totally. These expectations had particular consequences, especially in the way they shaped the emotions he allowed himself to feel and the direction in which he could feel them. In a traumatic moment, Gary felt like the only one left in an otherwise empty room.

For years, Gary had a long and successful career as a self-employed contractor, with his own tools, industry contacts, and client base. "My work has always been—I choose what I want to do and when I want to do it. So I've always been very free in how I make my living," he explained. Accustomed to meager means as a boy, Gary found the pay for his skilled manual labor usually more than ample. He traveled often and had as clients major hotels and other large businesses. But after about fifteen years, he noticed the industry changing around him.

"The self-employment was getting to be a little tougher around here than it used to be. It started getting hard to land the bigger contracts that I used to get. There was more competition in my field of work. Almost like the market was flooded with people," he remembered. At the same time, Gary became less geographically mobile when he separated from his son's mother and yet wanted to remain involved in raising the boy, splitting custody during the week. "The older he [the son] got and the more active he got, the more I started cutting back on what I did and keeping it more local. So I moved into smaller, higher-paying jobs, which allowed me to work very short hours and still make the same amount of money," Gary recalled. "But, again, there was more hustling involved, there was more searching for the work involved."

Gary started to have second thoughts about the self-employed life. "Even though I made pretty good money, it's always very stressful," he said. "It was—you always had to wonder whether or not you were going to make it through the next year. How long was it going to be before you just couldn't find work? How long was I going to keep getting lucky?"

Making the situation even more urgent was Gary's sense that he was supposed to provide some sort of livelihood, a future career, for his son Philip, who was getting older. Gary himself grew up in a fragmented family—he never knew his father, and his mother overdosed and lost her children to foster care for a few years before straightening out, remarrying, and calling them back home as teenagers. "I'm trying to break the cycle and start being normal from here on," he said matter-of-factly. "We do our best to ignore the past and try to act like a family." Even though his own inheritance never included one, Gary considered a vocation among the most important gifts he could give his son.

"I felt like I wanted to have something more structured for him when he got older," Gary explained. "Something that I might be able to offer to him other than just being a grunt construction worker. And that's not what I wanted to give him, you know." Instead, Gary wanted "to be able to offer him a job and offer him a future." He noted that he was not trying to dictate what his son did for a living necessarily, but that for him, leaving the legacy of a trade was part of good fathering. "Of course, everybody wants their kid to go to college and get their own future and do what their dream job is, but if for some reason that didn't play out, I wanted to make sure that I was in a position where I could offer him a position."

So Gary joined a firm as its second-in-command, an "established, solid company." He took a pay cut, and the hours were longer, but the money was guaranteed, and "somebody else [had] the stress of running the business." He thought he had made a good bet. "It was a young company with major, massive potential. So I felt like there was nothing to do but grow from where we were, and we were growing—growing rapidly in our supply of work, in the number of employees and everything, the size of contracts, we were, we were growing. I had no intentions of leaving. I thought I had found the last job I would ever have."

His future, and that of his son, was ensured, Gary thought. "I felt like I had nowhere to go but up in that company. I mean the only person above was the owner, so there was nothing but expansion. At least, that's what I thought." With a glad heart, Gary left behind the tools of his self-employment as if scuttling a ship he would never have to board again: he sold off all of his equipment and vehicles, finished his contracts, and let go of his old client roster.

For a while, business was good. "We were making great money. We were—our reputation was growing really fast. We were doing amazing work and the company was really functioning well," Gary recalled. "Things seemed to be good, and I know what kind of money we were bringing in because I saw it, I was the one that handled the contracts and collected a lot of the money personally, so I know what we were making."

Then, without warning, the guillotine fell. "I showed up to work one day and they told me that they were laying me off along with all of my crew and the other managers in the company," Gary remembered, in a wondering tone, still stunned many months later. "Just blindsided us. We had no idea."

We would not be surprised if Gary reported feeling betrayed by this experience, given that business was going well, his surprise and shock at the layoff, and the high stakes—the future he wished for his son—involved. And indeed, the emotional wallop was mighty. "It was devastating," he said, his voice hollow. "I was crushed. Oh God," he added, remembering.

But strangely, perhaps, Gary refuses to blame the company or its owner. Instead, when things went woefully awry, it was ultimately his fault. "I had spent so much of my working life depending on nobody but myself to find the work, and to make the money and to handle everything; my work was—everything was based on me, my performance. My hustle, everything was based on me," Gary emphasized. "I went to them and put my livelihood and my career in their hands and all at once it hit me: it was the biggest mistake I ever made."

STANCES OF OBLIGATION AND THE ONE-WAY HONOR SYSTEM

People adopt particular stances toward obligation, viewpoints that then serve to define a certain vision of the good, helping to shape what responsibilities they can even see and what is at stake in their fulfillment. When we see obligation through the lens of duty, like Gary, we have a more expansive definition of our mandate, and the stakes are high: either stepping up to our responsibilities or forsaking them. But when we see it through the lens of independence, we generally define obligation more narrowly, and the stakes shift dramatically: what is "good" is autonomy, self-reliance, and freedom as opposed to our vulnerability to others. These two stances predominated among people in insecure work, shaping what they see as their own obligations as well as those of their employers. (A third stance, pragmatism, captured the inclination of the stably employed to settle, defining obligation as endurance despite imperfection, and "the good" as being "realistic" about the flaws of others versus indulging a naïve narcissism.) Table 2.1 demonstrates the interplay of constancy and compromise that characterizes these stances, as explained in the last chapter.

Most people employed in insecure work, for example, view their own obligations at work from the stance of duty, in which they continue to have numerous responsibilities that they refuse to desert, while they adopt a different moral measure for their employers—one prescribing independence from fallible others—to evaluate their thin accountability.

Institutionalized in our social and economic milieus, such as the workplace, the courts, the military, religious institutions, consumer culture, and the like, these stances serve as ethical and emotional roadmaps to which people turn as they talk about when to leave and when to stay. Not infrequently, however, people discover that their own preferred stances are at odds with those permeating their surroundings, the mismatch generating powerful anguish. This book is in part a chronicle of how people manage the gaps between their own stances and those of the settings in which they find themselves.

Table 2.1 STANCES OF COMMITMENT

		Constancy	
		Low	High
	Low	**Independence**	**Duty**
Compromise	High		**Pragmatism**

THE LONELINESS OF BLAME

Asked directly if he felt betrayed by the company, Gary replies, "Absolutely."
But he quickly expands on his apportionment of blame. "I place it on myself
for letting—for allowing myself to get blindsided that way. I never should
have let my guard down. I never should have put my livelihood in somebody else's hands. I shouldn't have done that," he maintains. "But, of
course, I do blame them for not structuring things well and not controlling
the money well. So it's their fault the company fell apart, but it was my fault
for being in the position in the first place."

Gary doesn't take all the blame, as he concedes that the company should
have been managed better. But the offhand way in which he mentions that
"of course" they should have, when contrasted with his lengthy discourse
on "the biggest mistake [he] ever made," demonstrates the emphasis he
places here. And where he distributes the blame gives us a sense of the expectations he maintains for his employer and for himself, expectations
stemming from an acute sense of his own duty.

How do the expectations that we carry, for ourselves and for others,
matter? First and foremost, they tell us about how we see the world or-
dered in a certain way. Expectations are like coloring books as opposed to
blank canvases; they create empty shapes that wait to be filled in. When
people hold themselves totally responsible for what are in fact widespread
social trends, when they completely absolve their employers for what are in
fact tactics that are hardly inevitable or even proven to work, they invoke
those prefabricated shapes that demand narratives of personal accountability and fill them in with their own stories.

Yet expectations don't just reflect something deeper about the way
we see the world; they also *do* something to us. Expectations work to
shape our emotions, generating what we feel and also restricting what
we are allowed to feel. Expectations tell us who exceeded their obligations and who fell short, and thus about whom we might feel resentful,
grateful, or impressed. Expectations produce anger, guilt, or grief, and
they give those emotions a certain target. With Gary, that target was
himself.

"I could have turned the job down," Gary explained, in self-reproof. "I
had no reason to take the job. I wasn't doing bad. I had no reason to take
that job, other than I wanted to make things . . . you know, again, I justify
it as it was trying to make things better for him [the son]." For a second, he
steps out of himself to criticize his narrative for "justifying" the move, as if
his reasons were mere rationalizations. How was the layoff his fault, when
he was doing what he thought he should in order to provide a better future

for his son? "I thought in some twisted way that I was [making things better for my son] at the time. I thought I was going to make a more stable environment, you know. And I was wrong, you know, but that—that was my fault. I shouldn't have done it." Despite the best of intentions, according to Gary he was to blame for his lack of due diligence, his flawed market analysis.

The stakes of his recent layoff could not have been higher, from Gary's perspective. Since the layoff was his fault, so too are its consequences. The loss goes to his very heart: his inability to provide more for Phil in his teenage years is emotionally crippling. "Yeah, my son is now fifteen years old," Gary said, heavily. He sighed. "He'll be graduating high school soon." He paused, and then continued: "I would hope—I had hoped at this point that I'd be able to buy him a car as a graduation present. I had hoped that I'd have more to offer him in the way of funding his further education." He stopped short. "And I don't."

Without the buoyancy of a legacy from Gary, his son has only his own wits to rely upon, Gary mourned. "What most parents hope to do is provide for their kids better than they were provided for. Especially in situations of lower-class people. I think it's the whole goal is to get your kids out of that hole that you live in. And to be able to basically lay that path out for them. But now I can't." The impact of his layoff was severe, especially in an insecure economy; it severed Phil from Gary's protection as he embarked on his own trajectory. "Now, it's really solely dependent on him making the right choices and the right decisions in his life. And, if he doesn't, there's not much I can do for him."

Gary calls this helplessness his greatest regret, as he faces alone the steep emotional repercussions of seeing it as his own failure. "That bothers me worse than anything," he said, simply. "I've cried at night about it." It's not betrayal that he feels but a dreadful, powerful sorrow.

THE NEOLIBERAL SELF: HEROES OF THEIR OWN LIVES

Gary's story is a particularly modern tragedy, with the hero led inexorably to his downfall step by honorable step, carefully making a path through a thicket of precarious work, constrained opportunity for "lower-class" men, and involved fatherhood. His ardent, well-intentioned beliefs and practices come together in an insecure age to form a sort of doomed nobility. But both the nobility and its doom are rooted in his expectations of self and others, produced in part by the social, economic, and political pressures that impinge upon him and others like him.[16]

In his story, Gary calls upon some of the more foundational moral principles in the United States—personal responsibility, self-sufficiency, and
independence, themes with particular resonance now, in a neoliberal era
celebrating individualism and autonomy. Yet Gary is not just an unattached
cowboy; he is also dedicated to caring for others, staying involved, protecting his son from his own choices. His moral position invokes broad cultural
ideals, guided by a stance of duty. At the same time, his experiences seem
patently unfair. He joined the company, taking a pay cut and an increase in
hours, in order to do right by his son in an uncertain economy. He committed to the company, making no plans to leave and in fact jettisoning the
tools and contacts that might have provided an escape route. The company
laid him off without warning, even though they were "making great money
and . . . doing amazing work."

Anger, outrage, indignation would surely be reasonable in this situation,
even if we do not have his employer's perspective on the facts of the matter.
We see the tiniest glimpses in Gary's narrative, in words like "blindsided,"
which invoke an unforeseen attack, in the clipped and immediate way he
answers "absolutely" to the question about betrayal, or in the pauses sprin-
kled throughout his interview at key moments, such as when he talks about
how he was wrong—even "twisted"—in his belief that the company would
offer a stable environment.

But Gary also keeps a firm hold on his moral compass, which in turn relies
upon a vision of a self almost wholly responsible for its successes as well as its
failures. While his stance of duty is a noble one, it also leads to the intense disappointment and shame that plague him now. His worldview forces Gary to
focus the blame on himself and, in turn, inspires and elicits different kinds of
feelings: not anger but shame, not indignation but grief, not outrage but sorrow.

Expectations thus act as a sieve for emotions deemed valid or appropriate, a screen of available meanings through which feelings must pass in
order to be fully recognized and expressed. Low expectations for employers
and high ones for workers shape the emotions that people are allowed to
feel about the new ways of working, about workplace insecurity and the
ascendance of flexibility in an era in which workers are responsible for their
own careers, their own employability, and their own risks.

AFTER THE FALL: LOOKING ANYWHERE BUT AT THE
EMPLOYER

Nowhere is this emotional shaping more evident than among those who have
been laid off. Like Gary, however, for most who had lost their jobs,

their employers were not the target for their angry feelings. Laid-off people generally tried to maintain very low expectations for work, resigning themselves to "the way things are today." Like Gary, they considered their layoffs to be their own fault, or else they viewed them as opportunities to move on or regarded them with resignation or defiance. These were feelings that were apparently legitimate for them to have, ones they simply declared or proclaimed, ones that in our conversations they did not try to hide or suppress.[17]

Self-Blame

As we have seen with Gary's example, many laid-off people blame themselves for losing their job. Studies suggest that such self-blame is common, with the exception of those laid off from large firms en masse; layoffs can lead to depression, drinking, and drug-use problems. People report, wistfully or tragically, that they should not have taken that job in the first place. They argue that they should have come to the job with better training or education. They tell themselves they should not have complained about a problem or coworker.[18]

Resignation

Behind Gary's offhand characterization of his employer's fault lies an assumption about how little constancy we can expect from companies, and many of the laid-off people to whom I spoke adopted a resigned attitude when describing the limits of commitment in the workplace. Martha had been a high-powered marketing executive before she was let go from her job because, she says, her boss wanted to give it to a woman with whom he was having an affair. Even as she muses in retrospect that she should have sued to get her job back, she shrugs her shoulders.

> Well, it's a very competitive corporate environment. Few people were promoted, but we were also hired at the top of the pyramid, so there was no place to go. It wasn't like the company was expanding. . . . They would reshuffle and they'd save money. And if they would want to make a change then they just shuffled the deck and people are let go. And that's okay, they didn't care—they're there to make money, not there to hear complaints or problems.

Martha is now a single mother cobbling together a meager living from part-time retail service work despite her college degree and corporate experience, and her income is a fraction of what it once was. Still, as she describes the corporate culture she once knew, it is clear from her words— "and that's okay, they didn't care"—that she does not harbor any expectations of commitment on the part of her employer, or perhaps that she does not consider any resentment justified. The fact that they are "there to make money" absolves the company of any other duty, including to their employees.

In fact, she said:

> I think business bends over backwards to help people do their job well, or to give them reasonable doubt, because they don't want lawsuits. But if you don't have the talent for that job they have to let people—you've got to find something you're good at.

Embracing and deploying market logic, Martha is so understanding of the employer's problems—lawsuits, uneven personnel—that she even adopts their perspective, before readjusting her language to adopt the persona of the jobseeker: "You've got to find something you're good at."

Anticipation

People also talk about layoffs, surprisingly perhaps, as an opportunity for change they are glad to take, sounding as if they greet the next stage with some eagerness. Katherine, a financial services officer, considered getting let go a chance to grow. "Well, I would say everything happens for a reason, and the reason you got laid off is there's another opportunity out there for you," she maintained. In the meantime, the layoff was not personal, her managers were still her friends, and she was hoping for a new prospect soon.

Sarah, a white married woman, had been looking for a job when Carey, the director at her son's preschool, recommended that she try working for Carey's father's small business. Many years later, the business contracted, and Carey apparently encouraged her father to lay Sarah off. Sarah struggles today without a job, worrying about making her mortgage payments so her children will have a stable home. Nonetheless, Sarah took pains to tell me, she appreciated Carey urging her father to let Sarah go, since she had been there too long and wasn't "moving on."

> At one point, Grant [Carey's father] said to me, based on his daughter's urging, which actually was great, he said, "You know, I would never say I need to let you

go." But his daughter Carey said, "You know, Dad, you're not doing her any favors." Which I realized he wasn't. I mean the biggest favor was I had a paycheck coming every two weeks. But the other favor was I wasn't moving on. So, I said I understood.

Even though her employer had assured her, "I would never say I need to let you go," Sarah was laid off thanks to Carey's urging, we learn. Sarah protests that the daughter's intervention "actually was great"—the "actually" doing some discursive work to demonstrate that she recognizes that the daughter's advice sounds cold-hearted—and she says, "I realized [the boss] wasn't doing [me] any favors" by keeping her on, both statements that attest to her full acquiescence to her losing her job.

At the time of her layoff, she had been trying out two other money-making ideas in her free time, small-scale investing in the stock market and pursuing a dream of becoming a life coach; neither of these options had panned out, and instead all the money she spent on training seminars had been for naught. Nonetheless, her layoff was a new opportunity, she said. "In some respects, [after the layoff] I felt like, 'Wow, now I can step on the dock or on the boat.' And just concentrate on one thing," she recalled. "So, [losing my job] wasn't betrayal. It was like, 'Wow, this is a great opportunity.'"

Defiance

Christina was a nurse who left the hospital to work in home health care, providing private one-on-one care for ten years. When she came back to the hospital, she found medical care had become almost unrecognizable, with overwhelming caseloads and much needier patients. When clashes with her supervisor ended that job, she did not return to hospitals again. It just wasn't worth it, she said. There was no place anymore for the kind of nursing care she was trained to offer—compassionate, time-consuming, emotionally connecting with patients.

"I had too many responsibilities. It was not safe," Christina asserted. "And I was torn, because I couldn't be the compassionate nurse that I wanted to be when I had a lot of responsibilities. And it was very difficult for me to decide what was most important." She went into hospice care, then to a telephonic nursing facility, each experience a dehumanizing encounter with the contemporary organization of medicine, with its emphasis on efficiency, rationalization, and reimbursable task-oriented nursing. While leaving these jobs involuntarily was initially upsetting, in each case, Christina said, she wouldn't want to have continued working there anyway.

Christina's defiance, while critical, is different from anger or feeling be-trayed, from holding the employer accountable in any way; instead, the emotional focus is on moving on, with a sort of figurative head toss. Defi-ance is a way to deny psychological power to those earlier, hurtful experi-ences, by denying their meaning and, ultimately, by reducing their ultimate importance. Now, Christina is back delivering home health care in a one-on-one setting and, she reports, she is grateful.

WHEN EMOTIONS DON'T FOLLOW THE RULES

Sometimes, however, our feelings are not convenient, in that they do not fit well with prevailing ideas about what we owe each other. Our emotions are produced in part by our expectations of others and our sense of whether they have failed us or exceeded our hopes. Yet we also have a sense for whether those emotions are somehow justified, whether they are reasona-ble, whether we have any right to feel them given the dominant "feeling rules" that surround us. Sometimes the distance is greater between how we really feel and how we want to feel or think we are supposed to feel. These gaps widen when people are surrounded by current expectations—such as ascendant notions of flexibility and change—that violate some different, prior set of expectations—such as those of workplace commitment and loyalty.[19]

We come, then, to a final point about expectations: not only do they re-flect our inner worldviews, not only do they shape the emotions we feel, but they also generate how we feel about how we feel. We can feel angry about losing our job, but if we do not feel justified in that anger—say, be-cause we are surrounded by an ethos of independence—we may be ashamed or guilty about our feelings. These are cultural perceptions, moments when we use our inner antennae to ascertain how we *should* feel according to the operant rules and how that compares to how we actually feel. Are our ex-pectations of others widely shared in our current milieu, or, perhaps, do they reflect where we "came from," either a different time (an earlier, dis-credited age) or a different place (a rural community or a country of origin)? Sociologist Candace Clark dubbed this conflict "emotional dissonance," like "cognitive dissonance," a collision not of ideas but instead of feelings.[20]

We can be proud or sheepish or dismayed or rebellious—we have feel-ings—about our own feelings. These meta-feelings offer a powerful ac-count of individuals embedded in their environment, for it is a measure of the distance between how they feels and how they feel they ought to feel. Such feelings are the emotional expression of our relative ease with the prevalent worldviews that surround us, like the expansion joints that allow bridges to expand or contract with the prevailing weather.[21]

We can see and hear emotional dissonance when people express it. Those who have experienced job insecurity use different strategies to corral their feelings into what they think are their appropriate shape and intensity: they use "emotion work" to manage their feelings; they deploy cautionary tales to generate the appropriate attitude; and they invoke a mythic past to transform their disappointment into nostalgia. The feelings we have about our feelings offer us a window into the processes by which we yank and push and prod our emotions into submission, into being in line with where they ought to be, according to what we perceive of the feeling rules around us.

Emotion Work

Felicia, who worked for the same company for sixteen years before she was laid off, said her job was great until the owner's son took over. At that point "it became more of a lump-more-jobs-onto-fewer-people kind of a place," she said, describing a process by which the work was rationalized, sped-up, and deskilled. Ultimately, she ended up replaced by "cheaper labor." She was angry when it first happened, but then realized she didn't want to work there anyway.[22]

> Well, I knew at that point it kind of sucked, because there were several other people there who had worked for the company for that long and made good money and they were out, so it's not like it was only me. And it was wearing on my soul working there at that point too.
>
> It was time to move on because [*laughs*] yes, I was angry. [*Laughs.*] I hate to say no. Yeah, but at the same time, you know, sometimes it's best to know when things are done. You know what I mean? And nobody was happy there anymore, so, and a huge part of my life was trying to be happy.

In this passage, Felicia refuses to accept the stigma of the layoff—"It's not like it was only me"—and calls upon anticipation language, suggesting that it was time to move on, as well as invoking some defiance about not wanting to work there anyway. But feelings she regards as less legitimate break into her narrative, as she admits to being angry right in the middle of her reasoning. Her laughter is her unspoken acknowledgment that her emotional truth had not yet been corralled by her cognitive efforts. Yet she comes to some resolution about "being happy" and the work involved in that: "A huge part of my life was trying to be happy."

Witness the significant emotion work in Felicia's account, the wrenching steps she takes to get to the one-way honor system. She may have felt angry, but she is forcibly, almost consciously putting that aside as not helpful to her capacity to function, to train for another job, to look for work. Her feelings about her feelings—she's not necessarily embarrassed about her anger, but she is a little impatient with it—tell us about the relationship between how she *really* feels and the feeling rules she perceives. We may not accept that she is now "happy"—indeed, she is clearly even now a little angry—but we must take note of how she marshals her inner resources to turn down the intensity of her feelings so that she can function in the way she wants, or perhaps the way she must. In doing so, we can see the structural vise that grips those who are thrown aside in the postindustrial economy, and the emotional rules that prevail, making some feelings more available than others: the need to move on, to be upbeat and positive for one's own mental health as well as one's employability, juxtaposed with the betrayal, the rupture of relationships and self-worth at work, that comes with an involuntary departure from a job.

Cautionary Tales

Lily, a white divorced mother, supported her daughter on the pay she earned as a clerk in a large architecture firm. The job had gotten a lot more demanding of late, involving 20 percent more hours in mandatory overtime, she said. "They expect a lot more out of you these days than they used to. Because so many firms have cut back; my firm, too, cut back a couple of years ago. So, they've distributed that job among other people, split it up into little pieces and give everybody a little piece. So they have even more to do." The memory raised the constant specter of losing her position, and acted as a disciplinary force, eliciting her own dedication in the absence of any on the part of her employer. People used such stories as cautionary tales, to mold their own feelings so that they could do what was required to stay on.

Lily hated her job, she said, because the professionals she worked for were arrogant and peremptory. Yet cautionary tales she told herself about the pervasiveness of insecurity kept her from "griping," she said. Asked if she was afraid of losing her job just then, she at first replied, "No, I'm not." Then she paused and thought again. "I don't know, anybody could right now."

> That's why I don't complain about the hours or the work or anything. Although it's tough—I mean I got up at five a.m.; I was at work at seven. I don't have to be

there until nine but I want to make sure I'm getting the shit done. You know, because what if I lose my job? I mean truly, I'm just two paychecks away from being on the street. Then I won't be able to help my kid at all. And what will I do? Because jobs are so hard to find, I mean, I don't make a huge salary right now—forty-eight thousand—but that's a hell of a lot more than some people in this town make . . . and a lot more than nothing. I wouldn't make that working at Wal-Mart or Kroger, you know. So, I'm trying my best to keep this job, you know.

Visions of what she would be otherwise —unemployed or working at Wal-Mart—kept her compliant to employer demands, generating the fear that inspired her to get there two hours early, to be a more-than-exemplary employee.

Nostalgia and Acquiescence

In addition to emotion work and cautionary tales, a third process visibly mustering the "right" feelings for insecurely employed people is the invocation of the mythic past. People often referred to memories of their parents or grandparents, media images, or other cultural portrayals of "the way it used to be." Commonly, people talked about job insecurity with a certain mournfulness, and a yearning for the "old days"; thus the culture of flexibility was made to align with the future, but not the past. Nostalgia served as a shoehorn for acquiescence, in which insecurity was framed as lamentable but inevitable.

Clark was a white man who had even sought out jobs with major companies at their headquarters in the hope of finding security, only to endure surprise layoffs when the companies suddenly contracted. He mourned the loss of stable careers like his father's:

My father who was at the same one job for twenty years and then another job for twenty-five years, I had been brought up during the whole thing in the fifties and sixties where you worked for one company or at most two companies for the rest of your life and the company took care of you. Of course, concurrently with that in the sixties, seventies, and eighties, this of course all started transitioning.

Now, Clark was rueful as he compared the past and the present: "There's not that kind of stability in the workplace anymore."

When recalling the mythic past, precarious workers imputed their own meanings to it, so that it came to stand for the community or for family feeling at work, rather than the employment that buttressed those goods, for example. Others even considered that the twenty-year career was not about employer obligations shored up by state policies and union battles but rather was the outgrowth of a perfect match between employer and employee. Katherine, who had adopted a matter-of-fact tone about her layoff, warmly recalled a ceremony honoring several employees for working twenty years for the company that she had just left. "I think that is great; I would love to get with—to actually be with a company that long," she said, adding, "I don't know if it is possible now." But when she thought about what their twenty years represented, she used language to emphasize the workers' personal feelings, rather than a particular way of organizing work that enables such endurance. "I just think it shows commitment and that you love your job, if you're with an organization for that long. You love your job and the people you work with in the company. I think it's great."

The nostalgia felt by people who have experienced insecurity is like the emotional footprint of a different cultural paradigm, one that values long-term commitment. Yet by linking that paradigm to a mythic past, precarious workers offer an implicit explanation for the insecure workplace, one that relies simply on the passage of time. They call upon the inevitability of insecurity to dilute any critique that might be embedded in an alternative vision of mutual commitment. Like emotion work and cautionary tales, invoking the mythic past serves to generate the "right" feelings and suppress or manage the "wrong" ones by turning them into reminiscence. The feelings they have about their feelings—their embarrassment, their bitterness, their triumph—serve as clues for the ongoing effort underlying their acquiescence.

THE GRIM ARITHMETIC OF INSECURITY

In Wallace Stegner's *Crossing to Safety*, Larry Morgan, the main character, is dismissed from a job just as his wife has given birth to their first child. He grits his teeth:

> I shut away the bitterness of rejection. I sweep into the back closet of my mind the uncertainties and anxieties that are going to be with us now until I can find something else, in this wasteland of the Depression, that will support us. I sweep them all into the closet along with my anger and wounded vanity and punctured self-esteem and the grim arithmetic I will soon be working on. I say to myself, self-consciously and pompously, . . . the words of the Anglo-Saxon stoic: "That I have borne, this can I bear also."[23]

The stoicism that Stegner's character adopts with such resolve lives on in Gary, Katherine, Felicia, and the others who endured layoffs. But the characters that populate this book, as opposed to Stegner's, steel themselves not just against past losses but future ones as well, in the containment of their expectations at work. For those immersed in the world of precarious work, the one-way honor system suggests the battle over insecurity in the workplace is already over, and for many workers it is already lost.

The expectations we have for what we owe each other, expectations that we carry with us into work, have serious emotional consequences in shaping how we feel, and how we feel about how we feel. Much of the pain, triumph, or resignation of living with insecurity is borne in the workplace, in the way we get discarded or discard others. Some might predict that the ubiquitous nature of layoffs would help victims begin to move beyond blaming themselves. Instead, we see that victims of layoffs engage in self-blame and a host of other tactics to renegotiate difficult feelings. Expectations serve as a sieve for the "right" feelings about work.

By reshaping, defusing, or distracting themselves from anger—with emotion work, cautionary tales, and the invocation of the mythic past—people take part in a process of structural change whose contours are neither inevitable nor necessarily desirable. While they protect themselves from their feelings, they also protect their employers, they suppress what could be an important impetus for collective action, and they further a privatization of risk that brings the burdens of globalization to rest on their shoulders. In doing so, people employed in precarious work shunt aside a potentially important resource for social change: their own antagonism.

If insecurity is inevitable, then the best we can do is to adapt to it. Yet why would those adaptations end at the workplace door? For people who bear witness to the end of employer commitment, the question is an urgent one: What does commitment mean in the rest of their lives? In the next chapters, we see how they answer that question differently, depending in part on what job insecurity portends for them, their adaptations at work seeping into their intimate lives like muddy floodwater across a threshold.

CHAPTER 3

☙

New Economy Winners
and the Moral Wall

Robin Galbraith was a frank, friendly woman with close-cropped hair and a wry smile, who narrated a buoyant trajectory for herself and her husband, Ian, in which Ian's varied and well-compensated business career led them all over the country. Sitting in the sunny atrium of her expansive and comfortable home, Robin told stories of her and Ian's careers, punctuated by her sardonic laugh, that exemplified all the potential of the new economy, rife with opportunity and the possibility of the perfect match between worker and work. Like others of similar advantage, Robin's stories took place amid a culture of frequent wooing by potential employers, in which reasonable people continually weighed the short- and long-term costs and benefits of staying in a job versus moving on. I was struck, however, by the stark contrast between work and home for Robin and others like her: at work, they talked about the constant search for the better prospect and the heralding of the culture of flexibility, independence, and change, but at home, they were sticking it out in enduring, long-term relationships. Why don't they see marriage and family as another place to keep searching for a better prospect, a place where independence and change are positives? Instead they talk about long-term marriages as sites where expectations should be managed, where career optimizing is replaced by personal satisficing, where compromise or even surrender reigns.

Robin exuded a kind of unpretentious-but-assured competence that reflected the fusion of her Midwestern childhood and elite schooling. Until she left a promising career in marketing to work part-time in her children's schools, she and Ian had both moved from job to job, changing about every five years, evaluating their options, seeking out ventures that would capitalize on their existing strengths and add new ones. Now ensconced in the Washington, DC, suburbs, the family was living comfortably off of their portfolio while Ian tried his hand at a local start-up. Up here at this stratospheric level of advantage, "insecurity" looked more like "flexibility," and not just for the employer; like their peers, Robin and Ian reaped great benefits from being the ones whom companies try to lure away.[1]

These affluent, well-educated workers sound a different note than the workers we heard in the last chapter. What they "owe" the employer is their great dedication, best performance, and long work hours, but not their longevity, such workers maintain. They adopt an independent stance toward their obligation at work, one that makes it both inevitable and right that they should get the best deal for themselves that they can. For some, the primary consideration is compensation, but for many, the measure of a job does not stop there. Instead, work should offer a close fit between "job" and "self," including their particular skills and talents; in other words, work should be a calling. For these workers, one's career path can be as fluid as water and should be as personal as a fingerprint. If the "losers" of the new economy use the language of choice to restrain themselves from blaming others when insecurity descends, the "winners" use the language of choice to explain their own mobility when flexibility beckons.

But while workers like Robin and Ian exhibit little regret about moving from company to company in a quest for the best match of self to job, many of them are in long-term intimate relationships lasting twenty years or more. Like many advantaged couples, for whom divorce rates have been declining for decades to levels not seen since the 1960s, the ceaseless quest for "something better" that animates their behavior in the marketplace of jobs appears to be absent in their intimate lives. The very longevity of their relationships surely requires compromise and, to some degree, a surrender of the notion that there's a better option out there—the very same notion that lures them from job to job. Given their paeans to the perfect match at work, then, how do they manage to get beyond the idea of the perfect match at home?[2]

I found that Robin and others like her adopt a stance of independence toward their obligations at work but one of pragmatism toward their intimate life. At the same time, they use the language of choice to make moral sense of their actions in both realms—they choose to leave at work, while at home they choose to stay. They ignore or suppress the destabilizing implications of the language of choice in their intimate lives, and yet they rely heavily on that language to explain and motivate their mobility at work.

They thus call upon a vision of personal freedom to describe what are actually pragmatic practices in their intimate lives, which in all likelihood involve some concessions to endurance over individual desire. Given their own sense of self-efficacy, we might call their overall strategy "choosing."

EMBRACING INSECURITY

While job insecurity affects US workers at all levels, the significance of these trends for managers and professionals is entirely different than it is for lower-skilled workers. Changes in work since the mid-1970s led elite employees to increase their hours, to be sure, but they also increased their incomes and managed to keep their benefits over this time, and they report much higher job satisfaction. With the intensification of their work, then, has come increased reward. These benefits derive in part from their ability to take advantage of more flexible labor markets and switch firms; rather than insecure, it might be more apt to call their work itinerant.[3]

From Robin's perspective, as long as your particular combination of skills is valued, she said, there are always companies looking to lure you away. The family had moved four times, spending five to six years in each place, with each move precipitated by calls from headhunters luring Ian to new horizons. She remembered a recruiting dinner at a New York investment bank where the stakes were put rather baldly.

> They had the seating arrangement, there were like six of us. And the guy who would be his boss sits down next to me. And he knows that Ian is interested in the job and he doesn't know anything about me. He's like all over me trying to get me to be really interested in the job. And he goes—and I'm being very candid because I wouldn't want you to think—I don't really talk about this stuff. He was like, "Doesn't your husband want to make a lot of money?"

Although Robin thought this was the ultimate in tacky overtures, the story illustrates the constant courting that keeps a sense of a quest for something better eternally present at the workplace. Recall Holly's observation, from the introduction, that "the phone's always ringing with the headhunter, you know, waving money."

Advantaged workers feel like they enjoy the luxury of choosing—their jobs, their spouses, much of the contours of their lives. By invoking the language of choice, of course, these advantaged workers call upon a potent neoliberal ideology of autonomy and independence, one that hides the ways in which choosing is structured by existing inequalities. Their education and resources allow them and their families access to jobs and opportunities that are not available to others, to be sure. In addition, their financial where-withal allows them inordinate freedoms, freedom of where to live or send their children to school, as well as freedom from anxiety about supporting themselves or their loved ones—no small liberty, when we consider the sometimes desperate straits of those in the previous chapter. At the same time, however, "choosing" is itself vastly constrained, even at this level. The choices of advantaged workers are profoundly limited to the selection at hand, generated by powerful economic and political institutions. Such workers would be hard-pressed not to devote themselves entirely to a highly intensive job, for example, one that offered pecuniary rewards, to be sure, but that would not allow a partial commitment. Furthermore, these work-ers would find it difficult to divide their labor at home more equally. They don a mantle of "choosing," but even for these workers, what they can choose is limited, and they are not very free *not* to choose.

Robin had had her own meteoric rise in marketing, for example, but abandoned it after she had her second child; she laughed when she recalled the traditional southern CEO she was working for at the time and how he blanched when she asked him to accommodate her need to breastfeed. Her account reveals as much about her own easygoing practicality as it does about facing sexism at the office. "When I had my second child, I said, 'You know, we've got to get electrical outlets in the bathroom so women can pump'," Robin recalled. "I thought he was going to die. A good guy, very nice man, but he used to take these trips and he would only invite men and stuff like that, it was funny." The timing of the arrival of children coincided with Ian's career taking off, and as they started moving from place to place in service to his professional trajectory, they agreed that she would put her own career on the back burner, working part-time or episodically and hand-ling children and moving needs. While the details of this story may be unique, its very familiarity speaks to the demands of intensive work at the top and gendered understandings of who belongs there, bringing a little more nuance to the language of "choice."[4]

For advantaged itinerant workers, as we have seen for others, expecta-tions of job security are low. Belle's husband had worked for the same em-ployer for more than a decade, moving several times at their behest, but that did not mean they owed him anything more than a paycheck and two weeks' notice, she said. "I know he's been with the company for a long time—he's had a job for thirteen years. That's what his benefit is. I don't necessarily feel like they owe him anything. I think he works for what he gets and it works itself out. He's been with the company all this time, if we were to get a severance package or an option to leave, or if they let go of him, I don't know that they owe him any longer than that," Belle maintained. "It is what it is."

What makes these workers different, however, is that not only do they expect little job security, they also do not seem to wish for it. Their embrace of insecurity is informed by their sense of themselves as its beneficiaries. As Alexis recalled about their time overseas, "After the second year—it was a two-year commitment—it was kind of like every six months that conversation would take place. 'What do you want to do? Do you want to stay? Do you want to go? We would love to keep you.'" Adopting a narrative of personal responsibility for their own particular trajectories, these workers are careful to make the distinction between their dedication to achieving good results, which is one dimension of work commitment, and their decision to remain in a particular job over time. We might consider them high-performance, low-loyalty workers.[5]

Not all of the workers who talk this way are the elite managers being groomed for CEO-level jobs or their spouses. More midlevel white-collar professionals sometimes absorb and celebrate this narrative. Katherine, a financial services officer and a white mother of two, had recently been let go at work. She had been laid off from her job before, Katherine told me as we sat in a roadside café at midmorning talking over the noise of the television and espresso machine. As a long-time professional, she knew how it worked. You do not burn any bridges. You stay friendly with people; you keep a good attitude. You try and learn from every manager you have, you are grateful for new opportunities, and most of all, you keep looking. "You have to keep in touch with your managers; it's only going to benefit you," she said. "Plus, on a friendship basis, I have a lot of friends and I like keeping my friends."

Despite the fact that she "likes keeping friends," loyalty at work is not part of Katherine's mental landscape. Of course, she does profess to having a very strong work ethic, thanks to her father: "Yeah, he raised me to be a hard worker. Don't call out of work, you show up for work every day unless there's four feet of snow on the ground. That kind of instills in you . . . it's only helped me." But a few years back she left a family firm where she was employed—indeed, where she would still have a job if she had not moved on. "I know that when I was there I was just really happy; I loved my job," she remembered. "I loved the company, the owner—I mean, he's in his nineties and he'd come in the office and give me a hug. Family-oriented."

Two years ago, she was lured away by a larger, rival firm that offered $10,000 more in pay and the chance to learn new skills; she jumped ship. Today, despite the first owner's hugs, despite getting fired from the second company, she said she had no regrets. "If I hadn't gone here I wouldn't have gotten some of the skills I have now, in [my new] field," she said. "So, I don't have regrets because I know things happen for a reason," she said. Similarly, she thought good employers were those who offered recognition, appreciation, and respect, but not necessarily security. "I've been laid off several times in my life, and I've learned it's nothing against me personally. It's usually because of budgets or loss of contracts, and you can't burn your bridges," she said. With her careful rationality, her studied optimism, Katherine embodies the independent approach to work, where nobody is supposed to expect much loyalty and so nobody is supposed to get too upset.

Similarly, Florence, a white divorced retail manager, was careful to define the limits of what she owed her employer. "I feel like I owe my job the best I can give them in terms of the knowledge that I have," she said. At the same time, she noted, "I feel like I don't believe anymore—in this world of the way corporations treat their employees—that I necessarily owe my job a sense of loyalty. I think that I'm not the only person who says that," she added, ruefully. "That's really what I feel like I owe my job: is to do the best job I can when I'm there. But above and beyond that, I don't think I owe them anything else." She laughed shortly.

While more advantaged itinerant workers might agree, Florence also demonstrates a truth about her own cultural landscape in her slight discomfort in saying so out loud. Florence's laugh acts a signal, working as a sort of nonverbal acknowledgment that her language—when she says "above and beyond that, I don't think I owe them anything else"—sounded a bit tough or cold, not entirely legitimate for her. Florence's laugh tells us that in her world, this posture is still morally ambiguous, still a step forward across a new ethical frontier.

In contrast, Mary, a physical therapist married to an information technology professional, talked about job hopping as the de facto expectation of the tumbleweed society. With her husband and his friends, all in the same field, "the average is three to five years and then . . . it's really [fast] and you never plan on just staying," Mary said. "You do what's in front of you. And until this [recession] usually they were moving of their own accord. Moving up, you know, that's how you moved up. You didn't get promoted within." For high-performance, low-loyalty workers, particularly elite professionals and those working in fields dominated by external labor markets, the all-important work ethic applied to their dedication *on* the job, but not necessarily *to* the job.[6]

Most of those who embrace insecurity at work in this way are, not surprisingly, those who gain the most from it, those highly skilled, highly paid workers who benefit from companies' increasing propensity to hire from without. In one recent study, scholars asked workers who were largely satisfied with their jobs what aspect of their jobs mattered the most to them. Workers up to the level of middle managers tended to mention "job security" among their top five factors, while those respondents at the executive management level omitted it entirely. The most advantaged workers miss the social contract the least, welcoming the mantle of individual responsibility for their own career trajectories because they profit from it. As the heirs of the new insecurity, they are also its emissaries.[7]

LABOR AS A CALLING: AUTHENTIC WORK FROM IRON CAGE TO SILICON CHIP

In his classic *The Protestant Ethic and Spirit of Capitalism*, Max Weber argued that the Puritans grafted the religious idea of one's "calling" onto work, and in so doing produced the powerful notion of "labor as a calling," a concept permeating American culture. They suffused work with religious significance and financial success with divinity, as in the idea of predestination, through which God acknowledged the "elect," or those who would be saved. Weber argued that the ensuing equations trapped men in an iron cage, in which ideas such as the religious significance of work and the ensuing "care for external goods" forced them to participate in a system of overweening commitment to work. Yet the twin poles of Weber's argument—the notion of labor as a calling and the work ethic—have since pulled postindustrial workers in opposite directions in terms of their commitment. We can see this tug of war in the way these high-performance, low-loyalty workers talk about work.

On the one hand, the work ethic is a profound demonstration of commitment and focus that workers bring to their labor, and, as we have seen, it is still a powerfully salient evocation of honor, not just "the ghost of dead religious beliefs." By calling on duty, the work ethic summons ideals of longevity, reliability, and dedication. On the other hand, the notion of "labor as a calling" today involves a well-developed sense of the self, to which a particular occupation must cleave. Such notions sometimes act to dislodge people from their existing situations, invoking not so much duty as independence as they embark on a peripatetic quest for their own ideal. Even as the work ethic requires your unwavering dedication to the job, then, if labor is a calling, you leave jobs in search of a better fit.

In this tug of war, the contemporary vision of the changing self is part of what pulls workers from their jobs. While a settled adult self used to be one of the accomplishments of maturity, achieved when one crossed the threshold from childhood, the contemporary self—for those who still believe that the self exists—is more like a chain of projects, a series of linked but discrete growth phases. In this vision, we are always growing, always evolving. The pursuit of labor as a calling, then, may involve less a lifelong career than a string of possibly unrelated opportunities that express a particular self's changing "true" interests. The high-performance, low-loyalty approach to work reflects both of these ideas at once, the work ethic as the reflection of honor through duty, and continually changing work as a reflection of the primacy of independence. In retooling the work ethic in this way, high-performance, low-loyalty workers transform themselves into the flexible, mobile, dedicated employees ideally suited to the new economy.[8]

Weber's iron cage referred to the pursuit of material possessions, which he disparaged as an "economic compulsion," but a cage is not quite the right image for the very plasticity of the economic system, with its customized demands, that surrounds us today. The high-performance, low-loyalty workers seem to define as admirable those who give 200 percent *and* who know when to leave for a better match; by marrying the duty of working to the independence of the worker, insecurity culture hews closely, and relentlessly, to each person. Unmediated by otherworldly meaning, the new ways of organizing work act less like a cage and more like an implanted silicon chip—unique, customized, and adhering to the individual from within.

THE QUEST FOR THE PERFECT MATCH: EXCAVATING THE SELF FOR WORK

Ian was a successful executive who had worked in many different areas of business, from marketing to finance to business development. When she narrates their story, Robin calls attention to how their moves tapped into his constant search for a better fit. "He was a partner with [a high-profile investment bank], and he had been with them for a while, but, again, he's a Renaissance guy, he was tired and wanted to do something on his own," she said.

At one point when he was thinking about leaving a job, he visited an executive search firm that gave him a battery of tests to ascertain his best career choice.

> Yes, he went to—there's a company in New York that helps you figure out what you're good at. And so given that he has been kind of restless he went to this place and they did all these tests. . . . They will say you are a very good whatever and here are your interests. And of course, as we all know, if you can marry your abilities and your interests, you are going to be much happier. So he did this

thing, and the problem for him is that he has so many interests. Basically, what they said to him was, "You're going to have to follow certain things and then maybe other interests will have to be outside."

The very range and variety of his interests flummoxed the testers, Robin recalled.

These kinds of tests embody all the promise of the new economy for these workers, whereby work is supposed to reflect their particular skills and passions (with the onus on the individual to get a different job if it does not). Labor as a calling rests upon what we might consider a quest, akin to that for a soul mate or the perfect match in love.

That quest rests on three central ideas: the notion that we each have a unique inner self with particular wants and needs (that can change over time), that one's job (like one's intimate partner) should be as good a fit to that self as possible, and that there are a number of jobs (or people) available whom we might try out for this match. As in love, the first task in pursuing the quest is to know our selves well, to know what we prioritize so that we can achieve the best match. The battery of examinations that Ian took, the personality exercises that are sometimes part of the orientation or hiring process in a new job, the tests in the back of the perennial job-search bestseller *What Color Is Your Parachute?*—these are all about helping people locate their interests and abilities, to reveal their true selves on the path to finding personally meaningful work.[9]

While the notion of labor as a calling has been around for more than a century, what is new is its tethering to the itinerant work trajectories of advantaged workers. Scholars have documented the "portfolio career," in which any of multiple interests—expressed at work, in volunteer jobs, or in hobbies—may form the basis of a career change. For some of the most advantaged, interests fan out before them, beckoning them to make a decision not just once but several times; the quest is perennial at work. They often get to choose from among these interests, but they must excavate the selves to which the jobs must fit.[10]

THE MORAL WALL: KEEPING INSECURITY CORRALLED

Many affluent, elite professionals embrace insecurity culture at work as the conduit to the flexibility they prize and the opportunities they enjoy, and their narratives of independence mesh well with the reigning ethos of insecurity culture, that of a privatized, autonomous self with responsibility for one's own trajectory. Yet while most advantaged workers talk about work as a place where we owe each other little, they keep quite distinct expectations of others at work and at home. As a result, they cordon off their "private" lives from the insecurity that rifles through the workplace; their assiduous efforts to separate the two spheres build what we might think of as a "moral wall." On the other side of the moral wall, when they talk about their intimate partnerships, they largely adopt an entirely different stance, one of pragmatism, compromise, and stability.

"We actually have a really good relationship; we get along pretty well," said Tara, who had married for twenty-one years. "What do I owe him? I think I owe just to be pleasant and not complain all the time." Said Dorothy, married for twenty-five years, "We're pretty fortunate, it's a pretty joint kind of thing, we both get through the day, we have the same goals and priorities, and we enjoy each other a whole lot." "Be pleasant and not complain all the time" and "we both get through the day" are phrases of moderation, sounding quite a different note from their talk about the work world, over on the other side of the moral wall.

The moral wall is a wall because it is a symbolic barrier people construct to separate one set of relationships from another, and it is moral because it separates domains that people feel ought to be separate; it is the embodiment of their wish to keep insecurity culture at bay, corralled in the workplace. As a result, however, it loads "family" with all of the symbolic responsibility for enduring connections and humane practices. In doing so, people call upon years of historical precedent in the split between public and private.

People erect moral walls around different relationships, depending on their vantage point on job insecurity. For advantaged itinerant workers, their intense work commitment is assumed, allowing their employers to presume that they will forsake bonds to community and extended family in order to move where the jobs were. Their moral wall, then, encircles their nuclear families, but not friends or other ties; for them, the very private family, bolstered by the rewards of high wages and benefits and by the gendered division of labor, is still a functioning model for working and caring.[11]

Tara's statement "We get along pretty well" is striking not just because it contrasts so starkly with the language they use valorizing independence at work, but also because it contradicts what many Americans apparently believe about love. According to a 2011 national Marist poll, for example, 73 percent of Americans said they believed in the idea of "soul mates," or "two people who are destined to be together;" this figure rises to 83 percent of people of color, although the wealthier, more educated, and older among us are less likely to believe this.[12]

Advantaged itinerant workers, however, who seem to subscribe to the notion of a uniquely compatible job as worth looking for, are paradoxically less likely to use the extremes of "soul mate" language at home. Sometimes they even go so far as to say their relationships lasted, as one admitted, "*not* because we have this magical love affair," but instead through "ups and downs," because they "both get through the day." Their commitment talk suggests less a joyful leap and more of a low-key stroll. They emphasize the everyday nuts and bolts of a relationship, adopting a decidedly reasonable stance that prioritizes continuity and steadiness over passion and the perfect fit. Theirs is not the call to duty, with all the fervor of a pledge made on principle that envisions and rewards sacrifice. Instead, their pragmatism frames obligation as compromise, which they do not seem inclined to engage in anywhere but at home.

THE ASCENDANCE OF INSECURITY CULTURE

The pragmatism of itinerant workers is also surprising, perhaps, because they are clearly aware of another way of thinking about relationships: they often joke with a vocabulary of choice, change, and independence that serves to hide some of their compromises or play with the notion of insecurity. In this they are partially echoing the tones of an insecurity culture that they perceive everywhere, and that often seems to be favoring an attenuating of all kinds of social relations, such as contemporary metaphors that denigrate overinvolvement (and often in mothers) like "helicopter mom," "lawnmower parent," or "Velcro girlfriend/boyfriend." The talk of advantaged workers is flush with similar language, even when they are not talking about work.[13]

Marin Grumman's husband kept joking about them getting a "playa divorce," for example. An ebullient, charismatic woman, warm and friendly, with a wry sense of humor and a certain stylish flair, Marin was happily married to an entrepreneur she had met at an earlier job. The two of them both go on an annual pilgrimage to Burning Man, a famous anarchism-and-art festival held in the Nevada desert. In the weeks leading up to the event, she explained, "Justin keeps asking can he have a 'playa divorce,'" some sort of festival invention, a temporary separation good only for the duration of the event. "It's a joke because there's women everywhere and most of them are scantily clad if clad at all," she says, rolling her eyes but grinning. "So he's going, 'Yeah, we got to get one of them playa divorces for the week,' you know, 'I can go nuts.' You know, that sort of thing."

Justin is her second husband, as Marin had first wed her high school sweetheart, who then turned out to be a serial philanderer, leaving children behind like small memorials with each woman he subsequently deserted ("Like my husband says, he's setting up franchises," she said, laughing). She uses her witty, wry perspective to adopt an explicitly ironic stance toward commitment, and the jokes she and her husband make play with the dangers of precariousness. Beneath all her vivaciousness, Marin demonstrates the powerful everyday salience of insecurity culture.

Of course, the only reason their jokes can be funny, the only way they might work, is if they play with some existing anxious energy. Many of the people with whom I spoke made jokes about commitment and uncertainty, with their humor acting as a sort of footprint of insecurity, an impression left by the invisible weight of the precariousness they perceived. One professional dubbed a day of massive layoffs "the great bloodletting," while another remembered joking with her spouse that if they got divorced, they would split up their friends a certain way—"you get the Smiths and I get the Joneses"—only to find that when they actually got divorced, as she laughingly told me, he got the Joneses and she got the Smiths. If they did not already subscribe to an independent stance toward obligation, the jokes demonstrated the work they had to do to reconcile themselves to the conventional wisdom of precariousness. It was as if the pervasiveness of insecurity culture had become "common sense," shaping people's expectations, practices, and feelings, and offering up a medium for people to play with discursively. Jokes like Marin's were not just their personal solution to their idiosyncratic issues but also signaled the collective symbolic baggage that many carry.[14]

When the two of them fight, Marin said, Justin's son jokes about what would happen if they got divorced:

> The kids will joke, you know, we'll have an argument—Justin and I'll have a disagreement—and my son Karl, who's a smart aleck, he'll go, "Woo, yay, four Christmases—three Christmases, meaning, you know, Mom's, Dad's, and now Marin's" because we're going to divorce over whatever silly—you know, it's just a joke. And so, you know, with [my daughter] Hester, we go, "Fourteen Christmases," because she's got, you know . . . she's got, you know, my mother, my father, who—They're separated. Then there's my ex-husband's mother and step—and second husband. So that's—and then with his father, that's four sets. Then there's Penny, the stepmother's parents, which is five. There's my husband's father, who's the only one left, six. You know, those kids have got more grandparents. [*Laughs.*]

Jokes like this one, recalling a 2008 movie *Four Christmases*, about a young, sophisticated couple reluctantly visiting each of their divorced parents' households, do a sprightly dance with the very issues that insecurity culture makes salient, and sometimes fraught.

What might the jokes be doing for the teller? Through humor, people can prove they are in control, savvy, aware of the risks involved but not too swayed by matters of the heart to take them too seriously. Jokes are a way to say, "I don't care too much about this," and "I am still a cultural critic, even though we are talking about my heart." Jokes allow them to take part in an assumed cultural imperative, a form of what the historian Peter Stearns has called "American cool."[15]

Alexis had lived in Switzerland and New York City before her husband's company moved them back to Richmond. "So we came back and it was like coming home. We had been gone ten years, so that was kind of weird too. Sometimes it is nice, it is like an old shoe, but then"—she paused, laughing—"it's an old shoe."

ALEXIS: Yeah, and nothing has changed. The first Sunday we went back to church, I turned to Bill and I said, "Those people have been sitting in that same pew . . . "

AJP: For ten years.

ALEXIS: For longer than that, since we started going to church there. I said, "I just want to scream, you guys on the left move to the right, guys on the right move to the left."

Alexis's jokes communicated something of her derision for people who remained in their communities over time, fitting in the same roles like "an old shoe." Despite their pragmatic approach to intimacy, then, many advantaged workers seem to be demonstrating their fluency in the tenets of the insecurity culture they perceived all around them.

Other kinds of language use seemed aimed at the same ends. Vicky, who relocated to Kentucky from suburban Connecticut, said she was at first loath to make the move. "And everybody in Connecticut, all my friends and people I worked with, were like, 'Why would you want to move there?' But actually it turned out to be a really nice place. And it was really transient, it was remarkably transient." The admiring tones conveyed that Kentucky was not as bad as her Connecticut friends supposed, in part because the people were actually mobile.

Jokes, metaphors, new meanings—these, then, are the evidence of an insecurity culture that these workers felt was in ascendance. For those immersed in itinerant work, the vocabulary of insecurity prevailed on the job; for many, it was also a part of their language in their nonwork lives. Yet while sometimes the new language seemed to enable a certain detachment from intimate others, many of the advantaged itinerant workers enjoyed long-term marriages, some lasting well into their third decades. Given the prevalence of insecurity culture, how do they reconcile the vocabulary of autonomy and choice with the compromise and surrender that were the hallmarks of pragmatism? How do they stay together for so long, and yet assure themselves and others that they are not stuck, settling, or too sedentary?

THE LANGUAGE OF CHOICE, THE PRACTICE OF STABILITY

Lawrence Gottfried was a playwright, but he pursued his craft only part of the time, spending the rest of the day shepherding the kids to their activities and making dinner while his wife held down a full-time professional career with a good salary and benefits. They had been married contentedly for twenty-two years, through childbirth, occupational changes, and several moves. The children were happy and successful, with one in college and two still at home, all of them friendly, motivated, and smart. Still, when a barber recently asked Lawrence about himself, his reaction to the answer gave Lawrence some pause, making him reflect on the sacrifices, particularly in his career, that the couple's path together has required.

The barber, an ancient hometown fixture who had been cutting hair for almost seven decades, had been making small talk while he clipped, asking Lawrence what he did. "Well," Lawrence told the man, "I spend about half my day writing, and half my day raising children and chickens." The old man paused in his snipping. "You know, I don't hear so good," he laughed, "I thought you said you spend half your day writing, and half your day erasing."

Before the latest move, Lawrence held several part-time jobs that were not well paid but were very meaningful—working with incarcerated youth, teaching playwriting at a local community college, running a small nonprofit to connect poor families and local services. He dropped all of these to relocate for his wife's dream job, and still wrestled with the image of himself as a househusband. Lawrence recounted the barber story partly because it was funny, but partly because it was probably true, he thought ruefully. "That may be a more accurate portrayal."

The valorization of choice is one of the central tenets undergirding insecurity culture, but it also presents a challenge to the long-term partnered: how to explain their longevity without sounding like they are merely "stuck" or "in a rut" compared to the restlessness they perceive all around them. Many solve the problem by espousing the notion that, unlike those who "choose" to leave, they "choose" to stay. For some of the most advantaged, then, the moral wall does not mean that they are simply settling for their enduring relationship. They may be compromising, but they are choosing to do so.

As Lawrence described it, he and his wife were very deliberate about their choices. When they were first starting out, he thought about working in disaster relief, but she said she did not want to have to move all the time ("You don't get to choose where you want to work"). So they decided that they would settle down where she could work as an oncologist, and he would write plays, teaching on the side. When the children were born, they both reduced their hours to be home with them as much as possible, using no babysitters at all in the summer. In this most recent move, they planned for him not to work for the first year in order to help their teenagers transition to the new environment. But when a recent job teaching playwriting came up, Lawrence got all set to apply, until his wife sat him down.

> She says, "Let's talk about this," because she does not want me to have a job. She likes—I mean, I'm the cook, so we eat, you know, delicious meals every night that are, you know, carefully prepared with a lot of love and very healthy. She doesn't have to worry about if the kids are being picked up or taken to tennis or soccer or whatever. She loves my work. She continues to be an unflagging believer that, you know, my art is worth her effort. And so, you know. So that's kind of what we're thinking about, you know, I think what we really want to do is [watch our spending carefully]. And in the meantime, just do what I'm doing.

While Lawrence is careful to emphasize the "we" in these plans, his talk conveys more than a little ambivalence, and it is also clear that he feels that his career has taken a hit in their recent move. "It's like, you know . . . I've got a lot to be thankful for," Lawrence said, and paused. "You know, I think." He then sighed audibly before he continued. "I don't know if I was offered a full-time job if I would want one."

> I'm sure there're some folks who question my decision. Our family at large, generally, is pretty appreciative of what I do and have done. I have tried not to let that kind of stuff bother me too much. We have known—we've known people who've made all kinds of sacrifices just for them both to have a full-time, high-powered career, and we determined a long time ago that we had other priorities . . .
>
> You know, I don't have anything to be ashamed of. You know, hell, if I won a Pulitzer Prize, I would appreciate the acclaim. But the truth is most of the people that I know who've won something like that, it has not improved their quality of life at all, and a number of them, it's hurt it.

Lawrence recounts the cautionary tales of those who "have made all sorts of sacrifices" and others for whom professional acclaim has "hurt their quality of life." He also uses the first-person plural to emphasize that theirs was a mutual decision that nonetheless benefited his wife's career much more. He baldly, albeit defensively, makes the assertion: "I don't have anything to be ashamed of." Finally, he almost convinces himself that he would not want a significant prize for his writing, even if he were able to get one. Yet his sighs, pauses, and denials suggest he is fighting with himself and some unruly feelings, as Lawrence asserts that it was all their choice, and at the same time works to rally his own satisfaction with the decisions they have made, decisions that not only subsume his own public achievement but also challenge gendered conventions about breadwinning. Lawrence has made some compromises here, and his feelings about them are still a little raw.

Given that Lawrence has made what he feels were such important sacrifices for his wife, calling his marriage his "ultimate commitment," we might predict that he would say his most important decision was to choose the woman he married. But there he would disagree. It's not about choosing the person, he argues, because even if you have the right person, you can still derail a marriage.

> Choosing a commitment is just about as important, you know. I think that—a lot of people don't see that. They think it's about choosing the right person, and it's hard to talk about that with my wife. It's—I think I did choose the right person. I didn't search the world over. So, I found her but it's really then—it's—if you've got someone who's good, [there are] plenty of chances to screw that up. You've got to kind of invest. You got to put time and care and love into it. Then you're rewarded back with that. So the—it's not choosing the person as much as it is choosing to be committed. To seeing it through.

Lawrence implicitly casts aside the soul-mate ideology when he suggests those who "think it's about choosing the right person" have it wrong. If one chooses anything, one chooses to commit to the relationship.

When asked, these advantaged workers explain the longevity of their commitment as their own choice. Karen was an African-American entrepreneur whose nineteen-year marriage endured despite a major early crisis over her husband's infidelity. "Everything is out there, you know, you're exposed to everything. You have options, you know. Other people could be options, whatever, you know, anything could be options," she said. "You just make the decision, 'That's not what I want and this is what I want and this is where I'm staying and that's it.'" Anita, a white woman who had been married for thirty years, contrasted the purposeful act of those who choose to stay and those who leave. "Some people I have seen deliberately choose a rocky situation and say, 'Okay, I want to go off by myself, so I'm going to use this as a means to do that.' I mean you can set your own path by your reactions to events."

The language of choice calls upon a particularly powerful American theme with a very long history, one written into layers of meaning tapping into consumer capitalism, the dreams of immigrants, frontier history, and other stories we tell ourselves about ourselves. But it also evokes a particularly contemporary vision of the honorable self, one disciplined into being by insecurity culture, which devolves responsibility and risk to the individual. By describing their actions as "choosing," advantaged workers make it sound like everyone can simply "choose" to stay in their relationships, that endurance is just another option, as opposed to it being powerfully enabled by structural supports such as ample resources, jobs with dignity, and the availability of appropriate mates in the first place. The language obscures what makes it difficult for others who are perhaps less perfectly positioned to simply choose longevity in their intimate lives. Furthermore, the choosing language of the advantaged workers also obscures the ways in which their own choices are constrained—how many at this level are able to choose a partnership that can support two serious careers, for example?

Most important, however, the language of choosing obscures what is actually allowing them to stay in satisfying relationships over the long haul: the compromises, the sacrifices, the concessions that make for bending so the union does not break. By transforming their acquiescence into choice, they hide from our view a secret ingredient in the recipe for their endurance. Rendering pragmatism less visible, they conceal the real achievement that is their longevity.

BEYOND CHOICE: MAKING BETS AND TAKING RISKS

Advantaged itinerant workers are picky at work, lured from company to company with the promise of better pay or more fulfilling jobs, and without much incentive to compromise. In their intimate lives, however, the idea that there might be someone better out there, a soul mate with whom they would not need to compromise, is a corrosive one. Such a notion poses an existential hazard, either dislodging them from their existing relationships or making those commitments out to be misguided or a sign of weakness, not bravery. The idea of the perfect match threatens to transform Lawrence's career sacrifices, for example, from saintly (or at least generous) to foolish, since the compromises he makes might easily end up being for the sake of something that is not going to last. In this, Lawrence faces the traditional dilemma of those spouses, most often women, who put their careers on the back burner to support someone else's.[16]

Rochelle, a white affluent woman married for twenty-four years, knew she was taking a gamble by giving up her own employability to support her husband's demanding career.

> I gave up my career very early, and my commitment was to try to raise a great family and be supportive of his career. The level of responsibility in his career— there is no way we could have what we have, and I don't mean material[ly], I mean emotionally and mentally, if I were not here managing life. *His* life. He couldn't do what he does and travel like he does, but I committed to that really early in our marriage, and it has not bit me in the ass yet [*laughs*].

The risk she was taking was more than a hypothetical one, however, as we can tell by her humorous use of salty language, and her dropping in the word "yet," with a laugh. Rochelle told me how her brother-in-law had hobbled his own career to move for his wife's job, only to find himself paying a high price for those choices after their divorce, when he was trapped (by shared custody and the requirement that he stay near the children) in a small town and no career.

"He is kind of like, 'I have to pay all this child support and I don't have my business off the ground at all. Now that the economy has crashed I don't have a chance of getting my business off the ground.' He is here and he is pretty bitter about it," Rochelle said. "Truthfully I think that can happen." Her brother-in-law stands as a cautionary tale that haunts Rochelle with the similarities between his bet and her own.[17]

The quest for the perfect match enshrined in insecurity culture, then, is one that profoundly threatens the long-term partnered, suggesting their best bets might be foolhardy mistakes, exposing all the vulnerability in their will to trust. This is marriage in what sociologist Karla Hackstaff called "divorce culture." Affluent couples responded with strategies to actively suppress the quest for something better in their intimate lives. In so doing, they exclude "choice" from the room before it has a chance to lay out the array.[18]

SUPPRESSING THE QUEST

Thus far we have seen two strategies by which advantaged workers who embrace job "flexibility" fend off the precariousness that dominates their working lives: they construct a "moral wall" to block insecurity culture from seeping into their intimate partnerships, and they invoke the language of choice paradoxically to explain how they make the compromises necessary to staying in a long-term relationship.

While some talked about choosing to stay, however, ultimately many of the advantaged finessed the challenge of choice by refusing to come to the fork in the road where a "choice" was necessary in the first place. Instead people who stay in long-term relationships work to head off the moment when they might actually have to choose. They pursue strategies that actively stifle the searching quality of insecurity culture and its quest for a better match, such as doubting that "perfect" exists; suggesting perfect is overrated; predicting that the quest would not be successful; considering the risks too high; or dismissing the quest as not relevant in the first place.

Perfect Doesn't Exist

Many in long-term partnerships said they were "realistic," able to recognize that we are all imperfect, as opposed to the selfish idealism of those who continued to hold out for something better. Mary remembered hearing friends talk about divorce and thinking they needed to adjust their expectations downward.

> When they were in their late thirties or early forties, I would say, in some things I thought, "Oh, you're just not being real. This is as good as it gets. How much do you expect?" When it was more like "He's not my soul mate." And there were three women I know who got divorced, who I was pretty close to and I understand why they did, but also part of me thought, "Yeah but you've got to give some too. Men are human." [*Laughs.*] Men are men, really, be real.

"Realism," the classic pragmatic approach, meant adjusting expectations downward to suppress the search for something better.[19]

Belle tried to get her husband to adopt the "get real" approach, although it sounded like he was wishing for more. She recounted a conversation in which he asked her, wistfully, if she missed the passion they had in the early years of their marriage. Belle said she told him, "'You know, you can't . . . that's not real. We had that, but it's too much to ask that a relationship would have that for years and years and years,' and 'That was a brief moment, we weren't really who we were with each other.'"

Sometimes people with a "get real" approach ironically made references to media icons of perfection. Yet instead of pointing to televised happy marriages as examples to emulate, people used the media to stand for some sort of naïve ideal, an unattainable standard of dedication. Disparaging the media versions as unrealistic, people then curtailed their own aspirations. Karina recalled her disappointment with her husband's ability to be there for her, beginning when she was pregnant.

> Even though he was there for the delivery of both of the kids—in the room—but he just didn't do, you know, the caring part that I thought that I needed. But I got over it. I just say hey, everybody's not *Father Knows Best*, whatever that means.

In this case, *Father Knows Best* (a television show, although it sounds like she has never seen it) stands for the burnished image of the involved, caring husband and father, a dream that her husband convinced her was unrealistic and that she "got over." People used media images as stand-ins for unfeasible families, as impossible comparisons to the actually achievable, and thus as measures to suppress the urge to look for something better.

Perfect Is Overrated

Others use a different tactic: there may indeed be a more perfect match out there, they seemed to argue, but, for a variety of reasons, the quest for that person is still not worth pursuing. If you pursued that perfect person, Lawrence pointed out, you would lose the time you had invested in the long-term partnership you were ending. That time had its own value, working as its own ballast, over and above the value of any particular relationship ideal.

> And, you know, one thing we saw is that, you know, from marriages we admired, was that time creates a lot of a marriage. You know [*laughs*], after twenty years if you worked on it productively. You have twenty years invested in that. You don't start again with those twenty years. You start from scratch.

Ultimately, he said, the accretion of history is what makes a marriage.

Others noted that their partner and their best friend was actually the same person, and leaving their partner meant losing their friend. The perfect partner may be out there, then, but it was not worth this other potential loss. "It's not like a whole host of people that you have that are friends, that you kind of talk to about your marriage and things of that nature. The person you're married to is actually that person," said Karen, whose marriage had survived infidelity. "So once you're kind of thinking about walking away, you're thinking about not just a marriage relationship, but what you are actually founded on was the friendship. And so you're giving that up too, and how do you . . ." She trailed off. After arguments with her husband, she said, the two of them would joke afterward as friends, laughing at and with each other about it.

A number of people thought that even if a perfect match existed out there, he or she was hardly worth the horror of having to navigate the dating scene again. Tara said the specter of singlehood was one reason why there was never a moment when you could stop working on a marriage.

> I'm saying this because you can definitely be in love with somebody, but not like you're passionately, madly in love with them, but I think I'm still in love with him. But the flip side is I would never want to be on the other side, I would never want to be divorced. Not that that's keeping me married, because I'm happily married, but every once in a while if I think about that or get mad enough, I'm like I don't want to be out in the single scene again.

Her marriage was pretty good, she said, but even if she wanted to improve upon her husband, it was definitely not worth the trouble of going through another search.

Perfect Is Irrelevant

Finally, for some, the quest was fundamentally irrelevant, because marriage made you related to each other forever, transcending the measure of a particular match. When I asked Mary if there were any "dealbreakers" for her marriage, a question that some people answered with infidelity, others with drug addiction or abuse, Mary could not think of a thing. "I would put it probably on par with—and maybe it's not a commitment you have with family relationships—but it's a bond that's there because you are family. Like you can't really dissolve family relationships. You can not see them, but you're always connected in that family even if it's not physically or conversation or whatever. You're always—just because you were born. So I think I would say now after twenty-seven years," she laughed and continued, "that's the level of affection I have." Ultimately, she said, "I can't think of what it would be that there wouldn't be a way to fix it."

Thus the advantaged embrace insecurity culture at work, and feel its ascendance all around them, invoking the language of the quest to explain and justify their own itinerant approach to career. Yet they construct a moral wall to keep it away from their intimate lives, and practice a paradoxical form of pragmatic surrender to enable their enduring partnerships, nonetheless cloaking their actions in the narrative of choice to hide their compromises within the dominant vocabulary of insecurity. They also adopt other strategies to suppress the quest, strategies that call into question the point of searching for something better, and that justify what they see as their choice to stay.

PRAGMATISM AND THE DIVORCE DIVIDE

It is not that these long-term partnered were just the personality type to compromise, to surrender in their private lives what they refused to in their work lives. Advantaged itinerant workers adopted the stance of pragmatism only when it came to their very private families. When it came to friends and communities, they invoked choice and independence to explain their decision to leave. Tara had described her happy marriage as "a really good relationship; we get along pretty well," but said one factor she thought about sometimes is that she didn't want to be "out in the single scene again;" she tamps down the idea of choice with her low-key pragmatic talk. But it was different when she thought about leaving her community. As she recalled:

> Okay. I don't even remember the negatives, but major positives were, you know, we could learn a new language, see a new culture. We knew we were going to be in central Europe, so all the travel. The kids at the international school, every Friday, in wintertime, they go up with a ski instructor and they learn how to ski. They thought that was huge. New foods—I mean, those are all the positives. The big negatives were leaving friends. I mean, that was really—we couldn't think of anything per se here that we wouldn't like—couldn't live without in Virginia. There just wasn't anything keeping us tied down here.

While leaving friends was a big negative, Tara admitted, it was not big enough to act as a counterweight for the family, because ultimately "there wasn't anything keeping [them] tied down here." The prospect of moving presented them with choices—a community with old relationships, or a community with all these other "positives"—leading to a decision that was clear after an impromptu cost-benefit analysis. But when it came to their families—spouses or partners, children—advantaged itinerant workers turned into pragmatists who suppressed the idea of the choice, even one that might offer other "positives."

It is of course possible that they opted for endurance in their intimate lives because they perceived that they would be in a weaker position in the market for love than they were in the market for work. In keeping with this, the affluent workers were most often couples that featured a gross imbalance of jobs. Perhaps pragmatism dominated their talk in part because, like Rochelle and Lawrence, trailing spouses had risked their very employability by betting on their relationships' staying power.[20]

Most likely, however, these advantaged workers and their spouses committed because they could—because their financial and cultural resources, and the institutional settings that endorsed them, allowed for enduring partnerships that supported high-quality, personalized care, mostly by women. Advantaged itinerant workers established very private families—narrowly defined because their mobility served to shed connections to other kin—matching visions of the nuclear family that have been culturally iconic since the mid-1800s, although not realized by most since that time. These families depended on gendered economic inequalities that buttressed their configuration of domestic and paid labor, and supported a kind of unpaid caregiving that was abundant, nurturing, and tailored to the jobholders' needs. As we heard Rochelle observe about her elite professional husband, ensconced in the very top of his profession: "There is no way we could have what we have, emotionally and mentally, if I were not here managing life. *His* life." Their relative privilege protected them from the economic ravages of job insecurity; the intensity of their jobs at this level required an extreme imbalance in the distribution of working and caring in their homes; and their culture—in the form of the pragmatism that invoked and justified compromise and surrender—enabled them to sustain the enduring partnerships that generated a high quality of care.

Thus pragmatic talk dominated the language of those whose relationships endure, of whom many were among the most advantaged. But surprisingly, one other group also sounded the same pragmatic note when they talked about their intimate lives: those less advantaged stably employed people, whose talk about home and work I explore further in chapter 7. This convergence is a surprise, because scholars have documented a widening chasm between the college-educated, whose relationships are more likely to endure, and everyone else, a chasm that some have called the divorce divide. While researchers have considered this chasm evidence that class shapes one's likelihood of divorce, few have investigated the impact of precarious work on lower-income people's capacity to sustain relationships. The implication of this surprising similarity is that we have not adequately explained the divorce divide, and so it is worth looking more closely not just at its socioeconomic roots but also at the way those roots are shaped by the experience of job insecurity.[21]

THE COSTS AND BENEFITS OF PRAGMATISM

How do people commit to others over the long term amid insecurity culture? The elite professionals who benefit from the flexibility of the new economy adopt a stance of independence when they consider their obligations at work, but many use an entirely different approach for their intimate lives, a stance of pragmatism. The contrast produces quite a verbal struggle when they talk about their intimate lives, as they try to reconcile embodied practices of compromise and continuity with the ethos of choice and change they perceive as ascendant all around them.

The pragmatic approach incurs its own costs. By maintaining a posture that suggests that to some degree all relationships are the same—thus that there is no such thing as perfect; the quest is not worth it, because what you have is as good as it gets—the pragmatic stance limits our expectations for the kind of relationships we should have. These actions have consequences, however; just as they appear to enable us to commit to a long-term partner, they also may inhibit our capacity to envision something better. Without subjecting these relationships to some sort of arbitrary evaluation, we can surely assume some are perhaps not worth maintaining: we will bear witness in the next chapter to the heady triumph of disadvantaged women who achieve independence from men who are unfaithful, abusive, or controlling.

On the other hand, as we have seen, the pragmatic stance enables both the desire and the capacity to commit, by juxtaposing "realism" with naïve indulgence. This framing allows people to surrender a bit of themselves for the sake of the union. Pragmatism is the foundation for the compromises without which long-term partnerships are not possible.

When people care for and connect with each other with dignity and respect, the capacity to commit over the long term is a profound achievement, especially given their perception of widespread insecurity. The confluence of the advantaged itinerant workers and the less advantaged stably employed in how they talk about their intimate lives suggests it is an achievement supported by economic arrangements that defang the threats posed by precariousness, either through the affluence that cushions insecurity or the security that cushions disadvantage. Perhaps people are better able to surrender themselves to each other when they are not also surrendering the prospects for their economic survival. It is when people use the language of choosing to mask those compromises as individualism that they tacitly acknowledge the ascendance of insecurity culture in their milieu.

CHAPTER 4

✧

The Imperative of Detachment

Fiona Parker has little patience for compromise. The white technical worker whom we met in the introduction, who proclaimed, "It's me and [my son] Jimmy against the world," Fiona views standard notions of commitment as dangerous, too often roping women into endless caregiving tasks from which they are never free. That is not going to be her problem, she swears.

Part of her vigilance stems from watching her mother stay put despite an unfaithful husband, a high-conflict marriage, and a daunting caregiving load. "So what I saw my mom doing is commitment to the wrong thing and sticking with it," Fiona says. "And that's opposite of how I live. I'm like, if it's wrong, I'm out of there. Forget it."

Walking beneath the leaves in the city park as she narrates her story, she suggests we should pledge ourselves to particular standards, rather than people. "Maybe it's that you're committed to your values, right? And if you try to—if you're always making sure that what you're doing is in line with those values, then you should be committed to the right things," she said. Even then, however, commitment is temporary. "But sometimes you might commit to something and realize that it's not really what you thought it was, and then you have to reevaluate that and maybe not stick with it." In figuring out this line of thinking, she ultimately redefines commitment altogether. "I mean, you don't have to be committed to something just because you thought you should be committed to it initially."

Fiona maintains this philosophy for work, where she holds that an employer owes very little indeed to an employee. "I always believe that you should do the best job that you can, no matter what you're doing," she intoned. Using someone from her current job as an example, she said: "I believe if the person isn't willing to try and they're not being productive or as productive as they should be, then it's the time to reconsider the employment. And it's probably time for the person to reconsider the employment. They should probably try and find something more interesting or something." Work relationships should end if they are not mutually satisfying. While it raises questions of how and when to commit to anyone, her philosophy meshes well with contemporary trends in work and in intimate relations.[1]

Compared to the affluent professionals of the last chapter, less advantaged workers like Fiona derived precious little benefit from changes in employment relations over the last several decades. If at the top of the occupational structure insecurity has largely meant newfound flexibility, lower down the pyramid it has accompanied the cutting of wages, decreases in benefits, unpredictable hours, and less work satisfaction. Deregulation has fostered the ability of companies to slash benefits and lay people off, while the weakening of unions has crippled the capacity of workers to fight back. These developments have been accompanied by a simultaneous withdrawal of state provisioning and declines in such programs as unemployment insurance, welfare, and food stamps. In fact, scholars suggest, these trends have been part of the engine behind increasing economic inequality in the United States over the past twenty-five years.[2]

We have seen how people immersed in precarious work respond with the one-way honor system, expecting little from employers while avowing their own work ethic. Given the two faces of insecurity, however, we might expect that professionals and lower-paid workers would experience precariousness differently, both at work and at home. As explored in the last chapter, affluent professionals view their itinerant careers as an expression of their skills and interests, while erecting a moral wall to fend off insecurity from their intimate lives. How do less advantaged insecure workers—those "moderately educated" who have been laid off—conceive of what obligation means for them, at work and at home?

As Fiona suggests, the answer varies according to gender, as women have long been expected to meet the needs around them with invisible and unpaid care. Changing economic circumstances that generate greater need, particularly among their male compatriots, portend significant care demands that fall at the feet of less advantaged women. Insecurity looks different when you are responsible for the fallout.

Fiona and others like her prioritize their independence, from disappointing men, an unhelpful state, and relatives who fail you. They value work, as their cherished self-sufficiency rests upon their continued employment;

indeed, they sometimes see work as offering the straightforward clarity missing from the more tortuous negotiations of family and friends. But their expectations of constancy and their capacity for compromise are low; they meet job insecurity with their own mobility, and are at a job for as long as it is useful for them and not much longer. Though perhaps rare, Fiona and her ilk are powerful symbols of a possible future, because they represent a very rational response to employers' retreat from the social contract, matching withdrawal for withdrawal in a prisoner's dilemma of insecurity, the very response that employers fear and pundits anticipate.[3]

Theirs is also but one pathway of two taken by many less advantaged women adapting to insecurity: others prioritize the needs they face in their families and communities, calling on notions of duty to propel them to great heights of self-sacrifice in the face of their significant caring responsibilities. In contrast, women like Fiona rely on particular strategies of detachment to limit the needs of others to whom they must respond, because those needs portend their vulnerability to risks of exploitation and sorrow. Instead of nostalgic distress, their independence at home and at work generates a sort of triumph in the pleasures of freedom, freedom from the gendered trajectory of who responds to whose need at home: a trajectory of entitlement for men, and obligation for women.

Their very rebelliousness represents another kind of self generated and disciplined by insecurity culture, different and yet the same as the individual responsibility pledged by the elite professionals who lay claim to choosing. Less advantaged insecure workers like Fiona pursue a self that reflects and resists longstanding expectations for women. With their self-reliant approach shaped by expectations of insecurity everywhere, we might label their strategy: "defying."

THERE IS ALWAYS WORK

With autonomy their credo, less advantaged insecure workers valued work enormously as the means to the self-sufficiency they require. Lena, a health worker, put her husband through school, only to have him leave her and their daughters shortly thereafter; her job was the one thing that kept her going through the recriminations and doubt, she said. "It's empowering. It empowered me. It gave me my self-esteem back when it was really fragile. It was what I had and by helping other people, it helped me." As sociologist Jennifer Utrata has documented among single mothers in Russia, when men and the state prove rickety, women will put their faith in work, even that which is low-paid or discriminatory, as the path to self-reliance.[4]

Indeed, sometimes the job seemed to be a haven from other arenas that were full of conflict or sorrow. After years as a waitress and a travel agent, Abby, a single mother, found out about a temporary job based in Alaska, applied for it, and went away for a year, leaving eight-year-old Peyton with her parents. The money was incredible for someone without a college degree ($92,000 annually), she thrived in the job ("I really loved that work. I like the dynamics of it. I liked the satisfaction I got from it"), and she enjoyed her team ("I got friends for life"), so when she returned and found the local job market inhospitable, she went back to the same outfit again, this time for fifteen months, when her daughter entered middle school.

Now back and laid off from local low-wage employment, she wonders why she is even here (in the continental United States), in light of some conflicts with Peyton, now an adolescent.

> I'd say, "Mom, if I'm not doing anything, I'm not providing for her right now. She doesn't want to be around me. She tells me she doesn't want to be around me when we fight. Why am I here? I might as well be [in Alaska] working and at least providing money." Mom's like, "She really needs you here. She doesn't need . . ." you know. . . . But I do think about that a lot. Like, does she really need me here?

Sometimes paid work is more rewarding than the ephemeral and unappreciated contributions of unpaid caring labor in the home.[5]

Yet while they were committed to work, it was most often merely the means to an end. A single mother, Amelia had had many jobs, from yoga teacher to real estate agent to animal control technician, but she had never stayed in any one job too long, principally in order to retain control over her own schedule while her children were young. "All I know is, me personally, I have to work enough to pay my share, but not much more than that, because the rest of the time is going to my kids," she said.

Work was crucial for making ends meet, of course. After her first husband had ruined their finances, forcing her to declare bankruptcy, Amelia decided never to merge money with someone else again, and kept that vow through her second marriage, now going on seventeen years. Today they each contribute toward the bills, and neither carries the other, she said. "I believe that a woman needs to pull her own weight, you know." She described the conversation they had when her current husband first proposed:

> "You have your money. I have mine and there's house money, and that's the only way I'm doing this again. Love doesn't enter into that. You know I love you as a person, but financially I have to protect myself and my children." And he's like,

okay. And I've held to it to this day. You know if you come up and say, "Well I'm short on the house payment." "Well, find a way." You know, not to be hard-nosed, but I'm sorry, if I find a way to take care of my share, then you're a big boy, find a way.

Independence was orthodoxy for Amelia, and work its spiritual practice.

At the same time, these less advantaged workers knew employers had their own agenda. By keeping a steady career at bay, Amelia said, she had saved herself from being disappointed later when employers failed to fulfill their promises. She used cautionary tales to emphasize the point.

> A dear friend of mine was at a company for twenty-seven years. She went right out of high school and missed all of the time with her children. She said she did it so when they finally got out, you know, she could travel with them and stuff and then she found out when she got ready to take early retirement—no bene-fits, and here she thought she would have everything. Twenty-seven years and they said, "Sorry. There's no money." They did away with all the benefits for early retirement, so now she's still working, has grandchildren.

All work trajectories involve risk, and all workers make bets about that risk. The risk of a more itinerant work history like Amelia's is that she would not be able to support her family or to get a job when she needed one; her gamble was that she would be able to prioritize time with her chil-dren, retaining control over when she worked and for whom, without suf-fering too much financially. Her cautionary tale is the story of a friend who made a different bet and lost: that she could postpone being with her chil-dren in favor of a long-term, traditional career, in which she would make enough money to retire early and spend time with them then. Amelia car-ries this tale around, however, and repeated it to me, because it validates her own choices: to work, but to work selectively, eschewing a steady career to be able to control her own time.

Sitting on a picnic table in a suburban park, Amelia felt vindicated by the instability wrought by the Great Recession. "The times today have proven that people need to sit back and think about what's really important be-cause, yeah, you put in all these years at these companies and you've made all this money, and what do you have now?" she asked. "Your kids are grown, you can't go back." Work was important for independence, to be sure, but still had to be held at arm's length.

Fiona agreed, attesting to the work ethic—"I always believe that you should do the best job that you can, no matter what you're doing"—while regarding work with a baleful eye, ready to resist the greedy institution.

"I don't think an employee owes any employer their life. Like, I mean, or their happiness, like, you should be able to do your job, do it well, go home. Not be chained to your desk all the time and slaving away." While they valued work, less advantaged women who were insecurely employed protected themselves from employers just as they did from exploitative partners, friends, and relatives.

WHEN INDEPENDENCE AND INTIMACY COLLIDE

When it comes to what they owe other people, Fiona and those like her sound a bit different from the elite professionals in the previous chapter. While both groups adopt an independent stance toward work, the less advantaged are generally not undertaking a quest for the perfect job. Nor are they guided by a stance of pragmatism in their intimate life, choosing to settle for the imperfections of a relationship with history. Of course, these less advantaged workers do not generally have jobs that allow them to indulge in the luxury of self-actualization at work, nor do they have the financial cushion allowing for pragmatic concessions to romantic partners who might prove feckless. Instead, many—most of them women—consider their independence a core principle in both arenas.[6]

In intimate life, infidelity works like a tripwire for Fiona, a nonnegotiable reason to terminate a relationship. In one serious relationship with a coworker, the man earned a decent salary, had a son by a previous marriage, and lived in a nice house—all points in his favor, Fiona said. But two months after she moved in with him, things went downhill. For her, the story of the relationship's denouement is a priceless example of her son Jimmy's resilience:

> I found an email, like, to another girl that he was planning to go somewhere with. We were supposed to be going to this party, and I was looking up a recipe and I saw the email. And I was, like, "I'm out of here. See you later." Get Jimmy, get in the car. And [the boyfriend is] like, you know, probably yelling for me not to leave and we need to talk about it or something. And I'm like, "Whatever." So we get in the car, Jimmy's with me, and we start driving away. And it's June, but you know that Rudolph song? [Sings] "Put one foot in front of the other, and soon you'll be walking out . . ." He just started singing that in the back of the car. He's like four years old. I mean how perfect is that? [Laughs.]

In her recounting, Fiona remembers the transgression (the other woman), how she found out (the email), how she reacted ("I'm out of here"), and how

Jimmy responded (by singing). What she does not remember—what was not important, once the tripwire was triggered—was what the boyfriend was saying ("probably yelling for me not to leave and we need to talk about it or something"). Breezy, defiant, Fiona refused to curtail her independence for a relationship that looked like it was not going to go well.

Fiona represents an important group, those with a high school degree or some college, who are at the center of a maelstrom of family upheaval, with more divorce than the college-educated and more marriage than less advantaged couples. While some writers contend that these family patterns stem from unemployment, underemployment, or low wages impeding men without college degrees from supporting their families, others point out how members of the working class are increasingly separated from anchoring institutions and segregated from middle-class role models who marry, go to church, and keep jobs.[7]

These explanations downplay the importance of employer conduct, however; one's history of job insecurity matters in how class affects coupling, as we saw in the last chapter when we considered the similarities between elite itinerant workers and those who are less advantaged but stably employed. Job insecurity, the personal experience of the lack of employer commitment, makes it difficult to sustain other types of commitments; indeed, it calls into question the notion of commitment writ large. The affluent professionals adapt to itinerant work by convincing themselves that work is a separate realm, with separate norms governing behavior, erecting a moral wall that protects their intimate lives from its encroachment. Some less advantaged insecure workers take a different tack, however: some find themselves less able to protect their intimate lives from the ravages of job precariousness, some view the moral wall as out of reach, but in any case, they adapt by inuring themselves to insecurity everywhere. For Fiona and her peers, "defying" signifies the primacy of independence, their invulnerability to hazardous others.

Less advantaged women talk about being "picky," holding out for a better partner, even a soul mate, rather than compromising their ideals to make a bad choice. Abby, who had worked in Alaska, had gotten pregnant from a fling at the beach when she was twenty-three, and had not had a date in the fourteen years since. Upon learning she was pregnant, she returned home to live with her parents, who had been married for more than four decades.

> Both my parents, they just celebrated their forty-third wedding anniversary. I think that's a big factor in why I'm single. I'm not going to settle for anything less. So I'm really, I'm very strict about my relationships.

She viewed their four-decade marriage with admiration, but the lesson she derived from it was not about the compromises that allowed for its longevity but instead about how she needed to choose any future partner very carefully. The way to avoid divorce was to pick the best person and, until that person came along, to avoid messy entanglements, or to quickly disengage from partners who revealed major flaws.[8]

One might say independence is the best face they can put on a bad situation. Conventional understandings of gender charge women with primary responsibility for caregiving, for meeting needs that can seem unpredictable, expanding, and overwhelming. The family caregiving of women without college degrees was once supported, through marriage, by a combination of men, employers, and the state. Once this triad withdrew its backing in the decades after World War II, most of these women had no choice but to live off of their own low-wage work. From this viewpoint, those who declare their independence do so in order to limit the demands of others as they adapt to their constraints, shaped by the abandonment they have suffered as a group in the postwar era.[9]

Felicia echoed this kind of thinking when she talked about why she left her second husband: "He had severe problems with depression, because of the lack of being able to have children. . . . So, I didn't want to deal with this one person in my life being so incredibly—" she paused, and laughed, "a burden? I hate to say that."

Thus Fiona and others of her ilk articulate a stance toward relationships—cool, transitory, appraising—that rests on a principle of independence. They advocate a path of autonomy, flexibility, and resilience, of staying true to ideals of self-respect and happiness while maintaining light and loose associations. It is a stance that reflects and complies with the demands of insecurity culture.[10]

GENDER AND THE PLEASURES OF FREEDOM

These women sound different from those people with long-term commitments, who, as we heard in the last chapter, can seem a little beaten down, a bit resigned to the compromises they made in service to their union's longevity. In contrast, those who talked about leaving others behind, like Fiona, conjured up a sense of power, even triumph.[11]

Lena worked to pay for her husband to get a college degree, but was nonetheless very dependent in other ways during their marriage; when he left her, she learned how to be her own person, she said. "I learned to be independent, which I never was. I mean, growing up, my dad did all the driving, and then when I got married Scott did all the driving, and now if I want to go to [a local college], I just get in the car and, I mean, I can do it myself," she said, crowing happily. "I don't have to wait for somebody else to make a decision to do something."

Of course, some appear to be working on their feelings to emphasize and produce the rejoicing that they seem to think they are supposed to feel. Becca, a white single mother, recounted her own departure drama in which she drove down the highway away from her abusive husband, in echo of Fiona's story of Jimmy singing the song celebrating their exodus. The day must have been a frightening one, involving pulling the kids out of school unannounced so that the man would not be able to thwart her plan to leave. But she took drastic steps to make it a defiant moment, instead of merely a fearful one:

> The kids had to leave their TVs, their beds, their toys. They just basically had clothes, and I knew they were really upset, so I tried to make it fun. Let's bash Wyatt. "Here, Blake, here's my ring, throw it out the window." So he throws my engagement ring out the window.

While she regrets the gesture now, as she certainly could have used the money the ring would have brought, she does not regret trying to impart the feeling of independence to her children, a thrilling sense of grabbing onto a future without physical violence.

These women derive some pleasure from being free of the sometimes overwhelming obligations that have traditionally fallen to less-advantaged women, unfettered by expectations that they will always be the ones to serve. "I'm happy where I am, and as long as the kids are happy, I'm good too," said Amelia, adding, "And my husband's happy, as long as he's pulling his weight," as she laughed, her mirth perhaps suggesting some residual discomfort or sense that she might be violating expectations. Generally, these women were exultant about defying the expectations to take on burdens they resisted.

Amelia's relationship—with responsibility carefully meted out in equal parts, staving off vulnerability—points to a crucial point here: marriage might have to be remade into a different kind of partnership to appeal to these women who discover and cherish their new self-efficacy. Lena's gleeful taste for independence, for example, suggests it might be difficult for her to repartner successfully with someone of her ex-husband's (or her father's) ilk again. Survey researchers have indeed found a "self-reliance" effect serving to dampen the predilection for marriage among women. From the perspective of these women, however, it is not the dissolution of mutual commitment that is the central problem of contemporary intimacy but the intransigence of conventional heterosexual marriage, the rigidity of our cultural patterns of partnering, and the challenge of caregiving without support from social institutions. Freedom from any of these snares generates some of the pleasures of independence.[12]

Fiona, Lena, and Amelia illustrate the paradigmatic independent approach to intimate relationships in insecurity culture. The uncompromising standards, the tripwires, the defiance—their stance toward questions of obligation represents the epitome of the rational response to precariousness everywhere. What do we owe each other when flexibility is ascendant at work and at home? For Fiona, the answer is not very much. It is a cool emotional world that she inhabits. But she also demonstrates a powerful freedom, pride, and autonomy that look like the answer to another question: How might women have gained something with the onset of insecurity? In some ways, she embodies the future that some decry and others celebrate.[13]

WHAT WE KNOW ABOUT INSECURITY CULTURE AND INTIMACY: IS FIONA TYPICAL?

Surely Fiona is not typical. Most Americans report that they are "still connected," according to Claude Fischer, a Berkeley sociologist. Fischer reviewed statistical evidence to evaluate claims of declining American social connectedness and argued that concerns about such a decline are generally unfounded. Compared to the 1970s, about the same proportion of Americans thirty years later reported that they spend social evenings several times a month or more with relatives. Americans were just as likely in the early 2000s to say they could rely on a spouse or partner for help if they had a serious problem as they were ten years later, and they were much more likely to say that their spouse or partner understood "the way they feel about things." Americans also told researchers they found it relatively easy to be close to others, and they were not worried about being abandoned or about other's dependency on them, at about the same rate in the early 2000s as they had ten years earlier.[14]

Setting aside any concerns that people might want to tell survey researchers they are more connected than they are, these findings do not mean that there are no changes in how people approach their social lives, however. To take intimate partners as an example, we already know that people are marrying less and cohabiting more, and the marriages that remain are more intense, closer, and more satisfying than in the past. At the same time, except for those among the college-educated, marriages are more likely to break up than in the past. The idea that people still rely on their spouses or partners for help with a serious problem is not a surprise, then, since that and other measures tell us something about how close, how intense, or how satisfying an ongoing relationship is, not how likely it is to end.[15]

Given that intimate partnerships are shorter-lived, albeit more intense for the duration, we might foresee that some might use the moral wall to heighten their expectations of those in the private sphere in contrast to their low standards at work. But we can also predict that others might take steps to distance themselves from significant others, to shrink what they owe, to prepare themselves for their imminent betrayal, and to otherwise adapt to insecurity culture with independence. Fiona may not necessarily be typical, but she represents a way of navigating work and love in an insecure age that meshes well with evolving trends in both domains.

CONSTRUCTING WHAT INDEPENDENCE MEANS

Fiona dates her understanding of the perils of commitment to her childhood, in which she watched her mother and stepfather endure their high-conflict marriage. Despite the man's infidelity, Fiona's mother stayed by his side. "The cheating, the instability—so what I saw is a lot of situations—like my mom's still with my stepdad after all this stuff with them." Fiona considers this commitment her mother's needless sacrifice, her freedom curtailed even further by the fact that now, just as her last child has left the house, her husband's mother, afflicted with Alzheimer's disease, has moved in.

> And I love my mom but she's just given up a lot of happiness for—and now, like, his mom's living with her with Alzheimer's. And finally my sister's graduating from school, and she's got, like, Hank and Emma, and I feel like, "I'm out of here guys. See you later." So I respect that she's committed or whatever, [but] it's not the way I would live. And that's—I think that's what's driven a lot of my flexibility and adaptability, because I didn't want to get stuck in this situation.

Fiona's mother, in this vignette, serves as her cautionary tale, the foil for Fiona's own abiding philosophy, as evidenced by how she even refers to her mother's behavior as "committed, or whatever," the "whatever" doing some discursive work through which Fiona denigrates the duty to family caregiving that her mother takes on. Though perhaps laudable by the codes of traditional marriage, her mother's commitment—to stick by her husband, no matter the instability, the faithlessness—seems to Fiona to leave her mother trapped, ever vulnerable to the overweening needs of others. Fiona considers her mother's course the ultimate in self-abnegation. In contrast, she asserts: "I'm like, if it's wrong, I'm out of there."

Others who proclaimed independence as a stance toward their intimate lives had different stories—of responding to mothers who "had a lot of kids" but "just didn't properly take care of them," mothers who were overly controlling, even parents with long-term marriages who modeled endurance. Each had direct, personal experience of job precariousness, however, and understood insecurity as entirely predictable. They read their pasts for the meaning of independence—as righting a wrong, as a form of protection, as a safer bet, as a prudent move—and their interpretation framed their approach to obligation.

Fiona has chosen a different path since high school, when her mother kicked her out—a perplexing act when you consider the story of her mother's unwavering commitment to her cheating husband, but one that Fiona nonetheless credits with helping her find her way straight.

> If your kids are being really horrible, you have to really try to work with them to get them through it. But if it gets to a point where they're not helping themselves and they're not responding to it, at that point, you—you've got to just let them go, especially if they're teenagers. And I really strongly believe in that. My mom did that to me, and if she had not done that, I would be a much different person than I am right now.

Had she not been forced on her own, Fiona said, "I don't think I would have been as good at being able to pull myself out of bad situations." One cousin, now a heroin addict, had been consistently rescued by his father, and Fiona regarded that tack as dangerously misguided. "You just got to let him hit the bottom. If you don't, then they're going to end up like Jimmy's dad and his uncle. And, I mean, they'll just do it for—some people will do it forever." Fiona's fear of "enabling" is a fairly common framing that emphasizes the risk of overcommitment, the certain dangers of not curtailing our obligations to each other, that also serves as a distancing discourse for those faced with difficult others.

This philosophy does not mean giving up on children as soon as they get in trouble, Fiona insists. "So, I mean, I really think you have to try to give them a good foundation and make sure that they don't get there. And if they do get there, you've got to do everything you can to help them," she said. At a certain point, however, you do have to limit how far you will go for them. "But you have to make sure that they're really helping themselves too."

Even for children, then, the tripwires that generate Fiona's withdrawal are there, but they are put in place for the children's own good. As an example, Fiona mentions a "joke" that she and Jimmy share, which he brings up whenever she talks about how he will be supporting himself after high school. "He's like, 'I'll just move in with my grandparents [his father's parents].'" Jimmy's grandparents were nice but ineffectual people, whose children were slothful and addicted, Fiona thought. "I was like, 'You know, Jimmy, I love your grandparents, but there is no way you are ever living with them. And if you even try it, I will stop talking to you.' Like, 'I will not be associated with you at all if you go live with them.'"

Given her background and philosophy, it is perhaps surprising that Fiona actually got married five years ago to her husband, Hal. Why commit, when independence is the whole point? "Because I was pregnant," she laughs. But the relationship was going well, in part because of how much more secure Hal felt now, she said. "Our relationship's a lot better now that we're married and have a kid. I think it was really hard for me to finally commit to someone because I'd been so free and independent this whole time. And I think he really wanted that, like, to feel secure. So I think that that has actually improved." Hal is also very involved with the baby, even though Fiona is still the family organizer. Comparing parenting now to her decade as a single mother, she observes, appreciatively: "It's almost like having extra arms." Despite her convictions, Fiona is seeing some benefits to a long-term partnership.

Still, her wedding vows do not remove the tripwires in place for intimate others. The relationship is good now, but the stance of independence means that her stated tolerance for misbehavior before she abandons ship is lower for a spouse than for children. "If your spouse is being really horrible? That's easy. You just . . ." she laughed. "I'm committed as long as it's good. I'm not committed to anything bad."

CONTRADICTIONS AND AMBIVALENCES

Despite the seeming coherence of her philosophy, Fiona, like her peers, is not immune to inconsistencies and doubts. Jimmy, her son, is largely in a separate category, for example, as children are for most mothers. In addition, like many women, particularly those with working-class origins, Fiona keeps ties to her maternal relatives, even when those ties are stretched thin by conflict or struggle. When she talks about her mother, her mother's siblings, and her mother's parents, suddenly the "I'm out of here" toughness is gone, and instead she's being very careful to maintain relationships even when it is difficult.[16]

"We're very close, my whole . . . And I try to keep those relationships really close," Fiona said. This has not always been easy, she said, recounting multiple conflicts, including a recent one where they accused Jimmy of cursing at one of them, believing the worst of him, as they were wont to do. "There's a lot of fighting within the family, but I try, no matter what, to stay close with everybody and make sure that we see them regularly," she said. She remembered a recent year-long fight between her aunt and uncle that challenged her capacity to ignore it. "But I made sure that I was friends with both of them during the whole time and didn't take a side or anything like that."

Governed by independence throughout much of her relationships, Fiona does something different with her maternal relatives—suddenly connecting to others involves prioritizing their relationships over and above any fleeting conflict. Here, finally, we find Fiona's moral wall, beyond which insecurity will not go. Like other single mothers without college degrees who are immersed in the world of precarious work, to the extent that Fiona has such a wall, it is not between some fixed notions of "work" and "home" but between an outer core—employers, friends, spouses, and other intimate partners—and an inner core—her children and her maternal relatives.

Staying close to her aunt, her uncle, and her uncle's longtime girlfriend—despite the recurrent arguments she recounts about children, discipline, and other hot-button issues—demonstrates their unique status to Fiona as people with whom she will maintain ties even when they challenge her values, ties that are worth more than any particular fight, simply because of what they are. She might invoke independence repeatedly, then, but when it comes to her maternal relatives, Fiona calls upon the pragmatism that we saw in the last chapter, of the kind that might lead one to shrug and say, "You can't choose your relatives." Of course, given the intensely voluntaristic nature of her relationships, one might say that Fiona, and people like her, "choose" who counts as a relative all the time, like her uncle's girlfriend, and who does not, like Jimmy's father and paternal grandparents. Nonetheless, her pragmatism about her maternal relatives both forces and enables her to endure the sort of conflict—even cases of hostility, criticism, and petty disloyalty—that she refuses to stand for in the rest of her life. For those who fall outside the moral wall, however, Fiona and her peers are uncompromising.

THE PRACTICES OF INDEPENDENCE

Independence, pragmatism, duty—these stances toward obligation are more than simple philosophies of life that people simply proclaim and thus live by; they instead require the daily calibration of what we owe to others and what we can expect from them. Just as pragmatism entailed different strategies to enable people to compromise, those who adopt the stance of independence likewise work to shrink their obligations to others: they engage in a "needs reduction" strategy, convincing themselves that they or others do not *really* require as much; they deploy invented phrases and language that redefine their circles of commitment; and they invoke the absolution of other people, whom we might call "detachment brokers." In so doing, they find within themselves the capacity, feeling, and justification for defying.

In her most recent study of surrogate mothers, nannies, and other purveyors of outsourced care, Arlie Hochschild has documented what she terms the "emotional labor of estrangement"—their efforts not to care, to pull back from inconvenient feelings that would get in the way of the marketized transactions she chronicles. Hochschild found that people worked on their feelings, actively massaging them so that they would feel the way they were supposed to feel. Similarly, people immersed in the tumbleweed society sometimes used these strategies to feel the "right way"—in this case not necessarily to fit in with a marketized transaction but instead to enable, animate, and excuse their independence.[17]

The Reduction of Need

If there is less need, then there is less obligation, and thus those who approached obligation with the stance of independence often seemed to be redefining and reducing the need they faced, both their own and that of others around them. One example is offered by Stanley, one of the men who adopted an independent stance at work and at home, for whom the stance was less about defying than managing expected insecurity. Stanley, who worked in sales, was going through a divorce with his wife, with whom he had separated and reunited repeatedly. There are hints that he has been deeply hurt, particularly when she had an affair, during a time in which they were what he called "semiseparated." "That was extremely painful," he said. "In some ways, I'm probably still dealing with that in my own heart." He said he was proud of the way he and his wife had kept his daughter out of their conflict, however. "I think that's given her the confidence to be who she is," he said. "She's not dependent on her parents necessarily being together or being apart. She is her own person."[18]

In this comment, Stanley transforms the word "dependent" from needing care, as one might expect of a child, to needing her parents' marital commitment, which through the word "necessarily" he makes sound unreasonable. He manages to argue that his daughter is "independent" enough not to need her parents to be together. There are plenty of children of divorced parents who flourish, as the vast majority of them do, as do those whose parents stay together. Yet Stanley's language is a bit odd here, in that he appears to be working to recast dependence as a statement about family structure and then to dismiss it as unwarranted.[19]

His efforts at needs reduction are not as invisible as he may think, however. He tells a story of going out to dinner with his wife and daughter a few days earlier and having his daughter run off to the bathroom crying. Stanley recalls: "I said, 'Why are you crying?' And she said, 'I'm really sad because I still love you.'" Does he tell this story to point to deep emotions that cannot be reduced away? Is his daughter standing in for his own sorrow here? Does she serve as the repository of feeling, enabling him to withhold his own intense feelings from the situation? Regardless of the answers to these questions, we can make note of how the vignette contrasts with his earlier words about her, which explicitly valued independence and invulnerability, even to one's parents.

Needs reduction also allowed Abby to do what she had to do. Abby was the single mother who left her daughter Peyton with her parents twice for more than two years, in order to earn a living at a job she enjoyed in Alaska. In talking about the separation, she seems to reduce Peyton's need, and her own.

> So, missing her? You know, when I went into it I said, "Oh, we can email." You know I showed her how to email and she was real young. My dad had a computer and got everything set up, and the intentions were there to keep really in good touch. What we found was that she would be fine until she talked to me. . . . We found that when I was gone, if I called every day, she'd be fine, and then I'd call, and she'd be depressed for the rest of the day. She'd think about it and everything. It was easier—we did maybe once a week.

With her daughter "fine" before they talked, and "depressed the rest of the day" afterward, Abby thought that Peyton's yearning for her mother was somehow fabricated by their weekly phone calls, abetted by her father.

So, I really seriously feel like she played up, not—she didn't play it up—but I know my dad missed me terribly, but he projected that on my daughter. She missed me. Don't get me wrong, I know she missed me. But she always put on a brave face and so did I.

She always has been kind of like a mommy girl. When she was with me, she was very clingy, very lovey, and we have a great relationship. But . . . she doesn't miss me. She doesn't pine after me and I pretty much didn't either at the time.

Ultimately, the story Abby tells is of a two-sided relationship, one with all the loving connection but without the inconvenience of need, one in which her daughter is loving when they are together but "doesn't pine" after her. How did she solve any inopportune moments of longing, bubbling up unbidden after their regular phone calls?

I limited my communication home. We talked once a week, but oftentimes she'd get on the phone and we had nothing to talk about. She'd really rather be talking to her friends online. It was kind of like, "Okay, whatever."

Despite the intentions to "keep really in good touch," Abby reduces her daughter's expressed emotional needs to a "projection" from her father, which led to her decreasing their contact while she was away. She further managed any maternal desire by suppressing it.

I didn't let myself think about that too much. I'll be honest with you, all the time I was there, that was the big thing. If I talked to her every day I wouldn't have been able to do it. In the last few years I've recognized in myself this ability I have to kind of disassociate. She has, too, as an only child.

Without imputing some inherent need on the part of a mother for her child, we can witness in Abby's account a fairly explicit emotional strategy in which she "dissociates" to accommodate the requirements of her job, reducing Peyton's needs and her own to achieve the necessary independence.

Using Language to Shrink Our Obligations

People also modified or invented new language to minimize their obligations to others. Phyllis was a single African-American mother whose verbal play managed to redefine commitment in the first place, just as we saw with Fiona ("I'm committed to anything as long as it's good"). Left by the fathers of both her children, Phyllis viewed intimacy as a risk, a moment of costly vulnerability with an uncertain payoff. "As far as what we owe our mates?" she asked. "Yeah, okay, conditional love until I feel like you've de-served or earned unconditional."

People created new words and phrases to distinguish relationships from one another, along with the obligations that accompany them. They used the term "heart family" to signify unrelated people who actually care about each other, as opposed to unfeeling mothers and brothers; "bar friends" to distinguish from "real friends"; "the brother I love" to distinguish from the ones they did not. When they came up with new phrases to describe situations to which old understandings did not apply, people inadvertently highlighted the space between social trends and the means we have to describe them.

Manny Trigeros, a food service worker, used the term "live-in family," for example, to describe his vision for his second wife, now pregnant, as he sought to distinguish between that family and how he thought of his first child, who now lived in New York. Just saying "family" was not good enough, Manny felt, because he needed the mediating adjective "live-in"; how else could he convey that *this* family would be different, closer, than his first family living three hundred miles away? His invention disman-tled the assumption that families cohabit unless we specify that they do not, and his language both reflected and constructed distance in rela-tionships, highlighting his efforts to connect to some and to detach from others.

Stanley, the divorcing man who minimized his daughter's "dependence," also found new meanings of the common phrase "working on a marriage" that enabled him to turn away:

> Because the work changes. The work can be in letting go. That's the right thing to do. Or if something changes in the future where it can be saying yes, I can be your friend, even if you're dating someone else or you get remarried or whatever it is. The work is all in dealing with that, and if that's ultimately what happens and that she's happy about that, that could be part of it too. So, yeah, that's all the work. Because I think bottling it up or denying it, if that's what happens it's not going to work either.

In Stanley's formulation, "working on a marriage" has a new meaning, one that would perhaps surprise the pragmatic couples in the last chapter: leav-ing it behind, or working on being able to do so. Sometimes people who aim to adopt the stance of independence are not quite there yet emotionally; Stanley appears to be engaging in some cultural creativity (transforming "marriage takes work" into "the work is in relinquishing") to move his own heart.

Detachment Brokers: Seeking the Absolution of Others

Sometimes we want to limit what we do for others, but are uncomfortable with drawing those boundaries, for example, because the act would violate social mores that still carried moral weight. Lena is the single mother whose job in health care empowered her after her divorce. Her three daughters, now in college or just out, still blamed her for the breakup, she said. She had never explained to them the reasons for the breakup—which was catalyzed by her husband's affair, and culminated when he left them, taking the refrigerator and leaving a gaping hole in the kitchen, and then failing to pay a dime (but still showing up) for his daughter's bat mitzvah several weeks later. Instead, she said, she hoped that just by her behaving conscientiously, working, being responsible for them, they would see that whatever happened between their parents was not her fault. But Lena still feels some guilt, clearly—even though she certainly seems the aggrieved one in her recollections of the marriage, in which she worked constantly to pay for her husband's education and then was betrayed by his infidelity once he graduated and started a business of his own. The guilt Lena feels about breaking off the relationship emerges when she describes its end.

> Is it better to stay together and hate each other and then divorce when the kids are in college, or is it better to split now and be done with it? That's kind of what was going through my head, part of it. The other part of it . . . my brother was like, "You can't trust him. You've got to move on. You've got to let him go." I had a little bit of . . . I didn't know what to do . . . a very difficult situation. I mean, I wasn't thrilled with the idea of being a single parent. I mean, I don't guess anybody is. But I had to get an apartment. I had to . . . I mean, there were a lot of things . . . I had to get a better job. I had to take up an extra job.

Lena describes herself as momentarily paralyzed by the daunting task of supporting herself and her three daughters, and emphasizes that she kept her children's best interests at heart by weighing the impact of divorce versus a high-conflict marriage on them. Her brother's urging, she remembered, helped her make the difficult choice. By invoking her brother at this moment in her narrative, Lena brings him in as another witness to her humiliation, absolving her of guilt in deciding to end the relationship.

When they talked about similarly difficult stories, people frequently called upon the voices of others, who serve as what I term "detachment brokers." These were influential others—such as therapists, priests, or relatives—who were called upon to witness or sanction distancing behavior, particularly if the narrators were slightly uncomfortable, feeling that their actions might count as dishonorable because they signaled they were not committed enough. Most commonly, such narrators are mothers who seek to disentangle themselves from children, as that relationship is still widely perceived to be off limits to detachment.

Katherine was the white financial services officer who had been laid off several times in the last few years. When her ex-husband died unexpectedly after a routine knee operation, she invited her teenaged daughter, Jessica, who had been living with him, to return home and join her sister in Katherine's household. Yet Katherine and her fiancé, Lars, ended up kicking Jessica out after two months.

> So when he passed away, I said, "You pack your stuff up and you can come live with me." She lived with us for two months and then we caught her lying about several things and said, "That's it. We can't have you here lying and being deceitful; it's just not a good influence for your sister."

Two months might seem like a fairly brief grace period for a teenager who has just lost her custodial father, even for a teenager who is misbehaving. There is some evidence that a part of Katherine thinks so too, because she invokes the advice of her therapist here, who counseled her to lower the boom despite her feelings.

> And the therapist told me that if I kept allowing her to come in, she was going to keep taking advantage of me. And I had to stop allowing her to do that. She said she's going to have to hit rock bottom before she realizes what she has to do for herself. She's the only one that has control of that. And it took me a long time to realize that. Finally, I realized [the therapist] was right, and it was hard to do that because I love [my daughter] so much. And she's been through so much the last two years.

Katherine derived from her therapist the strength to draw the line around the extent of her commitment to her daughter, who was acting out in the months after her father's death. By pointing to the expertise of the therapist, whose counsel warned of continuing exploitation, Katherine reasoned her way to an honorable position ("Finally, I realized she was right"), which she underscored by referring to how hard it was to ask her daughter to leave, how much she loved her, and how much she understood the difficult position her grieving daughter was in.

For some people, stepparents—often fathers—seem to perform the same role, standing apart from the mother's relationship with her children and offering the judgment that they are too close. Katherine said she appreciated that Lars, her fiancé, let her know:

> Joanie [her other daughter] especially was kind of running all over me, and Lars, he just stood back and said, "Wait a minute. You're letting your kid run all over you? You've got to stop doing that." So, he kind of made me open my eyes and make me see I was trying to be her friend and not her mother. And he just—you can't do that.

Lars absolved Katherine of distancing behavior, the establishment of limits, the enactment of "tough love," actions that she was not entirely comfortable laying claim to on her own.

When Sylvia married Derek, they went through a difficult adjustment period with her son.

> Derek really saw him more as a manipulator more than I would see and I was more protecting of him, "He's not manipulating, he's just whatever," and I'll give excuses. I'll own it when I finally see it myself. Derek [is] more objective.

In Sylvia's view, Derek helped her to become more impartial about her son, by helping her to see when he was exploiting her allegiance.

Detachment brokers were emblems called upon to enable the socially risky distancing that people sometimes desired. The greater incidence of this tactic among distancing mothers serves as a signal of just how transgressive this move is for them, one for which they need the permission of witnesses. It was just one of multiple strategies people deployed to move toward smaller expectations of others, more finite obligations, shallower connections, or at the very least reframing their feelings in light of shrinking understandings of what we owe each other.[20]

THE PERILS OF INDEPENDENCE

Those who adopt the stance of independence toward their obligations sing a song of defiance to celebrate their triumphant autonomy. Like Elsa in the 2013 Disney film *Frozen,* they shrug off the pull of family warmth and responsibility and embrace their freedom; as Elsa sang in the ode "Let It Go," "the fears that once controlled me can't get to me at all." Independence promises a freedom from vulnerability and (other people's) need.

Fiona's defiance might in some ways be chilling, as independence severs connections in service to uncompromising standards with little room for vulnerability, for human mistakes, for dependence. But we can also see the devaluation of care work and job precariousness that helped to generate her situation, and we can understand her triumph as an echo of her freedom from a gendered trajectory of obligation that falls disproportionately upon lower-income women.

As we saw in the last chapter, many Americans reach for personal responsibility narratives that emphasize individual choice, and these accounts are particularly likely from more advantaged people. The problem with the language of choice, however, is that it becomes a moral statement about how others who do not stay together are "making a different choice." For some less advantaged workers, however, the choices on offer are all bad; the women declaring independence had few good options to support their caregiving, from faithless men similarly unmoored by unstable employment, to insecure low-wage market work, to the withdrawal of the neoliberal state. With nobody there, and buttressed by dominant narratives of self-sufficiency, is it any wonder they "chose" independence?[21]

The stances of "defying" or "choosing" reflect readily available meanings of obligation, and offer culturally understandable ways to explain them. Fiona's is another kind of individual responsibility, but one that fits in just as well with insecurity culture and its emphasis on personal autonomy and the devolution of risk. The next chapter explores the perspective of those with a gendered trajectory of entitlement, but who have nonetheless incurred great losses from the rise of job insecurity: less advantaged men and their twisted helix of duty and betrayal.

CHAPTER 5

✧

The Knots of Duty

Gary Gilbert, the laid-off tradesman we first met in the book's introduction, had shouldered the blame for his layoff like a resigned and sorrowful Atlas, but he faced his intimate life with an entirely different stance. With respect to work, despite the lack of advance notice of the layoff, his shock given that he knew the company had been making money, and his dismay at being left without an adequate livelihood to pass down to his son, Gary essentially absolved his employer of responsibility, channeling anger into grief and a shrugging sort of fatalism. We can recall how he proclaimed his own work ethic, his own dependability, as a statement of personal character that rested on the notion of unyielding duty, yet like many on the receiving end of precarious work, his was a selective sort of duty, one that applied to himself but not to his employers, whom he released from all but the barest minimum of obligation.

Where was the anger, the sense of betrayal we might expect from someone with this kind of job history, particularly one who decreed his own obligations at work with such fervor? Gary and others like him feel their anger not at work but at home. Borrowing a term from psychology to capture this shifting emotional burden, we might say they are "displacing." Displacing is a way for workers to feel their feelings, but without aiming them at the forces at work that they view as more implacable, impervious, and inevitable. Instead, they aim these feelings at their intimate partners, animated by a powerful sense of other people's duty at home.[1]

DUTY AND THE ANGRY WHITE MAN

Duty is a potent cultural force. A deeply freighted call to action, it can inspire people to put aside their own rational self-interest, enable them to give of themselves to meet another's need, and even lead to great martyrdom. Part of duty's might lies in the high stakes it lays down, stakes of sacrifice or abandonment: one either steps up to fulfill one's duty or is some kind of deserter. In this way, duty acts as a kind of high-beam spotlight, bleaching out the gray areas, intensifying the darks and lights. That intensity is reflected in the feelings that surround duty, certainly in the zeal with which people assert its necessity, but also in the vehemence of those who witness its neglect.

Duty also suggests a certain set of known tasks—and people—that one is obliged to satisfy, defined by conventional notions of gender, race, and other social categories, understandings inscribed in the interactions and the institutions that demarcate the wrong and the wronged. We cannot really invent our own duty out of whole cloth—when we try to expand or contract it, we run up against other people—witness the cooing surprise with which onlookers often greet involved fathers. Yet these conventional ideas—what we owe each other as men, as women, as employers and workers, as intimate partners, as parents and children—are shifting, starting with the social contract on the job.

Gary is on his third serious relationship, after his first two marriages imploded, the second one ending when his wife called him from home as he was traveling for work to tell him she was leaving him. "I have a very set opinion of relationships and how females handle them," Gary says rather flatly. "It's—what I've seen consistently throughout my life."

Gary's experience with "females" includes his mother's turning him over to foster care when he was a teenager and his two dissolved marriages, both of which produced children; he views his lack of contact with his first son, who is now a heroin addict, as a harrowing failure that plagues him to this day. While he keeps his language quite abstract, using general pronouncements about "females" and "people," in the introduction we witnessed the note of personal betrayal pervading his talk about "the hurt that's been caused to me by a lack of commitment on the part of other people" and his comments that "marriage can be tossed out like a Pepsi can." Gary may not be able to name betrayal at work, then, but he can see it clearly at home, at the hands of women. Perhaps, we might surmise, Gary feels tossed out like a Pepsi can as well.[2]

Much has been written of late about "angry white men," those whose race and gender privilege has not protected them from the economic ravages of the last thirty years. In a book that ranges widely over school shootings, battering, and fathers' rights movements, Michael Kimmel suggests that lower-middle-class and working-class men suffer from "aggrieved entitlement," stemming from their sense of having lost something precious that was owed to them. "Ironically that sense of being entitled is a marker not of deprivation but of privilege," Kimmel writes. "It is that spring—the belief in the system, having something yet to lose, and feeling like they're not getting what they deserve—that sources the rivers of rage that flow through America."[3]

What is the treasure that they have lost, and who has it now? White men on the lower end of the class ladder today are haunted by the echo of old expectations, of being able to support their families through jobs largely reserved for them, to hand such a livelihood down to their sons, and to count on women's personal care services in the home. The expectations stem from a gendered historical trajectory of such entitlements, in which men like them—indeed, often their own fathers and grandfathers— enjoyed these assurances.[4]

The treasure here, then, is perhaps a simple one: the chance to earn a modest but stable living and to head a stable family. Furthermore, while their privileges were shored up by crucial inequalities, they also entailed certain obligations on the part of the men—theirs was not simply a license for idleness. With the promise of a good life hinging on their participation in lifelong, full-time work, this "package deal" feels like an honorable bargain they are willing to strike, rather than a collection of undeserved advantages—hence the righteous tone of their hurt and outrage.[5]

This legacy has been chipped away, as many writers have noted, by a host of political, economic, and social changes over the last forty years. Primary among these, however, has been the erosion of job security and the economic platform on which less advantaged white men's privilege has rested. Yet social movements advancing feminism and civil rights helped to make visible the gendered and racialized nature of their privilege; among these groups they find the social targets for their ire. Of course, with regard to many characteristics, gender and race have declined in significance compared to class, as less advantaged men and women of all races face increasingly similar economic straits, since the real story of the last four decades has been the ever-widening crevasse in socioeconomic advantage. Take pay equity, for example: the distance between the average earnings of men with college degrees and high-school-educated men in the United States has increased by 36 percent in thirty years, so that now the median income of one is more than twice the other; for women, the spread has increased by 29 percent. In the meantime, even after we control for education, experience, industry, occupation, hours worked, and a host of other factors, men still outearn women by 9 percent.[6]

This collective displacing—blaming feminists and people of color for what are mostly economic changes undertaken by political and economic elites—magnifies what is happening on an individual level as well. Displacing happens when people uphold notions of their own duty at work but someone else's duty in their intimate lives. This combination is much more likely among men, of course, as orthodox understandings of gender outline extensive duties for men at work but not at home, where men have long been the beneficiaries of women's care and responsibility.

Gary's current girlfriend is a better match for him, he says. Nonetheless, he holds back from giving himself totally:

> She's important to me, you know. She's the longest-running relationship I've ever had. I'd like it to remain that way. At the same time, I got to say—I have kind of a hard heart when it comes to that stuff. If it ended, it ended. I mean, we don't have kids together. We're not married, we never will be.

Gary is stinting in this relationship, even when it is going well, which he communicates in tone, with how he says "you know" almost dismissively, with tepid conditional phrasing—"I'd like it"—and with verbal cues that delineate a moment of straightforward but perhaps impolitic honesty— "I got to say." Convinced that women will betray him, he says that if it does end, it will be because *she* was unable to sustain the commitment. "I am a very committed person," he said, of his reformed persona. It is other people—and by this he means the "females" in his life, but not his employer—who *should* be "very committed" but are not.

At work, then, notions of his own duty and how he has fallen short exact a powerful penance in the form of shame and grief. With intimate partners, however, he attends closely to the duty of others, specifically women. Betrayed by both, Gary recognizes the failings of one and not the other, using a very particular configuration of duty to displace feelings of anger, disappointment, and outrage away from work and onto his intimate life.

Less advantaged men have a unique vantage point on the job insecurity that rages around them like a storm. Long challenged to fulfill the provider role, they now face jobs with stagnating wages, no benefits, and no promise of stability. Scholars have found men's connections to their children are often mediated through their wives and expressed through material provisioning. Without steady work, however, men's contributions to families within typically understood gender roles are uncertain, generating a central problem for them to solve: What is their duty now?

The traditional definitions of gendered duty are what shape the feelings that Gary allows himself to feel; his displacing keeps his intimate life at once rigid and fragile. Others try to set duty aside, attempting to take a new, more malleable stance toward obligation. They seek to reconcile themselves to instability by adopting, however awkwardly, a more flexible stance, with different expectations of self and other. Still others wrestle with the dictates of duty, managing the expectations of others to reestablish the contours of the honorable, to redefine intimate life as an arena where their contributions are valuable. The fixity of gender for men, as opposed to women—what scholars have called the "stalled revolution," in which women have changed far more than men—may be written into the traditional notions of duty that they have been carrying around. Rather than discard it for a new ethos, however, some men are now redefining what counts as their duty in the first place, and along the way redefining what it means to be a man.[7]

THE USES OF BETRAYAL

Like Gary, those who could potentially be naming betrayal everywhere—people who have been laid off and who have been left by spouses, for example—instead often curtailed those narratives at work, while giving them free rein in their intimate life. This imbalance reflects the moral wall, the fact that the "home" is viewed as the realm of mutual aid and responsibility, where you can really count on others, where expectations of altruism prevail; the extent of the betrayal that people feel when these expectations are dashed is a measure of the height of that moral wall. Yet at the same time the absence of betrayal talk at work suggests that it is not just bubbling up at home unmediated. Rather, it is being allowed to emerge, in contrast to the significant effort people undertake (as we witnessed in chapter 2) to suppress and manage inconvenient feelings at work. Watching what people do at work allows us to see what they do not do with their friends and family and leads us to ask: Why is betrayal not an inconvenient feeling at home?[8]

Some people, particularly those who adopt the stance of duty, use betrayal stories to shape and explain their commitment. They seem to use betrayal as an emotional crowbar, helping to justify and explain their dislodging from close relationships. Betrayal acts both as a sign of the heightened expectations people maintain for their intimate life and as a means by which they pull back from those expectations. Finally, betrayal narratives provide the drama through which people reconcile, painfully, the contradictions of duty and independence, the primacy of sacrifice on the one hand and of invulnerability on the other.

How different the emotional tone is here, compared to the jubilant rebelliousness of Fiona and the less advantaged women in the last chapter, who prioritize independence, who are "defying." Rather than betrayal borne, there we heard more about traps escaped, the contrast serving as evidence of how historical burdens of need fall differently upon less advantaged men and women. Both groups reflect their gendered trajectories in their response to the ravages of contemporary insecurity, with men showing their disappointment, pain, and outrage stemming from a prevailing sense of loss of entitlement while some women evince grim triumph stemming from a prevailing sense of freedom from obligation.[9]

Of course, other women adopt the lens of duty as well, as we will explore in the next chapter; women thus seem to have at least two approaches—independence or duty—to managing the new insecurities. In contrast, however, less advantaged men seem to converge on the primacy of duty as a way to make sense of changes in their lives. On the one hand, the notion of men's duty has a longstanding history of roping men into dirty and dangerous jobs. But in an age of insecurity, duty also has a uniquely contemporary edge: it serves as a potent reminder that *they* were not the ones who left the table, a symbol of their continued honor in the face of the dramatic changes going on around them. Calling on duty bespeaks what these lower-middle-class and working-class men are still willing to do, as one country music song portraying a jobseeker put it, mournfully: "give you forty [hours], and then some, whatever it takes." For less advantaged men, however, "whatever it takes" is transforming all around them.[10]

WHEN TWO STANCES COLLIDE

Conventional ideas of gender have not been serving less advantaged men well of late. Yet by amplifying the failure of others in the home, by codifying disappointment, traditional masculine notions of duty can lead to the disillusionment, anger, and outrage that make intimate connections fraught, offering little comfort beyond the claim to honor. Some, like Sean Dunning, sought a different route.

Sean had been a merchant ship captain before he was diagnosed with a serious mental illness that interfered with his job, leading him to be laid off. He repeatedly reached for financial metaphors to describe promises, such as "Marriage is probably my ultimate commitment; it's like signing a mortgage." He joked about the compromises he has made in that marriage, lamenting that they moved away from his home in Illinois for his wife's new job, because he "didn't prenup a move to the East Coast." In calling upon the financial language, Sean imposes a contractual framework on his commitment, both solidifying it with institutionalized economic meanings but stripping it of more transcendent moral content. The jokes show that he does so wittingly, winking and nodding as he draws these slightly profane analogies to what is "supposed to be" the more sacred family sphere.

After Sean was laid off, the family limped along on his wife's salary and savings, while he struggled with the implications of his illness for himself as a spouse and as father to his teenaged son, Michael. After some years, his wife finally asked him to leave, although he had recently moved back in to present a united front when her family visited for Thanksgiving. Sean spent a lot of energy recounting how well he understood his wife's position, however chilling it may seem, since he had made her life very difficult.

> And I told her my family didn't understand why, how she could kick me out kind of thing, but *I* understood. I mean, all along, I said—I always kidded about seeking some "health clause" [out of the "In sickness and health" part of the marital contract], because if I had to live with the kind of crap that she's had, I wouldn't blame her, so—that's why it was an easy decision for me to move out, even though it was devastating and difficult with Michael.

In his narration, Sean blends together different notions of the good, of what his wife should be doing and how he should respond. While he seems to be invoking a notion of duty when he makes reference to the iconic marriage phrase "In sickness and in health," this concept is clearly no longer working for him, since it no longer successfully explains how he is supposed to approach his wife while he has this debilitating mental illness. His feelings of betrayal seep in, as when he refers to the moment of moving out as "devastating and difficult." At the same time, however, he maintains that because of "the kind of crap that's she had," he "wouldn't blame her" for kicking him out, and he even sounds a bit like Fiona when he suggests that the decision to move out was "easy," because there's only so much he can ask his wife to endure. Through this mélange, Sean demonstrates a coincidence of a sense of abandonment and (attempted) independence.

Later on in the interview, however, a plaintive query escapes. He asks: "If I had cancer would you do the same—would you kick my ass out if I had cancer?" Sean's distraught sense of being forsaken is bubbling up through (and despite) his attempt to reason his way toward a cool detachment.

Sean epitomizes the battle between two stances toward obligation: on the one hand that which involves high expectations of others, a yearning for deep commitments, and a keen outrage when these commitments are broken or not forthcoming. These feelings are rooted in a principle of duty, and are often more intense among those who feel buffeted by insecurity on the job, as they think "Well, we have to expect job insecurity, because that's just the way it is, but at least here at home people are not disposable. Outside of work, we're just not supposed to treat each other that way." On the other hand, there is a breezier emotional culture, resting upon a flexible stance toward commitment, a loose attachment to others, dictating a cool distance, a light touch. Some seem to think that the light breeziness of independence is how they are *supposed* to feel. They then can be heard laboring on their strong feelings to bring them in line with a more detached, constrained sort of approach, with low expectations for self and other.

Sean works hard to manage the distance between what he feels we owe our spouses—not to abandon each other in mental illness—and what he thinks he is supposed to feel—that marriage, perhaps like a financial commitment, can sustain only so much, and that it is unreasonable to expect that a spouse could withstand such an onslaught on her own happiness and fulfillment. Visible here are not just the core foundations of Sean's deepest morality but also his perceptions about other people's morality, which shape what it *feels* like for him to feel these feelings, to hold these ideas dear (for Sean, it is very painful). Note how his position in the final question changes as well, so he is no longer narrating what he told "her," but instead asking "you" directly, painfully, and thus giving the lie to his compliant stance. Sean's feelings—as captured in the poignant sorrow of "Would you kick me out if I had cancer?"—demonstrate the lengthy emotional distance between the two stances of duty and independence that he tries to reconcile. Dragging himself back from his plaintive note of desertion, he tells his wife, "*I* understood."[11]

The writer Richard Russo considers the interplay of duty and independence in his novel *Empire Falls*, in which Janine leaves her husband, Miles, the main character and—in her eyes—an overly dutiful man. "It was pathetic really, and when Janine decided to divorce him, she'd added watching-Miles-get-suckered-into-doing-things-he-didn't-want-to-do-and-swore-he-wouldn't-do to the long list of things she wouldn't miss." But when Janine contemplates her new fiancé, Walt, she sees the flaws inherent in a more "flexible" approach:

> The problem though, she had to admit, was that Walt wouldn't commit either to *doing* or *not doing* much of anything. The secret of his success, he was fond of reminding her, was keeping all his options open. There were times when zigging was called for, but on further reflection you might want to zag.[12]

Duty opened you up to exploitation, Russo seems to be saying, but independence, at least of this particularly flexible kind, was feather-light, a stance nearly indistinguishable from that of a conman.

As Russo suggests, these are stances that are difficult to combine in one person. For those who subscribe to duty, invoking independence can be an uneasy step. Sean embodies a collision between the two stances, at one point highlighting the dire stakes, at another trying to control his own feelings of betrayal. His emotional labor works—only partly successfully—to discipline his yearning for enduring support and unconditional loyalty, to construct a savvy posture of detached understanding.

DUTY, CONNECTION, AND THE IMPACT OF JOB INSECURITY

Standard understandings of men's duty, then, can extract a rent that becomes particularly high under the duress of job insecurity, as we have seen in some men's intimate partnerships, brittle with rigid expectations, suffused with betrayal and outrage. Yet the costs are potentially even higher for their relationships with children.

For Sean, his layoff interrupted his career trajectory, his ability to provide for his family, and his identity as a good father to his teenaged son. Now the family was worried about making the mortgage payments, drawing down their savings just to make ends meet.

> I tried for a long time to keep things as normal as I possibly could keep them, you
> know, in retrospect. And it then got to a point where—it just wasn't—more cuts
> were going to have to be made, and it was embarrassing for me and humiliating
> for me to have to come out and say that. Because as a father—[you're supposed
> to be a] *My Three Sons* provider . . . and then when you can't fulfill that role that
> you—society as well as yourself have expectations [about] . . . you're going to
> feel guilty. It was hard to talk about that, but . . . it got to the point where he
> knew that we just couldn't take off, and we didn't go skiing the last years and
> we've always had a ski trip together, and we couldn't do it.

While Sean has come out of the closet, so to speak, as a nonprovider, with the canceled ski trips, he is still struggling with the dictates of the duties of fatherhood—being the "*My Three Sons* provider"—that he cannot fulfill.

Scholars document how men have sometimes been so swept along in their work commitments, doing what they were supposed to do as men, that they find themselves without deep emotional connections to their family, or with shallow relationships with their children almost entirely mediated by their wives. Masculinities scholar Michael Messner identifies these as some of the "costs of masculinity," noting that "men tend to pay heavy costs—in the form of shallow relationships, poor health, and early death—for conformity with the narrow definitions of masculinity that promise to bring them status and privilege." Yet this raises a central conundrum about fathers in precarious employment: If you do your duty by attending to work, thereby letting your connections to your children attenuate, what happens when work grows insecure? Are dutiful fathers, those following the rules, then to be left with nothing?[13]

Recently, Sean and his wife fought over whether they should help their son buy a boat. "You know the whole thing with the boat thing—I promised that I was going to help him out and that we were going to do it," Sean said, soberly and painfully measuring out the meaning of the boat, which has begun, it seems, to represent his fatherhood. Without a steady job, however, he has to negotiate with his wife over the economically foolhardy but symbolically powerful gesture of giving a promised boat to his son. Sorrowfully, he recounted his bottom line:

> I said, "The only thing that I've got left is my word, and if you take that away, what have I got?"

Fathers have traditionally made connections to others through their duty to work, to provide. Yet these pathways to intimacy can make job insecurity even more traumatic for them, as they endure the risk it poses to their relationships.[14]

OPTIONAL FATHERHOOD AND THE CARE WORK ETHIC

Men thus face a trap of gendered duty, one from which they have garnered privilege, yes, but one that for some, particularly less advantaged men with increasing job insecurity, exacts a high cost. While men can cling to traditional notions of duty to justify the animus they feel toward their intimate partners, and others like Sean try to invoke independence instead, some men immersed in insecurity look to redefine duty, particularly with regard to their children. They maneuver within notions of duty to shift the configuration of what counts as obligation at home, to expand what they owe and thus what they contribute. While this change might seem like an unvarnished good, nonetheless active fatherhood can still be a struggle, one shaped by the rigidity of other people's ideas, as notions of duty are made and remade in interactions with other people and within institutions.

Men who rework conceptions of duty in their intimate lives battle against prevailing notions of optional fatherhood.

Of course, while media accounts frequently herald a sea change in masculinity allowing it to include active, involved fatherhood, the evidence is actually far more complex. There are certainly variants of masculinity that include the duty to care. An estimated 20 percent of fathers in two-parent households spend as much time as mothers interacting with and being available to their children, a significant increase over the 1960s. Still, father involvement has demonstrated a complicated set of trends: fathers in two-parent families are more likely to be involved, although on average their childcare time still lags behind that of mothers, while an increasingly large number of American fathers live apart from their children due to separation or divorce. Paradoxically, then, these trends mean that children are now less likely to live with an involved father, despite the increased participation of some fathers.[15]

The unevenness of our expectations for fatherhood mean that involved fathers are often confronted with people who are surprised by how much they care. Diane and her husband Alan had been married for eleven years before she had triplets. The ensuing fifteen years were extremely challenging, she recalled, particularly the early years, and especially for her husband, who had to stay home with them during the day while she earned benefits from her job as a teacher.

> It was rougher on him than it was on me really, quite honestly. It was funny, we were just out last week, and a good, good close friend, a girl that I've known since 5th grade, she was telling how she really respected him a lot for what he did at that time and dah dah dah. And as he put it, he's like, "You know what, I had no choice. They were my children," and she said, "Well, a lot of men would have just said—," and he was like, "Well I wasn't going to leave Diane and I wasn't going to leave my kids, so, the way I looked at it was I had no choice."

Similarly, Owen Coolidge, a white lower-middle-class man, told disturbing stories of taking care of a wife with a mental illness, but said he was insulted by "well-meaning people making comments like, 'Oh, gosh. Most men would have walked away.' Yadda yadda yadda. And that used to make me so mad. . . . I used to get offended by that." In the case of deeply involved fathers, the language of "choice" was not an emblem of culturally honorable autonomy, but instead more of an insult. Indeed, these comments felt like a stain, a sign of the elective nature of their gendered caregiving and that, to the rest of the world, what they were doing was above and beyond their duty.

As these bystander comments reveal, what we call "duty" is subject to the recognition of others, whose conflicting versions of duty may in fact be dominant, encoded in narratives of surprise and heroism when men simply show up to care. These dominant assumptions can even be institutionalized in the law. Clark Wheeler's first wife left him when she began using cocaine and moved in with her dealer; he ended up winning custody of their toddler in the divorce and spent the next two years as his primary caregiver. "All of my energies went into my son. Making sure that he was in a good preschool. Making sure that his life was stable," Clark recalled. "My whole thing was to take care of my son and to make sure that he had as little—there was as little impact on him as possible from all of this."

Yet when his ex-wife eschewed drugs, went through rehab, and got married, she won back custody of their son, who was three years old at the time, thanks to a "tender years" doctrine prevailing in the state of Connecticut that gave presumptive custody to the mother of preschool-aged children, barring extenuating circumstances. Clark was devastated. Nevertheless, what was his reaction, when his three-year-old son, whom he had taken care of every day for years, moved out of his house? Clark left the state and did not see him again for a decade.

CLARK: So they gave her custody. And that just was beyond my ability to cope with. So I wound up just deciding to leave.

RS: Leave?

CLARK: Leave my job, leave the area, and that's when I moved to Virginia.

RS: So your reasoning behind moving was just to, I mean, you know what I mean, why leave the whole . . .?

CLARK: Personal survival. Personal survival.

RS: So you thought you had to leave the area just to be able to cope at all, kind of have a new beginning of sorts?

CLARK: Right, that was absolutely essential to my well-being at that point, I just had to make a clean break from everything. It was one of those things where I said, where do—okay, I'm free of everything except financial obligations for my son, where do I want to go and what do I want to do with my life?

Clark had been a primary caregiver, doing his best to provide a safe and stable home for his son for years. He took on that responsibility by himself when his wife left the family, an unusual decision for the single fathers in this study and nationally (but commonplace among single mothers).

Yet the courts declined to recognize his actual fathering as equally or even more valuable than the potential mothering the son would receive from the woman who left him years before. The gendered assumptions embedded in the institutional environment—as reflected in the court's decision to take his son away from him—served to rend the ongoing caring relationship between father and son, as well as to diminish and discourage active fathering.[16]

In addition, however, we can read gendered notions in Clark's decision to leave the area entirely after the courts took action. Rather than submit to the humiliation of noncustodial visiting and the agony of daily contact with the person he hated in order to maintain his involvement in his son's life, Clark chose to abandon the effort entirely. The decision is understandable—to choose otherwise is to take a far more difficult, surely heartbreaking, possibly even soul-destroying route—but it is also one that prioritizes his own well-being over his relationship with his son. Furthermore, he does not feel that he has to explain much about this act, and it is only after repeated questions (from the graduate student interviewer, who sounds a little surprised) that he ventures an explanation. Indeed, once his son leaves his house, he considers himself "free of everything except financial obligations for my son." This statement, though a painful one, reflects the stance that men's caregiving is optional, a stance shored up by his ex-wife, the courts, and, in many contexts, mainstream culture.

What if we looked at the obligation to care as we look at the obligation to work? We might identify a "care work ethic," a system of values (like the work ethic) that prioritizes caregiving dedication and effort and that imbues such work with the moral valence of duty, maintaining that it reflects and enhances good character. If Clark demonstrates a care work ethic, then, its situational quality means it is a markedly attenuated one.

We can contrast Clark's decision to leave the area with the situation of Mindy, a single mother who lost custody of her four children to her ex-husband and his new wife. She described the slow, inexorable process of losing touch with her children, a process that tears at her heart today. It began with the "magnified moment" when she had to battle with her ex-husband and his new wife to take her youngest son to his dentist appointment:

> And I was like "This is my child." I said I took them every, you know, most of the time from the time they were little. I took them when they were two years old to the dentist. I took them at six months old for their eye appointment. I mean, "You're taking my whole purpose of living away."

"I'm devastated," she said, simply. "It's like somebody took my kids away, and that's what they did." Mindy's narrative centers on the sheer injustice of her loss. While the defeat defined her subsequent life, however, she still maintained their home as long as she could afford it, moved to just a mile from her ex-husband's house to make it easier for the kids to visit, and "always had to fight to be in their lives."[17]

Like Clark, Mindy was distraught when she lost custody. She called herself an alienated parent, and was full of grief and bitterness about the lengths to which she had to go to stay involved in her children's lives. Yet despite the mortification of her position—always scrounging for crumbs of contact with them, always the beseeching supplicant—she stayed in the area, and in fact moved closer to try (mostly in vain) to make connections with the children even easier.

> I wanted them, they were my kids. That's what I wanted to do when I had them was to be their mother. Another thing is that I knew what it was like not to have a mother and I knew all the things that I didn't have. And I wanted to give them those things. And when they took them away like that it was—they didn't care where I came from. They didn't care why I made those decisions. They just took them.

Wrapped up in Mindy's tormented narrative are many different themes of motherhood: of maternal desire, of passion, and of power and the lack thereof, but also of duty—the duty to provide care in a certain way, to give her children "all the things I didn't have"—a motive that powers her capacity to fight to maintain her relationships. Without minimizing the certain anguish he felt at losing custody, Clark's decision to leave reflects a different stance, a certain elective approach to care, even after his stint as a primary caregiver. Spurred on by the courts, Clark acceded to dominant notions of gendered duty that defined his care as optional.

MAKING UP FOR OPTIONALITY

Understandings of men's care as optional force men with a serious care work ethic to have to prove it constantly and with vehemence. Gary's story of displacement opened this chapter with the sense of betrayal that lies close to the surface of his intimate partnerships, predicated on traditional notions of gendered duty. Yet he is utterly dedicated to his son, of whom he shares custody with the teen's mother; he even switched jobs to give the youth a better shot at employment later on, and now feels great shame that he was laid off and thus will be unable to help him much in the future when he is looking for an occupation. "I did everything I—I based everything on my son," he avowed. "My work was based on my son. My lifestyle was based on my son. He came first in everything."

Yet Gary was not always this way. In fact, when he refers to "my son" as the person on whom he "based everything," Gary is referring to his second son. He and his first wife, married when she was just sixteen, gave his first son to her mother to raise, after they could not curtail their partying lifestyle, an act he regrets to this day. "Oh, I feel much differently now. I feel much differently now. I know it was just—everything we did was selfish. Every day of—every hour of every day, we lived selfishly." Gary vowed that he would treat his second son, born to a later relationship, differently.

> I think I was almost trying to make up for what I had done the first time around. You know, I think in some way I was trying to make myself feel better about what I had done before maybe. I don't really know. But I know for sure I was determined I was not going to let the same things happen again. I was not going to let this boy grow up in the—such an environment, turmoil and then disarray. It just wasn't going to happen. I wasn't going to allow it.

Gary's first son, the one he gave to his mother-in-law, is now apparently a heroin addict, after a life spent moving from place to place with his grandmother and mother, who was in and out of jail. Gary is tormented by his memory.

> And it haunts me and really on a daily basis I think about it on some level. Some days worse than others, but it's always, stuff like that never leaves your mind. It's always there. I feel bad that I've had so much involvement in my youngest son's life, and I feel like I neglected the first one. I wonder how, if he ever becomes aware of how close me and my youngest son are, how he's going to feel about that.

Gary feels guilty about the discrepancies in his fathering and the benefits he knows his second son has gotten from his active involvement.

Gary is also patently aware that caring is not just altruism, however, but that caregivers themselves get something important out of the relationship; for Gary, an important benefit is the sobriety inspired by being responsible for another person. He expresses some worry about keeping his former self at bay. He has been sober since his second son was born, and took an eight-year hiatus from dating when he and the boy's mother broke up. He's been focused on work and keeping his son on the straight and narrow. But what happens when his son leaves the house? Will he sink back into the old ways once his reason for straightening out is no longer there? Gary is afraid, partially because he is so ashamed of his prior self and what he was "capable of."

> It's always kind of looming over my head, what I—what I'm capable of. And I don't think—I think that's another one of those things that will never go away.
>
> I think one of my biggest concerns right now is that when he is old enough and doesn't have to depend on me—he's been my crutch that's kept me from living a life that I know I shouldn't live. And without him being there—what am I going to do?

Gary's son has acted like a tether for him, keeping him from being the irresponsible person he was before. It's as if now that he sees the world according to duty, Gary is afraid of the abandonment of which he knows he is capable.[18]

Gary's conversion to being a committed father has been total, he maintains. Asked what parents owe their children, he said:

> Everything. My life. Everything.
>
> From the day he was born he comes before me in everything. If—if we're both hungry and there's one French fry, he gets it. If there's—if he needs a schoolbook and I need gas in my car, he gets the schoolbook. I mean, everything. I owe him everything. I brought him into the world, you know, it's up to me to—to see that he, at least, survives his teenage years.

Gary's avowals are impassioned, but perhaps their very intensity betrays a certain anxiety about how his commitment is optional, lacking the taken-for-granted assumptions that prevail for women that conversely make not their caregiving but their detachment something to proclaim.

GENDER INNOVATORS: BEYOND BETRAYAL

When men in this study took on serious caregiving responsibilities, observers often underscored the optional quality of these commitments, much to their chagrin, by commending them effusively for doing what these men considered mandatory: stepping up to meet the needs of others in their care. But Clark, who had left his son as a toddler when he lost custody, invoked duty as he made his way to a new care work ethic with the daughter he had with his second wife. He wanted to be there for her, he said, in the same way that his mother was there for him.

> So when the bus came home, I was here for my daughter.
>
> And I felt that was very important. Again, that's part of my upbringing. I mean, when I got off the bus when I was in elementary school my mom was always there for me. And I wanted to provide the same stability for my daughter. I wanted her to have a secure life to where she knew there was somebody there for her.

Clark prioritized the care standard—*someone* there to greet the child coming off the school bus—but not its gender, so he took on this care responsibility as would, he maintained, any good parent (even one who happened to be a man).

In those moments when conventional gender expectations conflicted with care, then, some men innovated with new definitions of duty in order to prioritize the care work ethic. They eschewed the gendered "choice" that was assumed to be part of the mantle of masculinity; for these men, assuming responsibility for primary care was nothing more than their duty as humans (as parents, adult children, or spouses), and failing to do so was a form of abandonment.

Clark also cooked dinner for his daughter every night, again recalling his mother as he did so.

> I was brought up by a mother that always cooked at home, and going out to a restaurant was maybe a three- or four-time-a-year special event. Kids today, it's like, most of them—most of the parents don't cook anymore.
>
> And I think that will really help [my daughter] in her life, so that she'll remember, just like I remembered my mom always cooked for me; well, "Dad always cooked for me and I'm going to cook for my kids." It's something that I want to pass along to her.

Defining the work that is part of the care work ethic, Clark seeks to pass on the ritual of the home-cooked meal; the gender of the cook goes unremarked in the legacy of good care he hopes to bequeath.

In the past fifty years, women's lives have changed dramatically, so that what counts as femininity has broadened to include many configurations of caring and working. While media portrayals of the "mommy wars" might try to pit women with different configurations against each other, in actuality women simply have more honorable options for how they might live their lives than their mothers and grandmothers did, even as those options are constrained by available resources. Men's lives, and what counts as masculinity, have not changed nearly as much. Some of this "stalled revolution", I would suggest, stems from the fixed notions of duty that govern men's sense of the honorable self. And while some men might try to set duty aside as they reach for other stances like independence, the stories of Clark and men like him suggest that masculinity could widen to include more options when they work within the constraints of duty, and manage to redefine their responsibilities. And when such men are able to expand notions of masculinity to include caregiving, as studies from the Great Depression suggest, they actually help to buffer their families from the strain of economic uncertainty.[19]

Such kinds of gender innovation are not limited to those in insecure work, or to less advantaged men. Patrick Harlow is a police officer, a stocky figure, watchful, cautious, with the sturdy skepticism of one who has worked in law enforcement for decades. At the same time, he says he wishes he could have been a nurse ("I think it would have been nice to be a nurse. I know that sounds a little silly, but I like helping people like when they're sick or can't do things for themselves"), and talks about practicing his own brand of community care, in which he enjoys checking up on area retirees.

> And we have a lot of cops that have retired in the last eighteen or twenty years, a lot of them have passed away. Some of them have become very sick, some have had long drawn-out diseases. And I'm not tooting my horn or anything but I keep a check on as many of them as I can. And I go see them and I may stop by their house when I'm working, just to say hi to them. But I like helping people. I think a lot of people forget older people. I mean there are a lot of people that are sitting around at these nursing homes and different facilities. They may be physically deteriorating, but they still have a pretty sharp mind and, you know, they still have a lot to offer. And I like talking to those kinds of people.

Patrick is proud of his care work ethic, and gratified by his own high standards of care.

Patrick's wife has a high-paying professional job requiring many work hours. Early on in their family life, he took on the primary responsibility for their children ("One of the big reasons I kept working nights was because I wanted to take care of the children during the day. I didn't want to take them to the babysitter. And she certainly wasn't going to quit her job just to stay home"). Thus when their three girls were young, he undertook a fairly grueling schedule, encompassing almost the entire second shift: he would work the swing shift from 6:00 p.m. to 2:00 a.m., get home and sleep for five hours, and then wake up to take care of the kids all day until his wife got home at 5:30 p.m.

When Patrick talks about caring for the children, he sounds like many of the women I interviewed, as when he used "I" language to describe care responsibilities (e.g., "I had at least two kids in diapers for seven or eight years"). Ultimately, like some mothers, Patrick says he prioritizes his children over his spouse. "I think I put forth more effort where my children are concerned than with her. And I don't mean to be mean to her or anything, but it just seems like I only have a certain amount of energy. I hate to say it, but I think I owe my children more than I owe my spouse."

He recalls signing the children up for preschool, and his ambivalence there—grief at missing them, worry about how they were doing, relief at the break—echoed the way some of my women interviewees talked.

PATRICK: Finally we found a good school that her and Maya went to for a few hours, three days a week. And while I really missed being around the kids, it was good for them to be around other kids. It was also good for me to have a couple of hours . . .

AJP: Two seconds on your own.

PATRICK: Two seconds on my own, even if it was just to cut the grass and not have to worry about what they were doing inside.

Nonetheless, he declined to view those years—of swing-shift-plus-second-shift, sleeping five hours and then being the children's primary caregiver—as particularly admirable for a man, or even that unusual, compared to "a lot of people."

AJP: That's remarkable. I can't believe you did that for a really long time.

PATRICK: Well, a lot of people do it.

Without presuming men's care is optional, still, it is hardly true that "a lot of people" take on such a grueling schedule as a full-time job plus all the childcare, and certainly not too many men. Sociologist Anita Garey studied night-shift nurses who attempted the same punishing balancing act, doing so because they sought to maintain notions of themselves as intensive mothers even though they also worked for pay. For Patrick, his existing standards of care—no babysitters for his children, regular visitors for the area elderly—coupled with the inflexible demands of his wife's job, lead him to innovate around gender, attesting to the care work ethic and widening the care responsibilities of honorable men.[20]

Conventional ideas frame care as optional for men, rather than an integral component of their gendered selves, even for those who undertake primary caregiving responsibilities. Courts, schools, and other institutions reify this lack of expectation around men's caregiving. A few men, however, embrace the care work ethic, redefining good care as part of the honorable behavior for any good human. These men prioritize particular standards of care, based on memory or ideology, but refashion the gendered nature of those standards, so that what matters is the kind of care delivered—the early childhood without babysitters, the home-cooked meal—and not that it was a mother who gave it. Thus these gender innovators claim care as part of the fundamental duty of the honorable person, in this way "undoing" gender.[21]

While both stably employed and more affluent men can be found among these change makers, the shifting costs and benefits of traditional gender arrangements are rendered in stark relief by the experience of job insecurity among less advantaged men. Recall Clark, laid off time and again and ruing the insecure age, who made a point of waiting at the bus stop at day's end like his mother: "I wanted to provide the same stability for my daughter." Reinventing duty in the tumbleweed society, some reinvent gender along the way.[22]

THE BRITTLE FRAME

What counts as duty and for whom? While some may invoke duty as an overarching credo, in practice it is a specific mandate aimed at particular people and situations; in this, duty is less a sun for all than it is a floodlight for a few, less a big tent than an umbrella. The call of duty has long been powerful for men, particularly less advantaged men, providing a narrative throughout history that has both elicited and made sense of their sacrifices in service to risk, backbreaking work, and other masculine pursuits, as well as the gendered privileges they have enjoyed.

Yet job insecurity has rent the fabric of men's duty narrative, with its onslaught on the dependability of their provisioning, raising questions about what men can and should be counted on to contribute. As we have seen, some "angry white men," betrayed at work and at home, displace their feelings about work onto their intimate partnerships, in reflection of their gendered expectations of duty. Part of the birthright these men have lost includes many of the gendered and racial inequalities from which they derived benefits, to be sure. But another part was the notion of job security, the idea that their employer could count on them for their best, and they could count on their employer for their future. We would do well to also recognize why these changes might feel like injustice to them, given the primacy of work as a moral measure.

Although some may want stable jobs and stable families, by displacing their anger about one onto the other, they suggest that they have already given up their hopes, and their willingness to fight, for the former. Betrayal stories reveal where they maintain expectations, clinging to notions of what they are still owed.

If this book is charting the varying principles that people adopt toward obligation—independence, pragmatism, and the like—then surely all this talk of duty sounds very old-fashioned, as if here, finally, are the bulwarks of tradition holding back the provisional, flexible, resilient selves that others immersed in insecurity profess. Yet notions of duty, with their keen sense of accountability devolving to the individual, fit right into the calls for the neoliberal privatization of risk and responsibility characteristic of insecurity culture. People who call on duty ensure that individuals bear responsibility for the moral load, as they make moral sense of the destabilizing insecurity all around them.

Nonetheless, duty is a brittle frame, a rigid construction. The very rigidity provides the solid firmament allowing us to scale great heights, as we shall see in the next chapter. But it also leads to pain and outrage, fury and resentment, slash-and-burn emotions that give little room for the forgiveness or compromise that enables enduring ties. Duty can be like glue when it fixes our own hearts in place, but when we apply it to others, through the intensity of ensuing disappointment, it can dissolve our connections like turpentine.

CHAPTER 6

✑

The Giving Trees

Nicki Jones is an African-American single mother who already had three children of her own when she went to the hospital to visit her ex-husband's grand-niece, who had just had a baby named Karma. "I heard her talking about that she was going to give the baby up for adoption, and I thought that was devastating. I thought that it would be a decision that she would regret," she recalled. Despite some serious health issues, Nicki decided to step in. "So, I told her, 'I'll tell you what. I will take the baby for you, but if you decide later on you want her back, you can have her back.' I picked her, the baby, up from the hospital, took her home, took the baby home with me, and have had her ever since."

For Nicki, having one's baby adopted "out" to nonkin was a tragedy because it was irrevocable, and furthermore, Nicki defined herself, even as an ex-great-aunt, as kin, whose responsibility it was to step forward and assume the burden. Nicki has long suffered from fibromyalgia, a painful chronic condition that sometimes made it impossible for her to sit up in bed without her children pulling her up by the arms. Nonetheless, Nicki's definitions of family are rooted in such powerful notions of duty that she takes on significant burdens, such as raising Karma, whom Nicki describes as "my ex-husband's sister's granddaughter." Nicki considers herself responsible for meeting the desperate need around her despite the considerable sacrifice that it requires; in recognition of her commitment to saving others from their hardships, we might say that she is "rescuing."

We have seen how people view their obligations to others through different lenses, from independence to pragmatism to duty. Less advantaged men such as Gary, whose story opened the last chapter, rely on gendered notions of duty to make sense of insecurity, in which their own duty at work and other people's duty at home combine to shape a righteous anger—while a few men innovate to expand the caregiving that is expected of them. Among women in the same socioeconomic position, some eschew duty as a trap, evincing a triumphant independence at work and at home that protects them from the vulnerability they perceive as the worst-case scenario.

Others, however, run toward responsibility. Their lives made deeply meaningful by the call to duty, they step up to situations of extreme need, unflinching before the burdens with which they are met. While they might perceive that duty selectively, as applying to some and not others, like Nicki, they offer themselves up as sacrifices to the necessities they recognize. Amid the pull of insecurity culture, with its emphasis upon flexibility and change, loose associations and light obligations, they use the fixity of duty to pin their identities down. And while duty's rigidity can lead to anger when the expectations it brings are disappointed, its unyielding quality also generates the strength for great feats of devotion. We may find that devotion humbling, even awesome, in its scope, but it also serves to mask the social origins of those extreme needs, and the gendered scripts for who is to meet them.

Karma is now a teenager, with some attitude ("I try to tell her that I'm the last person that you should talk to like that") and some troubles ("It's constant issues. She's more than all three of mine put together and then some. I'm counting those two years [left until Karma becomes an adult]."). But the hardest part is that Nicki was recently laid off from her job, and money has become a struggle.

> When you have exhausted all of your funds, that's when you have a lot of stress. When you're not able to buy the groceries that you normally buy. When you're not able to put the gas in the vehicles that you normally put in there. When you're in jeopardy of—this was the first month I ever paid my rent late, you know, and literally have to go around from organization to organization. And also understand that the economy is what it is and it's hard for a lot of people, you know. And it's—it was like a rude awakening, a smack in the face. You can't do it, you know.

Adding to this challenge is Nicki's biological mother, who had given Nicki up as a child to be raised by a loving aunt and uncle. Nicki's mother had a stroke seven years ago that left her bedridden, and now she lives with Nicki.

In the beginning when she was like in the rehab hospitals and things like that, the way I was raised, you do what it takes for family, you know. My being an only child, I was the only one that could check on her. So I would go to the rehab hospital like three times a day, you know. And people were like, "You don't have to go that often." Well, that wasn't the way I was raised, you know.

Nicki's idea of duty is strong enough to move her to take on significant burdens, such as caring for her biological mother and raising a child born to her ex-husband's relatives.

Of course, in stepping up to care, particularly for the mother who never cared for her, Nicki is also able to achieve what her mother could not: an identity as someone who can be depended upon to provide in times of crisis. While it leads to some of Nicki's distress today, that identity has been a longstanding source of meaning and, within the context of her community, stature. The importance of that identity makes it nearly impossible to set aside when it no longer makes sense for her health or pocketbook, but rationality as defined by her material interests does not prevail here.

This chapter explores how some needs get met in desperate times by the heroes in our midst. We can define rescuing as facing the situations of someone else's dire and long-term needs, striving to meet those needs rather than walk away, and undertaking unusual struggle or sacrifice in doing so. People embark on rescuing missions, in spite of the alternative ways others conceive of their own obligations and the widespread perception of independence as an ascendant ethos, a moral rubric whose social validity is increasing. Given this milieu, the decision—and the capacity—of others to step forward when it is exceptionally difficult to do so is particularly striking.

We can find such "commitment heroes" in all corners of society, including among men, among the affluent, and among the stably employed. Nonetheless, some people are more likely than others to face the dire needs of others and to heed their call: mostly women, particularly women of color, embedded in insecure work. Laid-off, less advantaged people might see more need around them than the affluent, or than those who are securely employed but of modest means, who sometimes live in bubbles of stability. Most important, as we see here, those immersed in insecure work are most likely to use the moral wall to separate the insecurity they expect at work and the duty they anticipate at home.[1]

Trapped between two closing walls—both the gendered expectation that they would take on the burdens of care and the fact that those burdens increase under tough economic times such as those brought on by precarious work—less advantaged women use two different stances to make sense of their conundrum. As we have seen in chapter 4, some herald independence and use it to frame their defiance of the gendered trap of caregiving. But others find meaning in duty, whose dictates they believe they can still fulfill—even if at extremes of need it can look more like rescuing.

Yet while we might recognize their everyday care as acts of heroism, we must also remain clear-eyed about the social forces that produce such dire need in the first place, taking note of our systemic reliance upon their willingness to consider rescuing their duty. The tumbleweed society at once exploits, requires, and impedes those who make meaning out of intense obligation. Like choosing, defying, and displacing, rescuing is another way of disciplining the self to fit within the tenets of insecurity culture, by claiming individual accountability for social facts.

WHEN THE STATE WITHDRAWS: RELYING ON THE THOUSAND POINTS OF LIGHT

Sometimes that systemic reliance upon others who feel obliged is obvious, a sleight of hand slipping responsibility from institutions to individuals. Barbie Miller had escaped her parents' late divorce by marrying an unlikely bad boy ("just a big thug") but quickly came to her senses when her first son was born, leaving him and marrying her second husband, Ian, fourteen years ago. But Barbie's commitment to her new marriage was put to a horrible test one day early on when Ian suffered a gruesome accident at his worksite.

> It's a big—imagine a huge dumpster, three stories in the air, with a seven-hundred-pound steel metal door—and it threw him up three stories into another door and it came down on him. And it was crushing him—so it was like King Kong, just your head and your arms out—and it was going down his body. And he was screaming and wiggling and stuff. And they were trying to figure out which button to hit. And so then he said he made peace with God. And he was like, "This is how I'm going to die." That's when they hit the button and it released him. And he dropped three stories into the wet concrete. And he was out of work for two and a half years. He had a broken back, a broken tailbone, and a torn rotator cuff.

Barbie blames the accident on the engineer who was on site that day, who she says told her husband to go into the machine to shovel it out when it got stuck. "Ian was training to be a supervisor, so at that point he was the

guinea pig," she recalled. "Ian said, 'Has it completed a cycle? Has it finished blah blah blah?' They say 'Yes.'" But they were wrong, and the machine kicked back into gear, with Ian inside it, as soon as he cleared the
obstruction; Ian paid the price for this mistake with his body. In addition, however, the employer was using a dangerous machine, one that
violated safety standards. "OSHA fined them and made that machine ob-
solete," she said, with some satisfaction. "That machine hasn't run since
the day Ian got injured." While this step made sure no one else got hurt,
it did nothing to help Ian, even though it certainly suggests employer
fault. "In the state of Virginia, you can't sue your employer," Barbie remarked. "So we didn't get any compensation out of them, just workman's
comp."

Barbie had three small children at the time—her eldest in kindergarten
and twin babies. She worked as a waitress, cared for her bedridden husband
and small children, took him to doctor's appointments. She sought help
from local churches, the food pantry, from neighbors who would bring her
day-old bread from Winn Dixie. Speaking to me a decade later from her
comfortable dining room in the city suburbs, Barbie had clearly come a long
way, with her husband now working again and her own florist business
having gone well until the recession. But the memory of that time was sear-
ing. "I told my husband that was probably one of my lowest points in my
life," she told me.

> There was one day and I had twenty-three dollars in checking. And we were wait-
> ing on a workman's comp, and this was when the whole thing was first started
> happening. We couldn't get workman's comp, they were trying to send my hus-
> band back to work with a broken back. I mean it was just constant. It was crazy
> and we had twenty-three dollars to our name. I was waiting tables at night. The
> tips weren't being that great to me, you know, for whatever reason, and I called
> church after church. We had a 1997 Nissan Altima, and it was still too nice of a
> car at that time to qualify for Medicaid or anything like that so I couldn't get any
> assistance. I got no assistance from the government, and then I started calling
> churches because I needed food. I needed to feed my children and I couldn't
> afford to.

In Barbie's narrative, no one else was available to help: not the state, not
the employer, not the church, not even other relatives. Barbie was the only
one to bear the responsibility for caregiving after the terrible accident.

How did Barbie come to be the last one left standing? The privatization
of risk is one cost of the devolution of responsibility to the individual, part
and parcel of trends in state policies governing the mutual obligations

of employers and employees. Her experience has fostered in Barbie some old-fashioned class consciousness. "Virginia law sucks," Barbie declared.

> I mean, they protect the employer and not the employee. Well, there are a lot of employers that are sitting back here in their grandiose homes chomping on bon bons and just ringing in the dough. And then there's the poor man out there busting his ass for eight dollars. I mean that's just wrong. It's going back to the whole OSHA thing, they didn't even call OSHA, I called OSHA. I mean they didn't even do that as employers.

But Ian's company never admitted wrongdoing or offered any additional help, and by precluding Barbie and Ian's ability to seek any sort of damages, the state inhibited their capacity to seek redress for the industrial accident. The individualization of her responsibility recalls the "thousand points of light," the army of individuals volunteering to aid the needy invoked by George Bush when he accepted the presidential nomination in 1988; in this case, Barbie was the single point of light enabling her family to survive. Coupled with their distance from potential extended networks of support from other relatives, churches, or neighborhood groups, the burden of caregiving fell entirely on Barbie, whose rescuing, under these circumstances, felt not quite voluntary. Therein lies the magic of duty, in its capacity to make its bearer feel beholden.

PLAYING WITH DUTY

This power is even more magical when we get a sense of the pressures impinging upon people who subscribe to duty, which comes through in their language, particularly in their metaphors, imagery, and jokes. While we saw evidence of an ascendant insecurity culture in such turns of phrase in chapter 3, it becomes more surprising among people who make a point of sacrificing themselves at the altar of duty, whom we might expect to reject such talk altogether.

Some people motivated by duty manage to mock it at the same time, making distancing jokes that lampoon their own sense of duty as extreme, even ridiculous. Myra still felt betrayed by her parents' divorce, which followed what she remembers as an idyllic childhood. She maintained relations with both parents, even though she castigated them for their many faults. "Oh, I talk to my Mom. My Mom, I can't stand her," said Myra, chuckling, but somewhat bitterly. "I mean, you know, I love her.

I love her and she's my Mom and I talk to her every day, but I can't stand her." Her litany points us to some of the absurdities of duty, and lets us know she sees them too.

Similarly, Lola, a teacher, was caustic as she described feeling trapped and infuriated by having to care for the mentally disabled mother of her husband, Hank, a woman who had given Hank up when he was a child to be raised by his grandmother, but who then rejoined their lives after her husband died. Lola and Hank were entirely responsible for the woman's care, and yet all she had done to deserve this was to conceive and give birth to Hank, Lola said. "[Hank's] brother doesn't do anything for his mom, so we're completely and totally, entirely in charge of taking care of her," Lola raged, half comically, half seriously. "How much do we owe this woman for lying down?"

Stella, who worked in insurance, had bought a bigger house so her father and mother could move in. Because her father had Alzheimer's and her mother had a degenerative bone disease, she and her husband had not had a vacation together in three years, and she wept while describing her life with them. I asked her what lessons she thought her daughter, Tess, was getting from the choices she was making. "I don't know," she replied, and grimly joked: "Probably what nursing home to put me in."

In many ways these jokes are similar to those we heard in earlier chapters—about husbands wishing for a "playa divorce," old neighbors who are like "old shoes," and children getting "fourteen Christmases." Through these jokes, people are playing with the extent of their sacrifice, worrying, as jokes do, at the very nodes where anxiety lives. In addition, however, propelled by disquiet about other choices that are out there, alternatives to their care and devotion, these jokes tell us that the joker "knows better"— that she may be overcommitting, but she is not a fool—by making fun of "too much" commitment, pointing out its irrationality within a context of insecurity culture. The jokes tell us something about the dominance of insecurity as common sense, a backdrop that even these commitment heroes share, which makes their continued reliance on duty as a meaningful stance more striking.

To be sure, duty still calls on a strong moral heritage, one whose claim to honor continues to be powerful. Some commitment heroes point out how they do what others "could not," what others less able or less giving do not, or most often what they never thought they would be able to do. They believe that duty asks for their best selves, and they find their identities in how very much it asks. That their jokes sometimes ask the rest of us to bear witness to the farcical nature of duty's unyielding demands does not diminish the resonance of its call for them.

WHO DOES THE RESCUING

Rare as Barbie's burden is, remarkable as is Nicki's life-changing resolve to take on Karma's upbringing, the depth of their dedication is not wholly unique. I found a handful of other "commitment heroes," who faced situations of extreme need—challenging illnesses, special needs children, mentally disordered spouses, Alzheimer's-afflicted parents—and who defined themselves through facing them without shirking, rescuing others from their dire straits. Out of eighty, six others demonstrated self-sacrifice to a similar degree as Nicki, with stories testifying to comparable dedication. Another ten labored under less extraordinary conditions, practicing a kind of everyday heroism; examples of this self-described endurance ranged from long-term, dedicated single parenting in extreme poverty to divorced parents sharing custody with hated others but nonetheless working in close cooperation to raise children. While the circumstances varied—in the definitions of what counts as a dire need, in the situations that produced the need in the first place, and in the resources available—rescuing asserted the continued power of duty in an insecure age. While less advantaged, insecurely employed women were most common, people from all sorts of social locations took part in rescuing, including a few more advantaged women, men, and the stably employed.[2]

Mary and Peter Jordan were a married middle-class couple whom we first met in chapter 2 dealing with Peter's layoff from his technical job. They adopted their son, Eric, as a baby from a charismatic stripper and former teenage runaway, who met with them when she was pregnant and spoke frankly about her active sexual history, lack of impulse control, and recent substantial drug use. They were innocents, Mary remembered. "We were young and we thought you can love a baby, you can fix anything," she recalled. "It was a very idealistic—I had no idea the complications that come with that."

In the first ten months of life, Eric slept no longer than an hour and a half at a time. While awake, he cried constantly. "It was like colic to the tenth degree," Mary said. A physically adept child, when he got older he would get into extreme mischief, taking apart the toaster, climbing onto the refrigerator. He had next to no impulse control, so that even as he knew about consequences—natural or imposed by his parents—he could not stop himself. "So you could tell him twenty times, 'If you climb on the refrigerator it's going to fall over,' or 'You're going to get in trouble,' or whatever the consequence. And he would beforehand say that, 'Yes, what will happen, I will be in trouble, I will get a spanking, I will have to go to my room'—whatever it was, but the second that conversation was gone he would go do it. And then afterwards he would say, 'I know, I was going to fall off.'" At seven years old, the boy was hospitalized for two weeks for depression. He was diagnosed with ADHD, bipolar disorder, and a host of other problems. Doctors predicted that by the time Eric was nine or ten he would not be living at home.

Eric's sleep problems did not improve substantially from babyhood, and even in elementary school Eric slept no longer than three hours at a time. Doctors advised Mary and Peter to put a lock on his bedroom door. "And we just couldn't do it. I mean having someone being locked in their bedroom? I just couldn't do it." For more than a decade, then, Mary and Peter took turns sleeping outside of Eric's room. "So we took shifts. I think it was ten till two one of us would lay outside his bedroom door and the other one sleep in our bedroom, and at two we would switch. And we did that *for eleven years*. Which at the time—it seems ludicrous! But that's what we did."

Mary refused to put a lock on Eric's door because doing so was punitive, infringing upon his humanity, which she was dedicated to preserving and nurturing. The story she tells of the lengths to which she and Peter went to care for Eric is a dramatic one full of great personal forbearance, in which their commitment to accommodating his needs subordinated other, certainly reasonable, priorities, like parents wanting to sleep together in their own bed.

The ramifications of raising this extremely challenging child were dramatic. Mary quit teaching, staying out of the paid labor force for more than a decade because it was clear Eric needed one-on-one care, and the family downsized so as to be able to afford living on one income. They almost never socialized—"We couldn't. You couldn't get a babysitter. Who would do it?" It was not until Eric moved out as an adult that Mary described herself as having real friendships, calling the years he was at home the "Eric years." "Mostly we didn't go anywhere, we didn't do anything."

The heavy cost exacted by Eric's needs extended outside the home as well. Mary got used to reprimands in public by strangers witnessing Eric's tantrums and uncontrolled behavior. "We used to say, 'It would be easier if he was in a wheelchair.' We'd [at least] have people coming up willing to help us. He looked normal, so when he would have an outrageous meltdown you'd just think 'They're bad parents.'"

And every place in Richmond, there's not been a public place that I haven't had a person come up to me and feel like they can just tell me what was wrong with me and what a bad mother I was. I mean it happened. Rarely [did] we go anywhere, but if we went to the grocery or whatever and he would do whatever he would do—people feel very . . . It was awful. Initially, for many years, it just killed me. I just was mortified. And then I think you just get used to anything.

She and Peter made striking sacrifices by any normal standard, sacrifices even beyond the considerable ones required by more conventional parenting challenges.

Mary undertook intense negotiations with school authorities to secure the appropriate accommodations for her child—always a challenge, Mary said, because Eric "looks normal." Doctors helped to plead their case. "[They] would come to these IEP meetings [with school staff about special education needs] and say, 'No, you don't get it. . . . This kid should be institutionalized but he's not, but it's only because of the constant care and support that [he's] had.'"[3]

In middle school, new challenges emerged. Eric exhibited poor behaviors in school and low expectations for himself as a result of constant teacher reprimands—"He was becoming the bad kid because he was told over and over, 'You're a bad kid.' I mean it was like some little science experiment you saw happening but you couldn't do anything about it." Without any alternative, Mary felt homeschooling was the only option, but was afraid to take the plunge. "Because twenty-four hours with Eric . . ." It was almost too frightening to contemplate. She spent two weeks considering it: "I said to Peter, in fact I would yell at him, 'I can't do homeschooling!'" Somehow, over those two weeks, she made her peace with it, and she changed her mind, taking on the homeschooling she considered necessary for Eric to thrive. Two years later, she was proud to tell me, Eric was off all medications and at or above grade level in schoolwork, although high school would bring new challenges.

Of course, for Mary and Peter, Eric was their child, and the prohibitions against pulling back from children are great, especially for mothers—hence some mothers' use of the "detachment brokers" we saw in chapter 4, whom they call upon to absolve them of distancing. Mary and Peter's rescuing was also greatly aided by their available resources, especially Peter's job paying enough to support the family so that Mary could dedicate herself wholly to Eric. Still, there were repeated forks in the road where Mary and Peter could have chosen an easier path, but instead prioritized his enriched care. They could have locked his bedroom door at night without being seen as unreasonable. They could have kept him in school, even one ill-suited to his needs, as some parents resign themselves to doing, or are forced to do. Eric's case was so extreme, they could even have institutionalized him without being castigated.

Similarly, looking at other cases of need, there were people who took other routes and pointed to reasonable justifications. People sent their special needs children to a residential facility because they posed threats to others in the house, for example. They divorced mentally ill husbands for being too difficult to stay married to while they were also trying to care for children. They refused to care for their elderly parents because those parents were abusive or neglectful, because their own needs precluded their ability to help, or because they feared doing so encouraged a level of dependency they were trying not to model for their children.

Yet commitment heroes refused to take these other paths, even when the challenges presented people with plenty of justifications, and even when in some cases they were "allowed to," even urged to, by well-meaning others volunteering to play the "detachment broker" role. Rather, for them, these other paths were not viable alternatives: the stance of duty was for them more inflexible—risking the shame of abandonment—and their long-term identities were more grounded in its fulfillment.

This moment requires some delicacy, as we divide the world into commitment heroes and everyone else. Just knowing that some people assume these great and terrible burdens can make the rest of us seem selfish, shallow, or weak. Yet what matters here is not our praising of the few; we do better in not simply honoring the strength of commitment heroes (much as we might be inspired by their example) or blaming the rest of us for our supposed shortfalls. Instead, we gain by understanding more fully the complexity of rescuing: how people make sense of duty under these circumstances, what kind of selves they struggle to build, how they reconcile themselves to the limits of rescuing, and what we all face as the consequences.

THE POWER OF DUTY

How do people who take on the rescuing interpret what they are doing? While some view their practice as demonstrating the power of love, others consider it evidence of their own unique reliability, an identity made particularly compelling for them in the tumbleweed society. Most of all, those who subscribe to duty feel the steel at its core, its compulsory dictates: with an insecure world swirling around them, they think they have no choice.

Owen is a white contractor whose wife didn't discover her serious mental illness until after they were married. He told alarming stories of making sure she didn't hurt herself, of protecting his children, of suffering from sporadic employment because of his need to be available at all hours.

Despite his wife's profound need, however, Owen rejects the idea that he was motivated by pity, survivor's guilt, or even altruism. Instead, he said, he was deeply in love with her, in all her frailty. "There were some stories in which facts were very nearly irrelevant," the novelist Ann Patchett writes, in agreement with Owen. "In this life we love who we love."[4]

"The conventional wisdom around self-help is to take care of yourself," he said. "But my wisdom is just the opposite; it's not all about me, because some of my greatest joys have nothing to do with me. The greatest joy I probably have is the fact how much I love my wife." Of course, it is at least possible that Owen's strong feelings are not a cause of his dedication but rather a result, an example of his devotion to his wife, in which he refuses to patronize her as a pitiful victim but instead appreciates her as an admired partner. Devotion sometimes emerges out of rescuing, rather than being the reason for it.

In contrast, others did not generate these emotions as they complied with what they saw as their mandate. They spoke with some measure of grief about the burdens they faced, rather than being buoyed by a deep passion like Owen. Stella was the insurance agent who bought a bigger house so her ailing parents could move in. "We were like, you know, they are not going to be able to stay in their house. You know, something is going to have to change, Daddy's losing it, we can tell," she recalled.

"Yeah, I mean it's just hard for all of us, it's hard for my mother, it's hard for my daughter, it's hard for me, it's just . . ." Stella trailed off. Her parents could not be left alone at night because they could not handle each other's physical care. Stella and her husband had not had more than two evenings out alone together in three years. She got choked up while describing her vanishing marriage and the crushing of her financial dreams. "You know, so it sucks, now I'll probably die still owing money on this house," she said. "It's just the way it is". She anguished over the poisoning of her daughter's relationship with her increasingly combative grandfather. "Because, you know, she's seventeen, and this is how she's going to remember her grandparents. And that bothers me. You know, *I* can't even hardly remember my father before all this." Stella upended her life, her marriage, and her house for years to accommodate her parents' dire needs. She did so, however, without talking a lot about love or ginning up positive emotions about her dedication, which weighed upon her like a yoke.

Instead, many commitment heroes shared something else: a self-identity grounded in being uniquely dependable. "I believe that everything that happened to me in my life up until age sixteen prepared me for her," Owen said. "Because, you know, without being boastful, a small percentage of people would have been able to withstand what I did." Nicki, who was caring for Karma and her bedridden mother, observed that everyone looked to her for support. "Since my aunt and uncle have passed, it was like I was the family pillar, you know. I have some of their children come to me, you know, for help, and I'm younger than they are, you know," she said. "I am the more stable one, you know." As Lola, who takes care of her husband's mentally disabled mother, said: "He's like, 'Do you ever get tired of doing the right thing?' And it's like on both sides we are the good kid, we're the good ones."

Sylvia Jackson and her second husband, both social workers, had adopted a special needs child with reactive attachment disorder, who required constant, unremitting attention, guidance, and care.

> And my husband and I were very much on the same line as far as our passion for working with kids and such, and so we felt like this was our chance to take a child in who needed a family, rather than creating another child, you know, and so from the beginning we've been dealing with that. And he had a rough time before—we've had a rough time, but before he came he was like hospitalized psychiatrically several times, just really hard. So this was our chance to kind of put our money where our mouth is when it comes to our dedication to our work and in taking it home and just our dedication [to] people. So it's been a challenge, we really kind of challenged ourselves to the point like, "We thought we knew how to do this," and it was difficult.

Part of the appeal of rescuing here, as for others, was the very extremity of the case before them, the urgency. Sylvia's professional self and her rescuing bolster each other in her care for a particularly challenging child.

These kinds of statements reveal as much about their values as they do about their behavior. The very idea that one is one's best self when one is reliable, that being the "family pillar" is something one could be "boastful" about, contrasts with the invulnerability prized by independence and the less dramatic "get real" posture of pragmatism. Rescuing makes powerful moral identities from the raw materials of duty, the burdens it assigns and the sacrifices it engenders.

Most important, commitment heroes feel like they had no choice, that stepping up is the only way, because to do otherwise is to abandon their moral posts, to fail and to do so utterly. This kind of steeliness is supported, in part, by cultural ideas buttressed by social institutions that enshrine duty as noble, frame rescuing as expected and honorable (and anything less as shameful), and sometimes even give tangible assistance. These institutions include particular civic groups, the military, and churches; a number of commitment heroes derive an understanding of sacrifice from their

faith, although they may have stopped practicing. Duty defines the contours of honor, and like displacing—the other outgrowth of duty—rescuing brooks no compromise.

Owen said he decided early on to take on the responsibility of caring for
his wife. "So, I guess there was a point where I figured if my lot in life was
to try to keep her safe for the rest of her life, so be it, that's what I'll do."
Lola, the teacher who takes care of her husband's mentally disabled mother
and helps out with her own, views her caregiving as compulsory, even
though her relations are strained with both women. Her attachments
always come with responsibilities, Lola says. "Everybody that I love, other
than my children, they all have a 'but.' 'I love you, but—you can't say no.' 'I
love you, but—you have to do this.'"

Mary believed you "can't really dissolve family relationships," nor could
you "commit" to them per se—the very word involved too much volition
for a bond that was essentially inviolable. And with those connections
comes the unquestioning duty to serve, she said, recalling the "Eric years."
As she said, simply: "There was no other choice."

DUTY TO CHILDREN, DUTY TO PARENTS: GENDER, RACE, AND THE CARE WORK ETHIC

It is no coincidence that most (but not all) of these examples arise from
duties between parents and children, as widespread ideals still saturate
those relations in duty. Many of those who may have left duty behind in
other relationships still maintain it for these core connections, forged in
daily moments of intimate care. Of course, while one may view duty to
children as so fundamental as to be unassailable, it is true that even these
duties are fluid enough to be forsworn by others. People leave their children to other people all the time, and leave the care of their parents to
others as well: these are not necessarily even unusual paths. What are some
of the factors making duty particularly resonant for others?[5]

First, gender powerfully shapes the care work ethic that generates everyday sacrifices. Lola feels a duty to respond to her mother's needs, one
that stems in part from her notion of what a daughter is supposed to do. "I
do feel that I owe [my mother]. I do," Lola repeats like a mantra, and then
asks: "But why doesn't my sister feel that way?" Lola wonders at, and
judges, her sister's absence as she recalls how her sister fled the house early
on in a wayward adolescence. Indeed, she dubs her sister's refusal to help
now "very selfish," even as she has three brothers who could step in but
who escape her pointed ire.

Instead, Lola falls back on a gendered adage, whose cultural significance she at once honors and decries. "A son is a son until he takes a wife; a daughter is a daughter all of her life," she recites, remarking, "Once again, there's the embedding [of caregiving responsibilities in what it means to be a woman]." Lola feels the pressure of the gendered expectations of women's duty—even as she applies them herself when she calls her sister "very self-ish" for joining her brothers in their escape—the very same expectations whose weight Fiona and other women defied in chapter 4.

Gender does not only shape and encourage rescuing, however; it also generates—through the feminization of poverty, the distribution of low-wage work, and the like—the dire need and long-term struggle that make rescuing necessary. These difficulties make upholding a care work ethic the sort of exertion that can augur a form of rescuing. Of course, some of these everyday sacrifices might or might not actually be "rescuing"—given that in these interviews we must rely on people's own testimony of urgent needs, difficult conditions, and significant efforts—but more important than validating their claims is noticing the social glue that keeps them there despite the hardship they perceive: the power of duty, defined through gendered identities and inequality.[6]

Becca Wallace, a dispatcher, was living with her mother in Florida and taking care of her son, whose father had left her when she refused to termi-nate the pregnancy, when she met the man who became her first husband. "I thought I loved him, but I was in love with the idea of getting out of my current situation. He was a very much a caretaker. He wanted to take care of me. And, at that point, that's what I thought I needed," she said. A con-trolling, domineering man, he brought her back to Virginia and installed her in a trailer park with no phone, no car, no job, no friends or family; she stayed inside all day with her toddler, making weekly trips to the Laundro-mat where she could call her mother on the pay phone. At the time, how-ever, she had wanted her son to have a "father figure," and that led her to go along with the move, even though it stripped her of alternatives.

> It was horrible. But having been raised without my father because my father passed away when I was very young, I felt that my son needed that father figure and I needed the father figure. My husband was very controlling. He told me what to do and when to do it. For a while I was fine with that. So, that was like, okay, we're moving to Virginia, okay.

Eventually, she broke free of this relationship: when his pay improved enough for her to get a car, she started working during the children's school hours, and saved enough money to leave when he had an affair. After she returned to Florida, a second marriage ended up no better, with her in the hospital, having lost one fetal twin due to abuse. Leaving him, she moved in with her mother again, only to move back out again to live with another man for two years. Only after discovering later on that her second husband had molested her daughter did Becca swear off relationships altogether while she still had children in the house. She went back to school to earn a certificate while working, enabling her to get a pay raise and promotion in her job.

In one sense, Becca's story is a typical one of an undereducated white single mother in the United States, struggling to raise her children while trying to claw her way out of deep poverty, first through marriage and then through her own work. What brings her narrative closer to rescuing is the sheer endurance involved in facing the difficulties imposed by the gendered social organization of poverty and divorce in the United States. As she wends her way in and out of these relationships, any children she has with her partners become entirely her responsibility, as they do for most single mothers, while each move between Florida and Virginia becomes about finding jobs or keeping men who could help her better meet care needs, which she saw as her primary duty. "The main goal was to put food on the table and to provide a roof over the heads and stuff," she said.[7]

Yet women with care responsibilities are treated by employers as though they have no children, and by the state as if they have husbands on whom they can rely. The American workplace is still allowed to get away with assuming a rational autonomous worker without care obligations, whose needs are met by an attendant helpmeet; nevertheless, the American state assumes a married two-parent family in which many public benefits extend through the jobholder, while the hollowing out of "workfare" has made relying on public support no longer a viable option for the single, uneducated woman with children. These facts force mothers with little education, but who nonetheless derive powerful personal significance from their sense of duty to their children, into a trap out of which there are no easy escape routes.[8]

For many less advantaged mothers, their duty to children is what makes their lives meaningful. When overwhelmed and stretched beyond their capacities, the primary question they face, then, is not "How can I redefine duty so it matches what I can do?" or even "How can I eschew duty for another kind of stance that might help make sense of these quandaries?"— which appeared to be what the duty-bound men were asking in the last chapter. Instead, with duty unyielding, the question these women face is "How can I actually accomplish this non-negotiable duty?"

Sometimes, this question transforms into another one: "How can I get someone else to share this duty with me?" Boxed in at work, Becca sought out romantic partners who could share what she saw as her duty to her children. Each time Becca decided to move in with a man, she did so in part to give her son (and, as she noted, herself) a father figure.[9]

The notion that children, particularly boys, need a father to develop a healthy sense of masculinity, discipline, and good character is pervasive, permeating the cultural landscape and shored up by some research into the importance of fathers. But while children always gain from competent parenting, and on average children do better living with both biological parents, we now know that stepfathers do not always bring the same benefits, however, since children whose single mothers remain unmarried do the same as or better than those whose mothers remarry. Nonetheless, research on the benefits of biological fathers for children has been extrapolated to mean these benefits are provided by *all* fathers, a message that can also lead poor single mothers to rely on hope more than caution when choosing men to bring into their families. "I have a broken picker-outer," Lily, another single mother, lamented, giving a name to a worry that many less advantaged single women share.[10]

Time and time again in this study, women talked about having to walk the knife edge between good care for their children and financial support for their survival. Diane's husband was having a midlife crisis and going through affair after affair. Diane was in denial for a long time before they finally got divorced:

> I kept thinking he's going to get past this. He's going to get over it. I just didn't believe it, you know. My friends were telling me, "You need to, you know, kick him to the curb." And me thinking I'm working a part time-job, raising five kids, I can't do without him. What am I going to do? I can't. I've got to put up with this. I have no other alternative.

Similarly, Brianna was near homelessness, living off of her second husband's erratic wages with her children in a motel. But she tried not to ask her ex-husband for child support for his children, because that would mean increasing his visitation rights, which always coincided with her children exhibiting disturbing new habits.

> Every time I file the paperwork he goes from seeing them once every two months to every weekend. And my daughter's wetting the bed again. And my son's bouncing off the walls and he's acting out in school and won't pay attention. And

he's having night terrors again. And my daughter's pulling her hair out, she's grinding her teeth. And she's sick to her stomach to the point where she can't— and no, it's not worth it. There is no amount of money in this world that is worth my children feeling that. But then when I think about them getting what they need . . . [*pauses*]. And either way it seems cruel.

Many divorced people criticize their ex-spouses, and we do not have any way of knowing if these fathers are as reprehensible as these mothers think they are. The point here is that the women perceive the men as harmful and yet have few other choices. Compelled by her duty to her children, Brianna is faced with trading their time for money that would help them survive, a bargain she has not yet been willing to make because of the adverse consequences.

For some women, the dilemma was solved only by death. Felicia, a single mother with two kids, recalled that her ex-husband refused to pay any child support while he was alive. Then he was killed at age thirty-five when he drove a car into a wall with drugs in his system. She was unabashed. "He said, 'I'll pay child support over my dead body.' And so when he got in the car accident, they got social security. Ha!"

African-American women face an even broader set of caregiving expectations, as their perceived duty can extend beyond their own children or spouses to extended families, fictive kin, or broader racialized communities, as we saw in the case of Nicki, whose story opened this chapter. Furthermore, African-American communities ravaged by racialized poverty and high jobless numbers and incarceration rates are more likely to produce dire need that must be met by someone; African-American women who derive meaning from duty are thus more likely to face situations that call for rescuing.

Caught between the social facts of women's continued responsibility for caregiving and the extensive needs she faces in her community, Nicki is a powerful example of this bind, as she sees the world through the lens of duty, and considers her commitment a fundamental sign of good character that she does not feel comfortable redefining. The opposite of commitment, to Nicki, is abandonment, or a form of betrayal. Yet her chronic illness and bout of unemployment mean that her struggle to meet some of the needs in her community is a constant challenge to the duty she invokes.

The powerful significance of a wider definition of duty, particularly for African-American women, lives on in what Patricia Hill Collins called "othermothers," also captured in Michael Chabon's novel *Telegraph Avenue*, about race, love, and family in Oakland, California.

Mrs. Wiggins was strong then, furious and churchgoing, pleased to be known for and to advertise her own iron rule over the tribes of loose children who flowed like migrants through her door . . . taking what she could pay them in love and beatdowns, in clean clothes, food on the table. Years, decades, Mrs. Wiggins went on and on, like one of those Japanese soldiers who kept fighting in the Solomon Islands or wherever, nobody ever showing up to reinforce her, tell the poor woman to surrender.[11]

For those who find meaning in duty, however, "surrendering" is not a last resort, but instead no resort at all.

Thus the social organization of gender produces the everyday struggle of many less advantaged women. Some women perceived the problem as one of a "broken picker-outer," but it is also true that the anemic welfare state makes children (and women) suffer for that acutely, by making the fallibility of one's "picker-outer" so consequential. Such women derive larger meaning from the care work ethic, seeking to fulfill what they perceive as their duty under great duress. In assuming this duty, however, they make it difficult to turn aside tasks that are overwhelming; along the way, paradoxically, they also make the ravages of insecurity endurable for many.

THE LIMITS OF RESCUING

While duty brooks no compromise, even commitment heroes sometimes fall to the scythe of insecurity, their resources failing to cover the full extent of the need they recognize. While we may rely on less advantaged women to prevent the most desperate outcomes of insecurity culture, they are not themselves immune to its havoc.

Nicki has always been the "family pillar," her duty to others part of her core identity, but her layoff made it much harder to fulfill this duty, and she is now looking to others to help her out. "I constantly hear, oh, even from my son the other day. He says, 'Well, [about] Karma . . . all you have to do is call when she needs something,'" Nicki recounted. "And I have to tell my son the other day, 'I have been raising her for sixteen years. I don't think I need to call anybody.'" Nicki's position was that Karma's parents should just step up, now that she was unemployed.

> "Listen, they know I don't have a job." I said, "They know I take care of my mother and Karma. So they should pick up the phone and ask if she needs anything, you know, or call and say how are you doing." So I don't have to do it. I've done above

and beyond. There is a little hostility there, you know, because I just feel like, you know, she knows who they are. They know she knows. So why not do something? Yeah.

Nicki's "compassion fatigue," coupled with the diminution of her resources, has led to her talk of pulling back from the rescuing she has adopted in the past.

> It's always been the case, but it's changing [*chuckles*]. It's changing now because I'm finding that family is good, but you have to define the parameters of the family. Yes, because I would give my family my last dime. I would go out and borrow for my family. Yeah, but it came down to me, and if I had a need they wouldn't do it for me. So I learned that I can't give away all I have. I have to keep something for myself.

Nicki suggests her self-concept is changing along with her capacity to help others. She uses the present tense to refer to herself as "the more stable one," and to assert "I would give my family my last dime," but then pauses to reincorporate her new approach—"but it's changing"; "I have to keep something for myself." She is talking her way through the contradictions that bubble up through her conversation, using her experiences of insecurity culture to try on a new guiding principle—one of independence—and to counter the duty principle that she still clearly reveres.

Her identity as a "family pillar" perhaps serves as a cultural seedbed for her rescuing, but without the rain of available resources, it is drying up. At the same time, however, despite her talk, she is not actually abandoning Karma or her bedridden mother; instead, she simply counts the days until Karma leaves and refuses to take on new burdens. Her identity as one who adheres to duty may yet win out over prudence.

Even Mary and Peter demonstrate the limits of rescuing, in that their experience with Eric as a young adult was more variegated than the unfaltering altruism that characterized the early years. Often, as we saw in chapter 4, people find their way to a smaller obligation on the grounds that it is "better for everybody," frequently at the urging of expert others, the "detachment brokers." After years of being exceptions to this rule, in the end Mary and Peter came to embody it. The transformation casts doubt on the seeming choicelessness of duty.

After Mary homeschooled Eric as an adolescent, he attended the local high school. At once very good-looking and impulsive (much like his birth mother, Mary pointed out), Eric had a girlfriend in his junior year who got pregnant and had an abortion, sending Eric into a downward spiral into suicidal depression about replicating his birth mother's behavior. He started drinking regularly and staying out for several days at a time without calling home. By September, at the urging of a counselor, Mary and Peter told him he had to follow the rules of the house or not come back. Eric chose to leave.

"I know there were nights where he didn't know where he was going to stay, and that about killed me. In the long run, looking back I never could have done the tough-love thing without a lot of people saying, 'No, no, no, wait one more night,'" Mary said, invoking a chorus of detachment brokers. "And that's what we did for months," she said, sounding a little surprised, and a bit plaintive, even now. "He never has come back since then."

Eric survived the crisis, getting an apartment share and several part-time jobs and attending school just enough to stay enrolled. Now Eric lives with a girlfriend who is a pre-med student, and he is going to school to get his welder's certificate, with Mary and Peter's assistance.[12]

There's some rawness apparent in Mary's telling of the story of how Eric has ended up, some pain for her in the twists his trajectory has taken, in her flat statements of remembered desperation ("That about killed me") and in her forlorn summation ("He never has come back since then"). Eric achieved his independence by rejecting their care and supervision, a sorry recompense for Mary's years of self-abnegation in an effort to produce this functioning adult. But the rejection is not only Eric's; Mary conveys a palpable sense of having abandoned her own duty, in the "tough love" strategy that experts and others told her to pursue, even as she believes that strategy worked. If she had done as she wanted to, she confesses, "I would have caved and it would have been worse then." The refusal to let a lawless teenager live in the house shares some similarities with the tactic she rejected out of hand so many years ago, of putting a lock on the door of a roaming sleepless child—a setting of limits, a boundary for her commitment, a moment of intentional withholding after years of sacrifice undertaken because that is "just what you do."

"Tough love" and other cultural packages that counsel a more contained parenting are predicated on the guiding principle of independence, as we may recall from Fiona's example in chapter 4. And while they have been around for years, they resonate powerfully with the themes of insecurity culture, as a means of shrinking obligation in the name of love. Setting aside judgment of what parenting approach works best when, we can nonetheless notice how hard it is for Mary to move from duty, the principle that guided the first seventeen years of her mothering, to independence, which governed the last two. The anguish coming to the surface as she talks about the transition—"That about killed me"—is a measure of how difficult it can be to shift from one to the other. There may be some newfound choice here, but it is not easily grasped.

Here Mary's pain recalls that of Sean, who tried in the last chapter to reconcile the notion that a marriage can only sustain so much, as the independent stance asserts, with his yearning for his wife to stand by him as was her duty. Even when one stance no longer works to make moral sense of our dilemmas, even when a new stance appears to enjoy wide cultural support or practical utility, the switch is not a simple one—these can feel like core identities, shaping the habits by which we recognize ourselves. When the limits of rescuing cause people to leave duty behind, they feel like they see someone else in the mirror.

THE CONSEQUENCES OF COMMITMENT HEROISM

Rescuing brings very obvious benefits to the community, including the very fact that people assume these duties themselves, meeting needs that would otherwise require enormous effort by any social service system. Yet the heroes also reap some benefit. They can, as Nicki and Owen do, build a portrait of themselves as honorable, reliable, competent, even a "family pillar." They can maintain some control, as Mary and Peter do, over how their loved ones are cared for, since they do so much of the caring. They can rectify old wrongs to finally "do it right," as Barbie did.

Mary identified other benefits to raising Eric. She is much more confident in the face of others' judgment, she observes. "I never would have chosen it—but it's made me so much stronger, so much more confident and able to say [to criticizing strangers], 'I'm sorry you feel that way but you just don't know the whole . . .' I never could have done [that before]. I was a good girl, I always got all As, I wanted everyone to like me—this is not what I signed up for!" She says she has much deeper, more accessible stores of empathy, of compassion. "I do know it's made me the person that I am. It's made me way more compassionate and way less judgmental of other people. Where now if I see a kid losing it, I think, 'Oh, that poor mother, I wonder what I can do to help.' Instead of, 'Well she obviously doesn't know how to . . .' which is what most people think."

It certainly made her a much better classroom teacher, she said. "I was a way better teacher after Eric. Way better. Because all of a sudden you realize everything is not black and white. Everything is not because you didn't do something right. Unfortunately I had to actually experience that to—if I just had Ramona and Chris [Eric's younger siblings], who are two very easy kids, I would have been kind of judgmental."

She and Peter are also better parents, she says, able to handle—even enjoy—the teenaged defiance of their second child, Ramona. Ramona, whom she describes as generally outgoing, compassionate, and mature, was always very different from Eric. Mary recalled: "I mean really, we joked that after Eric, who you had to monitor every single thing, she came along and like when she was three years old if she did something she would [say], 'I go time out' and she would go." Now that Ramona is a teenager, there is more conflict, but they make jokes about being impossible to shock.

"Maybe partly because of what we went through with Eric we joke between ourselves. We're pretty good parents with our hands tied behind our back. And she was just starting to be like [a teenager, and we thought]: 'Yeah, let us have it, come on, show us what you've got.' And just nothing could compare, it just pales." We both laughed at her image of toughened parents saying, "Bring it on." Mary gets to know, and make jokes, that her commitment is unshakeable, given how it has been tested in the past.

Yet despite these individual benefits, there are some social costs. Without people like Mary, Owen, or Sylvia stepping up, perhaps communities would implement more programs to assist in the caregiving of special-needs children or adults with mental illness. Without people like Nicki filling in the gaps for her African-American kin, perhaps the nation would address the racialized patterns of incarceration and joblessness that produce children like Karma, whose desperate African-American parents could not care for her. Without people like Barbie, perhaps states would change the way they provide for victims of workplace tragedies. Without rescuing, perhaps there would be more of an outcry about the social costs of our pitiless economic policies, the ones that create the needs these commitment heroes struggle to meet, and that make that struggle even harder. They give a free pass to those larger social entities whose failures give rise to extreme individual needs in the first place: in this way, rescuing makes insecurity culture possible.

THE GIVING TREES: VISIBLE GIFT, INVISIBLE COST

In *The Giving Tree*, an illustrated children's book by the poet Shel Silverstein, a tree loves a little boy so much that she offers him more and more of herself as he gets older—first her shade to play in, then her apples to sell, then her limbs to make a house with, then her trunk to make a boat from. When he is an old man, he returns. "I wish that I could give you something," the tree says. "But I have nothing left. I am just an old stump."

"I don't need very much now," said the boy, "just a quiet place to sit and rest. I am very tired." "Well," said the tree, straightening herself up as much as she could, "well, an old stump *is* good for sitting and resting. Come, Boy, sit down. Sit down and rest." And the boy did. And the tree was happy.[13]

Rescuing is a gift proffered by people for whom duty still resonates powerfully, a gift of their struggle to care. While we have seen how notions of duty make intimate life more brittle, enabling some people to see and name betrayal in the home, such ideas also help to propel others to the great heights of self-sacrifice documented in this chapter. Given the choice, as duty frames it for them, between martyrdom and abandonment, some do all they can to shoulder their burdens.

While commitment heroes are not unique to our times, rampant insecurity both generates and impedes their efforts to hold duty sacred. Most important, they represent another crucial variant of the self that insecurity culture enables and cultivates—the self that takes on individual responsibility, that sees social trends as personal challenges. Like displacing, like defying, like choosing, rescuing features the self at center stage, adapting to forces of insecurity that lurk behind the curtains, but that cast the parts and write the script.

The facts on the ground—that these tenacious people are met with important needs, that they recognize those needs as such, and that they have to struggle to meet them—are all structured by social configurations of gender, the economy, and the state. Less advantaged women practice defying and rescuing in service to great expectations; perhaps for some, the need they refuse to take on is freighted with the departure of men, the state, and the employers, making independence particularly resonant, while for others, duty still makes moral sense of their lives because it still can.

The sacrifices required by commitment heroes are so extreme, however, that these are gifts perhaps no society has the right to expect of its members. These are gifts that absolve the rest of us from having to undergo serious change, from having to bolster a social safety net or a court system against the institutional failures that produce dire need, from having to address social inequities in divorce, poverty, and other calamities: gifts that enable the insecurity culture that surrounds us. These are the gifts of the giving tree—profound, humbling, deeply moving, even awesome, but perhaps also on some level dangerous, certainly for the giving tree, and sometimes for the rest of the forest. We can be inspired or awed by their example, but we surely cannot (and we might not want to) ask for it.

CHAPTER 7

◦◊◦

The Stable Oasis

Regina Hunter has been an art teacher for a decade and married for more than twice as long, but when she looks back on her early years, all she sees is uncertainty, years of floundering before she started studying art and turned it into a career, first as a graphic designer, then as an art teacher. Her intimate life was the same way, a few affairs with unstable free spirits, including one "really, really talented painter," until she met her current husband, an older man with a daughter already to whom he was a patient and dedicated father. Now happy with her work and marriage, Regina derives comfort and even joy from the small pleasures of an interesting job and a kindhearted spouse. At the same time, she is open about the compromises that are a part of making long-term arrangements, even satisfying ones, stick.

She spent a year doing serious painting, but she thinks that being "immature" and "insecure about not having a great art background" steered her toward graphic design, which she described as "intensely boring," although it paid the bills. She now relishes the autonomy of running her own classroom and, with two kids in college, welcomes the money and the safety net of her secure job while her husband labors in precarious work. At the same time she wonders whether she can survive the tough classroom environment until she retires. "If I can last twenty years, that's good. You know, I mean, because the [students'] behaviors are troublesome, you know," she says.

She talks about her happy marriage in the same way, with a long view that recognizes some blemishes but is bolstered by an appreciation for the everyday. "Yeah, you get mad, and, god, you know, frustrated, and stuff like that . . . Go through your rough patches, for sure," she concedes. "So, yeah, but . . . we're good together. He's not demanding or, you know, 'Cook me this,' or 'The house is a mess.' He's not that kind of guy. He's not critical, at all. He's very supportive." While this is certainly positive language, it is nonetheless hardly soaring or rhapsodic. Pragmatic at work and at home, Regina expresses a moderate vision of gratitude and compromise, in service to a life of pleasant stability and calm; given the priority she makes of staying put, we can say Regina is "settling."

On the one hand, we might not expect to find great differences in how the stably employed act or talk about obligation compared to insecure workers, since, in the United States, are we not all immersed in insecurity culture, transcending the boundaries of our particular workplaces? The same movies (say, *Up in the Air*, with George Clooney as a one-man corporate firing squad), the same books touting the latest management fad, the same news reports of mass layoffs once again, all of these cultural artifacts swirl around Regina and her family as they wrestle with how to make a college payment, just as they did around Fiona and her son as they left another man's house, or around Gary as he predicted his girlfriend's likely betrayal. Why should the specific experience of job insecurity matter when we all swim in the same precarious sea?

Furthermore, if there are differences to be found, perhaps they lie not in whether or not one's job is insecure but rather in the relative advantage with which one faces it: we have heard the echo of inequality in the way those at the top talk about "choosing" their itinerant work and their enduring intimacy, and in how the less advantaged engage in defying, displacing, or rescuing those whose need they recognize. As income inequality has risen over the last twenty years, we know it has also become more consequential; shouldn't class trump job insecurity in shaping how people see and fulfill their obligations to each other?

Yet we also know stable employment with a livable wage matters. The more secure your job, the greater your job satisfaction and your work performance; job security brings better physical health and improved psychological health, including less anxiety and depression. Why, then, would we imagine that its potential impact stops at the workplace door? When one can reasonably expect that an employer is beholden to job security norms, how might that shape how one makes sense of one's own obligations? What is the effect of stable employment on how people approach commitment, at work and in their intimate lives?[1]

Like Regina, many stably employed workers, particularly those at the less advantaged end of the spectrum—those lower-middle-class or working-class people who do not fear losing their job—adopt a pragmatic posture toward both work and their intimate lives, a flexible stance that generates everyday gratitude but makes allowances for disappointments along the way. Like duty, pragmatism involves high expectations of constancy, which generate an obligation to stay when the going gets tough. Unlike duty, however, pragmatism combines constancy with the habits of compromise; it says we can have faith in ourselves and each other, even while we are also fallible. Most of all, pragmatism eschews the idea of the perfect match—the dream job, the soul mate—as the misguided fancy of the self-indulgent.

Aimed at work, pragmatism means that the stably employed are unique among workers for maintaining high expectations for loyalty from their employers, and for not assuming the inevitability of insecurity. Aimed at home, their talk about intimate life bears a pronounced similarity to that of more advantaged insecure couples, whose choosing language masks a persistent matter-of-factness. In both realms, the stably employed demonstrate an assumption of mutual responsibility, in sharp contrast to the fervent insistence upon individual accountability—what has been called "neoliberal subjectivity"—that we have seen insecure workers profess in myriad ways. Insecurity culture only reaches so far.

"WORK IS KIND OF LIKE A MARRIAGE": SETTLING DOWN, OR SETTLING FOR?

Settling, of course, has two primary connotations: first, the sense that Regina is settling *down*, eschewing the wild headiness of an unpredictable love affair and the unstructured life of a working artist for the stable confines of a reliable man and a regular paycheck. Regina would in all likelihood fully embrace this characterization, as she only partially admires the path not chosen. Explaining why she left an early boyfriend, she laughs. "I decided I needed a little stability in my life," she remembers. "I'm not that, you know, live-in-the-back-of-a-van kind of person."

The other connotation, however, is that she is settling *for*, supplanting higher goals of achievement and passion, for which she would have to assume risks of poverty and isolation, with the stability she can get here and now. While not all of the stably employed would admit to this exchange, it nonetheless captures the habits of compromise, the sense of a bargain being struck between what's desired and what's realistic, that imbue the pragmatic stance.

Ed Case, the firefighter we heard from in the introduction, offers a potent example of these habits. Recall his words about his work, which reflect his approach to intimate life as well: "[Work] is kind of like a marriage," he said; "you kind of give a little and take a little."

The pragmatic stance gives workers the means to endure even when a job is unsatisfying, to soldier on despite its imperfections. Patrick is the police officer whom we met in chapter 5 taking care of the second shift at home. Compared to new officers just hired, he said, "When I went to work there and somebody asked me to do something, I just did it and that was it. I might not have liked it, but I didn't and I wasn't going to stand there and ask why." Honorable behavior, his words tell us, is when people suppress their own desires and simply acquiesce. Stella, who has worked for the same insurance company for two decades, feels herself replicating her father's persistence on the job. "My father would come home, you know, [and say,] 'I'm going to quit my job,' and—of course he's not going to, he didn't do that. He worked for the same place for thirty years," she remembered. "You know, but [I feel] the same, you know, I think similar, I think the same, similar frustration. Yeah, you know, so and so's an ass . . ."

The stably employed work in settings of low turnover and significant reciprocity. These settings can surely generate passionate conflict, as new disagreements layer onto old ones; history intensifies feelings in the present with meanings reverberating from the past. Yet the habits of compromise seem to flourish in these environments, as people experience conflict as something to withstand.[2]

Jayne, who has worked in a law firm for twenty-six years, said she "worked to live" rather than vice versa. "I still don't think of it as, like, you know, this is a fabulous career, I'm so happy to go to work every day, that kind of stuff or anything like that. When I retire I'm not going to look back." But she has her own mantra to help her get through the bad times. "You know, people panic and they change things, and if you pretty much just ride it out, you're going to be fine. I mean there are certainly going to be better times and less good times in every relationship and every job and every everything." Like others, Jayne seems to surrender to the imperfect match of her self and her job; rather than leaving or seeking to change things at work, Jayne evinces a certain acquiescence, an approach that also sustains her intimate life. The same tactics in one arena allow her to endure in another.

BEYOND THE ONE-WAY HONOR SYSTEM

Stably employed people sound just like workers immersed in precarious work in one crucial sense: they proclaim a work ethic that seems almost universal and practically required. "When I go to a job . . . I [am] very loyal, very committed, because you have to be," declared Stephanie, a medical paraprofessional. "You have to put in a hundred percent, or the job's not worth being there. If you're not gonna do it, and you don't like what you do, you definitely don't need to be there." James, a teacher, agreed:

> What do I owe my job? Well, the reflective me says: Nothing that's beyond the contract. But that's not the reality. The reality is, I want students to walk away enthused about education. I want them to be creative and look at things in a different way. Maybe because I'm a workaholic and I believe so strongly in some of these tenets, I think I'm a very, very strong teacher. I know that students rate me very high. I'm getting kudos for what I'm doing professionally. So what do I owe my job? Probably, the realistic answer is, anything that contributes to education, I should be on top of in doing.

"I'm just a workaholic kind of guy," said Barry, another teacher. "So, I don't have any problem jumping in and working and doing odd jobs or whatever I need to do to make things work out." Sylvia, a social worker, said, "If someone just comes to work promptly at 8:30 and leaves promptly at 5:00 and they just go through the motions, that is not a good worker to me. A good worker is someone who achieves goals, wants to do well, and is passionate about doing a good job."

Even those teachers who feel indifferent to their employers can often feel bound to their schools by their affection for their colleagues and motivated to work hard by their commitment to their students and their professional identities. Nalani was a little burned out by the stress of working in an urban school, and did not feel obligated to perform beyond her contract, she said. But her ties to the children in her classroom—and her professional duty to students—roped her into trying harder. "I owe the commitment of following my contract, following through with my contract but beyond—I guess I owe the kids to be there—not be there but to—I owe commitment to the kids," she asserted, finally. "I have a commitment to the kids. If I took on the job, then I have to be committed to teaching or working."

Stable working-class jobs are rarer today due to the decline in manufacturing, as well as the increased use of temping and outsourcing to solve staff needs; thus obtaining one of the remaining positions in police or firefighting is sometimes the result of a long effort of strategic moves, which might include military service, volunteering, or extra classes or training. Once they are in, firefighters often consider themselves fortunate, which feeds their sense of total dedication. "I wouldn't do anything but this job," said Jake. "I'd be crushed if I lost this job." Firefighters joined teachers and other professional workers in evincing a certain allegiance, even a love for their jobs.

Other kinds of stable workers also proclaimed their work ethic, however, even when they were not as passionate about their work. Although she said she was "not going to look back" when she retired, Jayne maintained it was important to live up to expectations at work, as she counseled her son, who was thinking of calling in sick.

> I said, "You don't do that, period. You don't call in sick, you know, certainly not a half an hour before you're due at work or whatever." It was—I said, "You go." I said, "You can go in there and say, 'I don't feel well,' if it's true. You know, 'I had a headache, I have a stomachache, I need to use the restroom every five minutes'. "You can do that," I said, "but you go." You show up, you do your job, and you do what's expected of you." And, you know, I'm probably disappointed more often than not because so many people don't do what they're expected to do.

Jayne laid out for her son what it meant to have a good work ethic: overriding whatever you might actually desire or need in service to being reliable at work. When we find our moral purpose in work, it matters less how we feel about our jobs than how we act in them.

Where the stably employed differ from those immersed in precarious work, however, is in their expectations of employers. In contrast to the one-way honor system, whose adherents shrug away employer obligation as the residue of a bygone era, all the while intensifying their own responsibility, for people with stable employment, high expectations are a mutual affair. Stably employed workers consider job insecurity as neither inevitable nor advisable; employment practices, they feel, are far from the anonymous outgrowth of global social forces but instead the reflection of an employer's decency and a company's honor.

Asked what employers owe their workers, the stably employed can sound a little anachronistic, in sharp contrast to the sort of answers—"a paycheck," or "respect"—that we heard in chapter 2. "Security, if at all possible," responded Ed, the firefighter. "I see that as being responsible, because obviously nowadays I feel if you take care of your employees then they are going to take care of you."

> That is kind of the same concept we have here. I look after my captain, my captain looks after me. I've got his back, he's got mine. But that is one thing, some responsibility to your employees. Okay, you hire them today, don't think just to hire them today and fire them in two weeks. As long as the employee is doing

their part, I think the promise from the other end is they have to do their part to help you. It is a two-way street. That is the way I see it.

Ed viewed obligations as fairly equal on both sides of the employment relation. Coupled with the compromises that enabled endurance, this mutuality of expectations constituted the pragmatic approach to work. With neither boss nor worker excused by references to social or economic trends beyond their control, neither is free of the moral gaze; both are subject to its unapologetic measure.

THE USES OF FAMILY METAPHORS

In part because they retain workers over decades, during which time births, deaths, and the care needs of others can intrude on and recede from the workplace, stable employers often seem to make allowances for people's personal lives. Jayne, for example, who had worked at a small law firm for more than twenty years, recalled how over that time, as various life events intruded, the firm was very understanding.

> They were very good about, you know, "Take what you need." They—actually they've been good about all that kind of stuff, "Anything . . ." You know. When my father-in-law died, when my mother-in-law died, anything like that, it's been, you know, "Take the time you need. No problem." There's been no pressure; nobody, like, "Get back to work," "How much time are you going to take? You need to be back here." They've always been good about that.

Wes, a firefighter, described what happened when home problems arose for whatever reason.

> This place is very family-oriented. They really—they are really—really family-oriented there. You know, you call and say, "I got to go home" and you tell them what the deal is. They stand by you. They'll come get you and then they call someone else to come to work to finish up the shift. They're very open to everything.

Workers in these sites feel human, as if they can be imperfect without sanction, which then serves to nourish their dedication.

Yet "family" is more than the catchall term for those life events that occasionally impinge on the workplace; sometimes it is the reigning metaphor for an employment relationship, one that enlists mutual obligation.

Theresa Hirsch lived her life as an exception to the culture of flexibility: she resided in the same city in which she had grown up, and she loved the fact that her daughter, Gillian, went to school with the children of her old schoolmates: "It's like a little miniature reunion every time we go to a basketball game or something. I mean these are the guys and the girls I went to school with," she said. She was suspicious of people who switched jobs frequently. "I don't know, they're not people I know," she said. A small-business owner, she maintained long-term commitments to her employees, even when their jobs threatened to disappear, as it did for her nanny, Carly, when her children grew older. Theresa worried about it: "I'm like 'What am I going to do with her when Gillian starts driving?' She'll be fourteen in October, so, like, I've got to find a job for [Carly]. Yeah, bringing her right in."

The nanny is a paradigmatic example of Theresa's approach to relationships. I asked Theresa why she did not just let Carly go, which would have been perfectly justifiable, since the children were now teenagers. "I would," Theresa replied. "I mean I would if I had to, but if I can use her here, and I love her, and she's like my oldest child, and she's also kind of like my wife."

Theresa has to invent new language use here, to blend together two different words to capture the emotional significance of the nanny. The language she reaches for, the metaphor that best captures their closeness, the care and the assumed nature of her obligation, is that of the family. The nanny is both as dear to her as a child in her care and as profoundly important, for years as useful and dependable to her, as a wife. The family metaphor both expresses a relationship and establishes a responsibility for Theresa as the employer.

Many stably employed people call upon "family" to describe their work, particularly if they find the work meaningful. Without a moral wall distinguishing where insecurity belongs and where it does not, they view both arenas as subject to the same ethical principles of what counts as good character, when to keep trying, when to call it quits, what we owe each other. Even as our families can be sites for disappointment, displeasure, and even danger, the family remains among our most powerful metaphors for care, warmth, and reliability, and the stably employed invoke it as the highest compliment.

"People here are like my family; they're a great support system," said Linda, a white married teacher. "It's a huge plus. They're like my family in a way, and my boss is great. I love what I do; I love the families that are here. We're really a support system for each other." Another teacher, Juliet, agreed. "I love it here. I absolutely love it here. And my best friends are here. The parents are just so great," she said. "So I look forward to coming to school; it's my second home. Actually, I probably spend more hours here than I do at home. So maybe it's my first home, I don't know."

Firefighters, who rotated on overnight shifts with the same teams, sometimes for years, can be as close to their colleagues as siblings. Said Jake:

> It's the camaraderie with the guys. The job we do, it's just, basically, every aspect of it. I have a whole separate surrogate family, I guess you could say. Because we spend twenty-four hours a day at it, twenty-four hours at a time together. So, I'm with those, some of those guys, the same as I am with my family. . . . One of the guys I work with at the same station, we came out of the academy together. We've been together the whole time. Another guy we work with is one of my best friends. Some of these guys I've known my whole career. So, we know each other's families, we know each other's backgrounds, we live together. It's just having another family.

While sometimes the rotating shifts or the constant on-call duty exacted a toll on his participation in his children's lives, Ed takes solace from the fact that his "work family" would end up taking care of his "home family" should something happen to him, if he were to become incapacitated or die. "It's tough on my biological family, but, like I say, no matter what happens, there is a bigger family that will somehow or other, the girls will go to college. They will get things that they need."

> There is one thing with this that you won't see elsewhere is the firefighters are a family to a certain degree. If I died in that wreck out there, my kids and my wife would have been taken care of. There wouldn't have been anything else they would have ever needed that something wouldn't have been done for them. Everybody from [the town], if she needed the yard mowed, the yard would have been mowed. Need a new roof? The guys from [the town's fire company] probably would have showed up or [the county] would have showed up and put a roof on the house or whatever.

This unspoken promise made up for all the inconvenience and sacrifice that a firefighter's family ended up making, Ed said.

Crucially, family feeling does not always mean that workmates actually like each other, that they are well matched, or that they would pick each other as friends if they had the option. Just as in families, the sense of mutual obligation and of a certain history together is supposed to transcend their affinities, no matter if individual personalities do not mesh well. Instead, just as in a family, an idealized dependency is rooted in relationships that go beyond the fleeting qualities of affection or choice. As Ed maintained: "You know these guys, we argue. I hate some of these guys sometimes, some of the stuff they do, but when the chips are down, they're there. They'll come drag my butt out of a fire if they have to; I'll do the same for them." For Ed, the family metaphor is not just about loyalty, but also about a certain sense of pragmatism, expressed as an involuntary resignation—he "hate[s] some of these guys sometimes," and thus if it were suddenly up to him he would not choose them as colleagues. Stable workers invoke the metaphor to highlight two beliefs about their work: that, like family members, we do not select our workmates, but also that we share a history with them that involves tolerance for differences and generates reciprocal obligations.

WHEN STABLE WORK BETRAYS

Set against the backdrop of the one-way honor system, the high expectations that stably employed people maintain for their employers stand out in sharp contrast; there is no moral wall allowing insecurity free rein at work. How might all this family feeling affect how they handle grievous disappointments, job loss, or a "divorce" from these "families"? Stably employed people have highly elaborated penchants for compromise, which make them different from the less advantaged men engaged in precarious work whose brittle expectations shatter in the face of others' fallibility at home. But while their propensity to compromise enables work relations of long endurance, the high expectations of the stably employed, when finally dashed themselves, can lead to an acute sense of betrayal that sounds quite familiar. What is unusual, we might note, recalling how the insecure workers in chapter 2 evinced anything but anger at work, is that this outrage is aimed at their employers.

Diane was particularly angry at the pay freeze that teachers in her area had endured for years, comparing it to the annual increases they had gotten "downtown." Her alienation had increased to the point that, uniquely, she was openly rejecting a strong work ethic:

> That's right. I'm not giving the extra mile. I know that's bad to say and it might be negative and stuff, but I'm older and I'm tired and I just feel like we are not paid what we are worth to begin with, but then when you look and see what's been going on . . . Without a pay raise, how many years without a step increase, and downtown they continue to get pay raises whether it's 2 percent, 5 percent, 10 percent, you know. We might be in a recession, but everything I buy is not

staying the same or going down. So, yes, it's leaving a bitter taste. I think the climate and the morale—it's not just me. I feel like I have been a dedicated, good, professional employee for twenty-four and a half years, and I feel like I'm being shit on, to tell you the truth . . . I've always said I worked two-and-a-half jobs. I'm going to leave on time. When it's 3:40, I'm walking.

While professional standards established the minimum job requirements, she withheld any extra work. "All that's said and done, I think [I owe the school] always to be a professional. To do my job to the best of my capability and get my reports and everything done on time. Just basically do what's expected of me. But I don't strive to exceed anymore," she said, and laughed, her laugh letting us know that she knows her proclamations are shocking. "They don't pay me to. That sounds really bad, I know." Diane's acute alienation has led to a rarity: someone openly defying the work ethic.

We read gratitude, value, and character—very personal meanings—into money, the impersonal medium of exchange; this emotional translation can be heightened in the long-term settings of stable work and the expectations they generate. Audrey had worked as a recruiter for a small family-owned firm for more than a decade before the owner's child developed leukemia. For a year she and another employee, Farber, did much more than their share to ensure the business stayed afloat. She went above and beyond, she said, because that is what you do in a small firm, where relationships were close and obligations high. When the owner returned to the job, however, their year-end bonus was insulting, Audrey said.

Then he gave me some crappy bonus that year? Are you kidding me? And not so much as a thank you. You know what? You do that for people that you care about. You step up to the plate. You could have told me thank you. Take the money out of it. You could have called me in and said—especially your daughter almost died. We ran your business while you were there. Farber was pissed when he got the bonus. He actually had the nads to go in and say something. He said, "Are you kidding me? Audrey and I ran this business for a year, Fred, and this is really all you feel like I should have?"

Audrey left shortly thereafter, still fuming about the betrayal. Her current job is also at a small firm, and her coworkers are like sisters.

There's nothing but us three chicks, whether it's complaining about our men or our children—it's such a stress reliever. I can't imagine having to come into work and hold that all day when you're about to stroke out. [Laughs.] We come in

some mornings, it's just, "Wah, wah, wah, wah, wah, wah." I'm very lucky I work
where I do with who I do.

As the economy contracted, she could see their business suffering significant losses. But she was not leaving, even though recruiters were easily
employable, she said.

> Right now I'd never—I am [staying] because I like my boss—bosses. I respect . . .
> the owner, I love him to death; and I work for Lorraine. I couldn't have some-
> body better to work for. Her and I are best friends, but it would never interfere
> with work, because I respect her too much to ever let—I have a good work ethic,
> anyway.

For Audrey, the lines between "work" and "family" are blurred: in addition
to her stories of the boss's child's leukemia and her notion of her current
supervisor as her best friend, she also met her longtime partner on the job.
These integrated domains invoke similar notions of obligation, similar expectations for what employers and employees owe each other: loyalty, dedication, their best effort. The family feelings that cloaked her intense feelings of betrayal at her previous job were at work again, enlisting her heart,
embedding her in relations of high obligation and high compromise.

Those employed in stable workplaces, then, generally reject the one-way
honor system, and instead embrace similar standards of commitment from
their employer to those they expect of themselves. For those few of these
workers touched by the reverberations of insecurity, however, such as layoffs or pay freezes—even in a familized environment—their sense of alienation and anger is strong. The tactics we witnessed in chapter 2, by which
precarious workers manage their feelings and keep their expectations
low—through resignation, shame, or the language of opportunity—these
options are less available to the stably employed. We can view their fury as
a measure of the cost that the rest are trying to avoid; for those living in
insecurity culture, their detachment works like armor, donned in a context
of inevitable insecurity. From this landscape of feeling, we can surmise the
emotional impact of the moral wall: when they use it, it protects people
from their own feelings in insecurity culture.

The pain of stably employed people when their expectations are dashed
also tells us about the reciprocal view they harbor, a mutuality belying the
one-way honor system prevailing among the insecure. Forsaking the paeans
to individual accountability, instead they insist upon a working relationship with shared obligations that contests the universality of insecurity
culture.

"IT'S TOUGH, BUT WE KEEP TRUDGING ON": PRAGMATISM IN INTIMATE LIFE

Stably employed people display a remarkable congruence in their approach to their work and intimate lives, an internal consistency we also saw among the less advantaged women in precarious work in chapter 4. Unlike Fiona and others defying the expectations of others at work and at home, however, the stably employed make sense of their obligations not through independence but instead with the same pragmatism with which they contemplate their work lives.

Ed, the firefighter, had been married for more than two decades, his wife, Janice, working as a part-time bookkeeper out of the house while she shuttled their three children to their activities around town; the family lived in the same town she had grown up in, blocks from her mother and grandmother. At first, she had wanted them to put down roots there. "I swore when I got married that I would never move next to my in-laws," Ed remembered, chuckling ruefully, "but we bought the house right behind them, put a gate in. I swore that I would not put a gate in."

But now Janice wanted to move to a more rural area, where they could buy a bigger home, partly because her childhood friends had married lawyers and architects, and the contrast with those families stung, Ed said. "So I think she would like to have more, but then again, I have difficulty letting go of being steady," he said. "Especially at this point with the economics the way it is." The move, and his resistance to it, was the biggest disagreement of their long marriage. Recall his summary from the introduction: "So it's tough, but we keep trudging on."

Ed's language—"It's tough, but we keep trudging on"—draws a picture of endurance, of compromised dreams and imperfection, that exemplifies the pragmatism of settling. Of course, we would do well to notice here that Janice is perhaps the one most obviously compromising her dreams; men's stable work can shore up conventional gender arrangements that weaken women's bargaining power in marriage.

But the bargains are central to pragmatism, no matter who is the stable worker. Theresa, who had run her own small business for more than fifteen years, dismisses the compromises at work and at home even as she recognizes them. She started her business with a partner, Garth, with whom she argued more than with her husband, and she was a little concerned about what her children thought of all the fighting: "So Garth frustrates me, but that's why it's good that Mommy can say, 'Alright Garth, you know what? Just kiss my butt.' And come home and not deal with him. I mean, that's why Mommy's not married to someone like Garth," she laughed. We might also observe that she remained in the business relationship anyway, despite the grinding of ill-meshed gears.

At the same time, Theresa described a marriage that involved making space for each other's differences. Dating had been "very comfortable—I would like to say it was just crazy, but it wasn't that crazy. It was just kind of right, obviously," she said. Now, they maintain an unusually independent relationship, with separate vacations, jobs, hobbies, and interests. "Well, you can't change people. If they don't like [to do something you like to do], they're not going to like it regardless," she maintained. "And it doesn't mean they don't love you, they just don't [like to do that activity], and that's just the way it is." Theresa adopts a consistently matter-of-fact approach to her work and intimate relationships, one that minimizes the importance of any mismatch of self and other.

It is certainly possible that we fall into two categories, those who can compromise and those who cannot, with the former finding themselves in steady work and relationships and the latter pinging from arrangement to arrangement, driven by their internal states of independence or outraged duty. We cannot know for certain which comes first, or which causes the other: the stable job or the ability to compromise. Yet the increasing rarity of stable work, especially for less advantaged people, means that even those who want it are often hard-pressed to find it. Furthermore, stable work has powerful economic effects—the predictable paycheck allows for long-term horizons that encourage planning.

What, then, is pragmatism, independence or duty? I argue they are stances by which we adapt to the degree of job security with which we find ourselves, given how our gender and class bestow upon us particular resources and obligations. These are stances that shape the extent of our commitments and how it feels to have them at work and at home; they are the means by which job insecurity wields its broader impact beyond the confines of the workplace. In this case, pragmatism entails a particular vision—how trifling this or that disagreement is, compared to the long-term meaning and pleasure here—and hence it allows us to settle.

THE LANGUAGE OF INSECURITY, THE PRACTICE OF COMMITMENT

It is not that those employed in stable work are not aware of the larger insecurity culture around them. Their awareness is written into their language, as they sometimes adopt the perspective of a more itinerant critic to mock their own settling behavior. "It's probably twenty-three years now in this particular school," said Juliet, a teacher, embarrassedly. "I live a boring life." Stella talked about sometimes wanting to leave her husband. "Well, you know, there's probably been times when I would have wanted to just go ahead and say the hell with you and take off too. But it was like, you know, you got the kid, and is that the thing to do? And I guess, because I'm more of a wimp than other people, I don't know." "Boring" and "wimp" judge the acts of staying put negatively; people who remained in place were sometimes sheepish about it, suggesting that they were painfully aware of the ways others might assess their behavior.

Others seemed to try out an independent stance, to show they "knew better" than to commit too much. Theresa, who strategized about hiring her nanny in her small business to avoid severing that tie, and who thrilled at the continuity between her daughter's childhood and her own, claimed that she rejected "enabling behavior." "I'm a big fan of ending relationships when they are too much work," she said flatly, discussing a friend's husband with a drinking problem and calling upon "enabling" language, often a vocabulary of detachment. In this way, she momentarily invoked an itinerant ideology that prevailed widely, even as the details of her narrative capture how much her daily life is devoted to settling.

We are few of us cultural isolates. Our task is to somehow make sense of our current surroundings, our current challenges, with the ideas and practices we have accumulated over time that render meaningful the route we have taken and the path ahead. Even for the stably employed, it seems, insecurity culture is like a rising moon, shedding a certain light on those paths, offering a way of viewing that feels increasingly powerful, a cold light that nonetheless provides a certain clarity. Even for them, to a limited degree, the vocabulary of insecurity finds its way into their talk.

ENGENDERING COMPROMISE

Stably employed people are thus aware of the broader environment of insecurity culture, share a sense of ascendant flexibility, and know that other people, at least, are engaged in a quest for the perfect match at work and in their intimate lives. In contrast, settling requires fine-tuned habits of compromise, which sometimes feels like surrendering to someone else's desires or, worse, like cowardice in the face of risk. In chapter 3, we saw several different strategies through which advantaged itinerant workers managed to eschew the quest for the perfect match in their intimate life, in service to their own pragmatism there. Stably employed workers invoke similar arguments to disparage and discourage the quest for something better, suggesting that perfect doesn't exist, perfect is not worth it, and perfect is irrelevant. Missing, however, compared to the more advantaged itinerant workers, is the choosing language of will and autonomy; fundamentally, stably employed, less advantaged workers do not seem to worry about whether or not their settling behavior taps into some neoliberal imperative of choice.

Perfect Doesn't Exist

Georgette, a proud, poised African-American woman, had grown up in Washington, DC, in an upper-middle-class family with ties to a number of prominent black achievers. While she had a master's degree to go with this privileged background, however, she was adaptable enough to take on a job as a supervisor at a local factory when she had trouble finding work, and there she met her husband, Sam, who still works on the line. They had been married for twenty years. "I always probably thought I would marry some-body who was a little—probably more educated," she said. "And I certainly dated guys who were doctors and lawyers, but the thing is, he was a nice person and works hard."

Looking back, Georgette describes the occasional serious conflict in her marriage, most of them stemming not from the class disparities in their background but from the gendered division of labor, because Sam's work on the night shift and his introverted nature made her the default care-giver and manager of the household. "But yeah, it's been hard and there are times when, I mean, we've had some knock-down drag-outs because I'm like, 'I didn't plan on this,'" Georgette said. "But I'm sure if I were married to a doctor it would be the same thing. You know, he'd be up and out, and it is what it is. I mean you would be the caregiver and the person who took care of the kids."

Georgette contrasted Sam with the man her sister married, a physician whom she disparaged as snobbish and lazy, who would rather not work at all than work at a job he felt was beneath him. "But this guy [her brother-in-law] is too good to do anything. I mean, what the hell is wrong with you?" Georgette asked. "And see, Sam and I, I think we share the same phi-losophy about a lot of things." She continued:

> And I'm just more realistic. I'm like this: Sam is not a perfect person, he can have an ugly, ugly temper, which pisses me off and I think sometimes can be irra-tional. But *they all fall* into that irrational category. But the thing is he has been a good provider. He loves his son; he will do anything for Nicholas.

In the end, what matters is not how perfect the man is but whether you make a pretty good match in the areas you think are important. One needs to be "realistic" about when to hold out for something better and when to adjust one's expectations; meanwhile, the quest for the perfect man is not worth it, because all men "fall into that irrational category," and "perfect" does not exist.

Perfect Is Overrated

Most often, the stably employed make jokes that sardonically hint at the pragmatism enabling couples to stay together. They point, jokingly, at their imperfect match, at the "trap" that is their unbreakable relationship, at the compromises they have had to make. In doing so, however, they also mock the very idea of perfection.

Several couples made jokes about death being the only way out of their marriage. Melissa and her stably employed husband adopted several children while also having four of their own; in addition, they serve as a foster-care family.

> I always used to joke to David when we would argue, like when we were resolving the conflict—not in the midst—I'd always say, "Go ahead and leave me. I've got eight of your kids. You'll never eat again." [*Laughs.*] And he'd just kind of roll his eyes because he knew. He'd better work it out because he can't afford not to. [*Laughs.*]

Notice how Melissa makes sure to tell us when this joke happened—not in the midst of a fight but afterwards, when they were resolving it—because otherwise it becomes more of a threat than a joke. Similarly, Sylvia said she and her second husband laughed together about why they would never divorce.

> Like we joke sometimes about that—"I could never divorce you because I wouldn't want to date anybody." That's just such a pain to have to date anybody. And so we joke back and forth about that, and it's serious but it's joking. I don't ever want a divorce again. He'll joke with me, "Well, I was your second choice."

Joking here works like the old trick in advertising, stoking an anxiety only to resolve it. Jokes about how awful it would be to divorce, told by stably employed couples to each other, also make fun of their own surrender to each other's imperfections.[3]

Pragmatic talk often takes on the same emotional tone as the jokes and invented words stemming from the stance of independence; both lead people to mock, however gently, the commitment that they or others make. Despite this surface similarity, however, the language performs a very different task. While the verbal play of independence serves to enact or commend distance (or pretend to), those who invoke pragmatism highlight the compromises, the very disappointments that are integral to their understanding of themselves as realistic, as opposed to self-indulgent. Pragmatic jokes, metaphors, and phrases play with both the notion of imperfection and its inescapability; in doing so, it reflects (and possibly generates) some of the capacity to endure.

Perfect Is Irrelevant

In a more frontal assault on insecurity culture, some stably employed people in long-term partnerships deny that the quest for perfection has any value or appeal, regardless of the potential of a more perfect union, and regardless of their chances of finding it. Their explanations are a bit more inchoate, as if the quest goes against something as foundational as their very identity. Recall how Regina, the art teacher now married for twenty-four years, describes why she had left an early boyfriend: "I'm not that, you know, live-in-the-back-of-a-van kind of person."

Grace had been married for twenty-six years to a man with chronic depression. She stayed because he was family, she said simply. "I think even though our kids are grown, I think it's just being a family. You know, the kids really—I mean, you know, their dad's their dad and this is just the way he's always been, and just, I think, being a family," she said. "Well, we've been together for so long now at this point, so . . ." Grace stayed with the man, despite years of being the primary breadwinner as well as absorbing the emotional impact of his mental troubles, but the task of explaining why was not really even within her verbal reach. It was like having to explain why she breathed.

Sometimes other things matter more than whether or not a spouse, or a job, was the perfect match. Victoria was a teacher who lived with her husband in the same house that he grew up in, where both sets of grandparents still lived, where both sets of great-grandparents had lived, with godparents, fictive grandparents, neighbors, and friends all still living in the same town.

> My daughter just graduated from high school, and we want her to have that same feeling when she goes away to school. I want her to be able to come home to her room, to her stuff. And, that's the—I just wouldn't move. Although this job is not my dream job, I can function until my dream job comes along.

Victoria was prepared to submit to the job's imperfections for now, in service to settling.

Instead, Victoria valued her family's deep embeddedness in their community. "It's that support group; the people who have watched me grow up or have grown up with me are all still there. There's a support group there you can't create anywhere else," Victoria said. In fact, Victoria explicitly cherished the very sameness at church that Alexis had scoffed at in chapter 3. "And our church is there, and I still sit in the same pew I've been sitting in my entire life," she said happily. "It's just one of those deals where the connection with our family and friends is way stronger than anything that may be trying to pull me away."

She had known her husband since she was on the swim team with him in middle school, and after getting together in high school they had a long engagement because he was patient enough to wait for her to graduate, she said. "And I guess because we're best friends, there wasn't a period of having to get to know you. Because we had known each other forever." When he went through a rough spell of adjusting to their son's departure for college, Victoria knew better than to take it personally.

> And for a week, he was a bear, just a bear to be around, because it was a change in life that he just wasn't sure how it was going to happen. Or how he was going to react with it. And that was the way he reacted and so I didn't take that personally; I knew exactly what he was going for. I had friends that were like, "I just don't know how you live with that." I'm like, well, it's a small phase and we'll get through it.

Victoria's stories feature a celebration of sameness, portraying a continuity that she relished, for which she cultivated the habits of compromise.

People who deployed a certain pragmatism at home—both the affluent and those less advantaged but stably employed—shared many of the same strategies for suppressing the quest for something better. There was one exception, however. We saw in chapter 3 some of the advantaged cloaking their compromises in the language of choice. "You have options, you know. Other people could be options, whatever, you know, anything could be options," said Karen, a middle-class black woman married for nineteen years. "You just make the decision, 'That's not what I want and this is what I want and this is where I'm staying and that's it.'" Yet only a few of the less advantaged secure workers made any such efforts to emphasize just how voluntary their compromises were.

In the absence of these claims to autonomy, even when sticking with a bargain made difficult, say, by someone newly disturbed by an empty nest, stably employed workers reveal how much their own experience with job insecurity matters. They demonstrate that merely living amid a widespread cultural sense of precariousness is not enough to generate the same stance toward obligation, couched in the same language of responsibility and risk—that in fact the stances depend in large part on whether or not one has personally experienced job insecurity and whether one's relative advantage transforms that insecurity into threat or opportunity.

WHO SURRENDERS? COMPLICATING THE DIVORCE DIVIDE

Both advantaged insecure workers and the less advantaged stably employed share the same approach to their intimate lives: the pragmatism that simultaneously maintains expectations of self and other, and includes a well-developed capacity for compromise. The combination allows people to still have faith in the endurance of their intimate relationships and to have some habits to help them endure. Yet as we learned in chapter 3, for these two groups of people on the opposite ends of advantage, existing scholarship predicts very different outcomes for their relationships: robust research has established the class difference in marriage and divorce rates, a sociological truism that has earned the moniker the 'divorce divide.' The divorce rate of people without college degrees is the engine behind the high divorce rate in the United States overall—indeed, the first marriages of "moderately educated" women (those with some college) are twice as likely to break up in the first five years as those of women with college degrees. How, then, is it possible that we find such overlap in how people talk about marriage and what we owe each other when they belong to social categories with such consequential differences?[4]

Yet those who evince pragmatism are not just different by class but also by their relationship to job insecurity, and there's the rub. While less advantaged people on the whole demonstrate a greater propensity to divorce, the job security of the stably employed conceivably protects them from the ravages of resource deprivation and its impact on coupling. Perhaps, then, the divorce divide is actually an account of the impact of job insecurity on less advantaged people, since so many of them labor in precarious work, rather than of the impact of socioeconomic status per se. Assuming that the partnering trends of these two groups—the affluent insecure and the stable less advantaged—do indeed overlap, we may have thus identified a mechanism (their pragmatism) for a finding that scholars have not yet sought (the shared endurance of their intimate partnerships).[5]

How might that mechanism work? Most of those who adopt a pragmatic stance have enjoyed relationships without significant hardship, either because their class advantage protects them from the vagaries of insecurity or their job security protects them from the privations of unpredictable disadvantage. Indeed, both groups stand as either the winners of insecurity culture, the beneficiaries of the external labor market that made them sought-after employees, or the remaining inheritors of the old social contract, with its promise of a stable life, modest to be sure, but one for which you can plan.[6]

As such, more than sharing a common class background or educational status, those who forged long-term relationships with a pragmatic approach shared a certain luxury, the fearlessness about the economic uncertainty that plagued the others, brought on either because they had not experienced much insecurity or because they benefited from it. In contrast to the laid-off who suffered from the predominance of precarious work, these relationships were grounded in an economic arrangement that enabled private caregiving and dependence—either through affluence or stability—amid anemic public support. This position did not guarantee the endurance of intimate ties, to be sure, but the fearlessness surely made staying put easier: easier to predict and plan for the future, easier to withstand minor indignities in service to reliable care and provisioning, easier to subsume one's individual interest to the larger whole.

IS SECURITY A FEMINIST ISSUE?

Sometimes compromises are not worth making, of course. We are not able to evaluate the extent to which people are settling for too little, whether these are jobs or intimate unions that require too high a cost for their stability—in part because what makes a cost too dear varies from person to person. The cost one is willing to bear is shaped by what one senses is the going rate, a calculus in which gender as a social structure—a collective, institutionalized experience, instead of a personal identity—figures prominently. Regina's appreciation of her husband ("He's not demanding or, you know, 'Cook me this,' or 'The house is a mess.' He's not that kind of guy. He's not critical, at all. He's very supportive") was based in part on the sense that (many, or at least enough) other husbands demand women's unpaid caring labor as part of their due. Furthermore, as we have seen, men's stable employment, which is often in jobs emblematic of working-class masculinity, seems to support conventional gendered arrangements of work and care.

Yet when women are the ones with stable work, they sometimes support families whose configurations allow for fluid gendered arrangements in which both men and women work and care. Their work enables that of men in precarious jobs or in full-time nurturing roles, and their families can reflect a diverse array of practices and adaptations to the needs that present themselves. Of course, some stable jobs for women—teaching, nursing—are also archetypically feminine work. Yet the value of women's stable work to less advantaged families has surely increased, as jobs become more precarious and their attendant benefits shrink. Regardless of what their families look like, stably employed women seem to derive some profit from all that mutual compromise. Compared to the less advantaged women in insecure work, who either shunt off their burdens or do all but collapse under the weight of them, some of their peers with stable work seem to share those loads with others.

SECURITY MATTERS: DECODING THE MYSTERY OF SETTLING

The less advantaged stably employed sound different than other workers when they talk about work, because they maintain high expectations for their employers, who are bound within a net of reciprocity that seems as involuntary, as assumed, as that of a family. Workers combine these high expectations with a propensity for compromise, with a mandate to "trudge along" even when they do not want to.

Many who consider their workplaces to be like a second home reject the one-way honor system. Yet the high costs of doing so become clear when they actually experience job insecurity, when they suffer the rare layoff or downsizing that is not supposed to happen in those kinds of jobs. Their anguish helps us understand the submission and self-blame of the laid-off: perhaps those low expectations for the employer actually help by offering an emotional shield, protection that the stably employed, most of the time, do not need. Unarmed as the stably employed are against flexibility culture, their emotional descent at these moments is steep.

In intimate life, these less advantaged workers sound different from their class peers, with words of resignation and moderate pleasures in the same tone they use at work. Could it be that these very tones reflect a stance that helps people stay in long-term arrangements? Could it be that what we hear is the vocabulary of commitment—not the brittle fervor of the duty-bound, which can lead to such heights and lows, and not the rebelliousness of the independent, but the mundane gratitude and contained anticipation that bespeaks and enables endurance? Minus the language of choice and autonomy that peppers the speech of the affluent itinerant workers, pragmatism among the stably employed appears to accompany the same lengthy, mostly satisfying but sometimes disappointing marriages evident among the beneficiaries of the divorce divide.

Ultimately, the experience of the stably employed suggests that job security matters, particularly for less advantaged workers, by protecting their capacity to plan, to endure disappointment, and to care without the total sacrifice required of those who face greater need. But the argument here is not simply one in which all outcomes are determined by economics. Instead, the story of the stably employed suggests that their pragmatism at work is also that which enables their endurance at home: the high expectations, the propensity to compromise. The mechanisms at issue here are cultural ones: the stances that make sense of people's obligations, that make certain practices visible and possible, that give validity to their yearnings, that generate their judgments and their emotions. Thus we can begin to decode what insecurity culture makes into a mystery: the desire, and the capacity, to settle.

CHAPTER 8

cᐱɔ

Duty and the Flexible Child

Marin Grumman is the woman whose husband Justin teases her about getting a "playa divorce" at the Burning Man festival, and whose stepson jokes about them having "fourteen Christmases" because of their assorted parents, step-parents, and step-grandparents. She likes to rib Justin, saying, "I keep telling him, 'You're leaving this marriage feet first. That's the only way you're getting out, buddy.'" Notwithstanding the insecurity from which it arose, however, their twelve-year marriage is a largely joyful affair, in which each of them makes happy compromises to gratify the other. Despite the jokes, for example, Marin spends hours working on Justin's project of modifying their van, saying with a mocking groan: "It's his dream to have it solar powered and not my dream, and, you know, all my time, my Saturdays are spent there helping install the stuff, and I'm going, 'Oh, God, I can't believe I'm working on this bus again.'"

When it comes to work, Marin and her husband Justin do not embrace insecurity exactly, but they surely benefit from it. Justin left a firm to start his own company with Marin, high-profile clients following him like imprinted geese, and while some of his employees feel like family, they have had to fire a few along the way "for various incendiary reasons." Pragmatic about her marriage, detached about obligations at work, Marin is typical of many advantaged people immersed in work flexibility. When she talks about her daughter, Hester, however, her language takes on all the fervor of duty.

"So she's, you know, my universe. She's kind of the center," Marin said. "You know, if something happens with my husband, yes I'm still going to go on and—and I'll take care of the kids and all that kind of good stuff.

If something happens to her, I'm going to throw myself off the roof. I could not handle that."

Insecurity is a powerful force, for some eroding the capacity to commit, for others shoring it up; the experience of precariousness shapes what obligations people can even see, and what honorable paths seem available to meet them. People differ—by their exposure to insecurity and by their relative advantage—in their notions of what they owe each other as adults. Yet for many, particularly mothers, when it comes to children, those differences seem to fall away, as newly insignificant as yesterday's argument. Children deserve only duty.

Marin's dedication to her daughter is total, she says, and in this regard she is similar to many women, either inspired by the profound experience of motherhood or constrained by the steely dictates mandating maternal devotion, or both. But while she herself is ardent, she is careful to raise her daughter to be more "flexible," saying she is concerned about Hester's inability to "handle change." She recounts her husband's jests that "some people see the glass as half full; some people see it as half empty; Hester sees the glass as on fire." She laughs. "You know, and, 'Every silver lining has a cloud.'"

> It's the way she looks at life so, you know, we try to—you know, I want her—so flexibility is something she really needs to learn. She doesn't like to give up anything. I'll show you her closet. I mean, the child—we had—at ten, she was bawling because we had gotten rid of her rug. Cats had given *birth* on this rug. It had to go!

Marin jokes, but her jokes express the sentiment that Hester's problem is that she is too attached, that she needs to learn flexibility to be able to give up what needs to be relinquished, to be able to handle change appropriately, to become more independent.

Childrearing is deeply cultural, a collection of beliefs and practices that we might interpret for meaning as we might a poem or a painting; we can read it to understand not only how people conceive of their obligations to children but also what kind of world they are raising their children to face. The paradoxes of parenting in insecurity culture, however, mean that even though many parents say they withhold nothing, they seek to teach their children to be a bit more withholding. At the same time as children seem to deserve only duty, drawing devotion, even self-abnegation, from many— including from people who might be more stinting in their obligation to the adults in their lives—the children themselves are not supposed to grow up to obey its strict dictates. Only the stably employed seemed to be raising children for a world you can count on; conversely, Marin speaks for others immersed in insecurity when she says: "I want her to be resilient, and I want all of them to be resilient."

Insecurity feels differently to people at the top and bottom of the class ladder, and to men and women; the different expectations and opportunities they glean from insecurity shape the way they see their obligations. Yet despite all this variety, they converge on the kind of children they are trying to raise, for the kind of world they expect them to face. Most of these parents predicted an insecure world, and hoped for their children to adopt a certain independence, and to develop the capacity for flexibility. Yet all this unanimity raises the question: If we rear children for insecurity, are we protecting them, or are we just lowering their expectations?

FOR PARENTS, ONLY DUTY

Lola Mason's jokes, like Marin's, braid hilarity and sorrow. A teacher without a college degree, she had just survived a rare but shocking layoff, and talked more like an insecure than a stably employed worker, saying a good employee should be grateful just to have a job, although perhaps "not to the point you have to sleep with the boss or anything." A Catholic and Latina who had moved from New York City to Richmond in high school, she never intended to get divorced, trying everything to stop her first husband's infidelity, to no avail: "There was no amount of fishnet hose, I tried that, it was just embarrassing."

Lola was acutely aware of insecurity, as if it were a roiling sea tossing her little boat, and her embrace of duty in all its fervor—taking care of her mother and mother-in-law at some sacrifice—was in part a response to the deck pitching and rolling. (Recall her husband's exasperated query in chapter 6: "Do you ever get tired of doing the right thing?"). Yet so much of Lola's life had not worked out as she anticipated that planning for the future, making decisions that felt "permanent," seemed very risky. Her children, however, were another issue altogether. For Lola, as for many mothers, her moral wall encircled her children like an old city fortification. She could not envision pulling back from them under any circumstances, she said. "I love them regardless."

Mothers like Lola often consider children as a category apart. Most women can envision a path by which they might leave an intimate partner, although just how dire the circumstances would have to be varies—from any infidelity, to drugs and alcohol addiction, to "when he stops trying." Yet while they suggest that maternal detachment from children is permissible in particular cases, such as rejecting stepchildren or troubled teens, most demonstrate some sort of fealty to a care work ethic that, when children are involved, is unyielding.

Though she is now happily remarried, Lola's story draws sharp contrasts between what intimate partners owe each other and what parents and children do. She wed her high school sweetheart, she says, partly because he was another New Yorker stranded in the South. They had three children in quick succession, but she knew something was wrong when he greeted the news that she was pregnant for the third time with actual tears ("I mean, he literally dropped to his knees and sobbed like a baby"). Telling her husband the date that the doctor was going to induce her labor, Lola was bewildered when he asked if she could reschedule. "When they say they're going to induce you on Monday, you say, 'Okay,'" she said, caustically, with a scandalized laugh. "You don't say, 'What about Tuesday?'" As it turned out, he was having an affair, and the scheduled date was his girlfriend's birthday; they married later.

With three children under three, Lola spent most of her time at home breastfeeding, she said, but she met her second husband the very first night she went out, urged on by her younger brother, in her best friend's clothes ("All I had was a muumuu"). From the moment Hank pulled up in her driveway with three Happy Meals, he included her kids in their courtship. They met in July, and he proposed in December, but when she worried about "ruining it," he too backed off, and they hemmed and hawed for five years. Only after they decided to have a child, after she got pregnant, after she started to show, when the due date was just days away—only then did they decide to get married. Why do it at all? "Honestly, it was the baby, it was Natalie," Lola said. "He said, '[Marriage is] just so permanent.' And I said, 'Well, you know what is really funny is that this [the coming baby] is permanent. This is here for the rest of our lives.'"

The day before Natalie arrived, with Lola on medication to delay her labor, in a white dress her excited children made her buy even though she was twice her normal size ("I can say, 'Just so you know, I can still fit in my wedding dress'"), she married Hank.

LOLA: So I had every-twelve-minute contractions and . . .

AJP: While you were saying . . .

LOLA: "I do, I do, I do. I'm good, I do."

Eleven years later, when I asked her if things were different now, she answered: "Definitely." Yet when she elaborates, the uncertainty creeps back in:

AJP: So is it different than when you first started and were like maybe yes, maybe no?

LOLA: I say that and parts of my brain are like, yeah. My heart says that this is my deal and I'm in it to win it and I'm going to be here for the long haul. But I can't control his thoughts, and my brain knows that. So my brain really goes, "Hold up, don't say that out loud. Don't jinx yourself." And so I say that my heart says that, my brain says no. My brain says, "Hopefully."

Lola is still cautious about her new relationship's future.

> Though I would like marriage to be lifelong, I would like it to be like we're two orca whales out in the middle of the ocean, it's not. And I did come to that realization the first time, that it takes two to make it work, or it takes two—or it *took* two, but it was [him and] his girlfriend. So I didn't have any clue, any idea, any thought that it was going to go away, and it did.

Lola tells this joke about her first marriage ("It *took* two, but it was him and his girlfriend") to make fun of her own dreams of a happy, guileless monogamy—as represented by the absurdity of the animal reference: "two orca whales out in the middle of the ocean." Despite her hopes for her current union, then, she mocks herself and the high expectations she used to hold for intimate relationships. Lola appears to be almost lecturing herself to adopt a more independent stance, convincing herself that she is newly savvy, in contrast to her past naïveté.

What she *is* sure about are the ties between parents and children. She complains about having to take care of her mother, a controlling and difficult person, but she does not feel free to walk away. "My mother, at least, did raise me, so I do feel in debt," Lola said. "I do feel that I owe her. I do." As for her own children, she calls her kids her "four favorite people in the world." She feels especially beholden to the older three, as children of her divorce. "I want them to have better than I did. I think I always wanted it to be a lot better," she says. "I felt that, especially the boys, I owed the boys more, because I never knew, I never even thought that my children would be caught up in some divorce and all this. And so I owed them."

For some mothers, jobs might be unpredictable and spouses temporary, but children are forever. Phyllis, an African-American single mother laid off several times, thought out loud about what she owed her kids versus a partner. "I think for my kids, unconditional love would be for them. For a partner, unconditional love to a degree. I don't know," she laughed, at the irony of limiting the limitless, then grew serious. "But definitely, kids, un-conditional love, that I owe them."

Even the stably employed, who normally sound a bit more matter-of-fact, share these notions of duty to children. Diane, a white teacher who had been married twenty-six years, similarly brought up the idea of uncon-ditional love and how she would apportion it. "I have unconditional love for my children, but it's harder for me to do with my husband," she said, laugh-ing with discomfort at her own admission. "It's just different. I don't know. Because I picked him, but they are mine. Do you know what I'm saying? I didn't have a choice with them. They were mine, they were born to me [*laughs*]. But him . . ." Somehow the "choice" to love means that she could always choose not to; to Diane, mothering love was more powerful because the relationship was involuntary.[1]

Lola and others immersed in insecurity tamp down their hopes for job and marriage, even if they are happy and hopeful in both domains; insecu-rity shapes their low expectations of others at work and at home. Yet chil-dren are cordoned off from this phenomenon, enclosed by a moral wall that forms a tight little circle. For these women, the tie between parents and children is fundamental, even though, especially for adult children of com-plex mothers, it can be a grievously unhappy one. As Lola intones: "A daughter is a daughter all of her life."

THE MISMATCH OF CONTEMPORARY MOTHERING
AND CONTEMPORARY CHILDHOOD

What Lola feels she owes her children has roots in historical changes in motherhood and childhood, changes that have been paradoxically aided and abetted by insecurity culture. For centuries, the meaning and mandate of childrearing expanded and intensified, in turn shaping what we thought of women and mothers.

Before the industrial revolution, children and wives were the property of fathers and husbands. Women and children were valued according to their participation in the economic unit that was the family, and childrearing was principally focused on leading children away from their condition of natural sin. When men's work left the home in the nineteenth century, however, women and children began the long process of slow (and uneven) emancipation. Middle-class women found considerable social and symbolic power in their roles as mothers, and the progressive movement called upon women's moral authority to fuel political campaigns such as those for wom-en's suffrage, temperance, and child labor reform.[2]

Children's symbolic power increased alongside women's power as mothers, with children becoming cherished less for their economic contribution and more for their emotional meaning. Slowly, over the twentieth century, in Western developed countries, they became recognized as individuals within the household, with needs and desires that were worthy of consideration. Makers and sellers of children's goods and experiences—from clothing to toys to entertainment—encouraged the discovery of the active, desiring child through marketing to mothers and ultimately to children directly. The organization of children's lives, increasingly spent in peer environments and in single-parent homes with more media and fewer parents, expanded children's collective identities, their consumer clout, and their cultural visibility.[3]

These developments in the measure of both woman and child took place in tandem and generally in the same direction—as the growing importance of one fed the growing importance of the other. Yet a major contradiction hides within the folds of this pairing: mothers' increasing social power has depended, paradoxically, on increasing conceptions of children's need.

On the one hand, the notion of what a child needs has indeed grown over the last century and a half, particularly for some children in some contexts. Today, childrearing standards in affluent families—dubbed "concerted cultivation" by the sociologist Annette Lareau—dictate that advantaged children particularly need to have their talents developed in focused and careful ways. Contemporary mothers must cultivate their children's interests and talents at very early ages, and their intensive involvement extends well into the teen years and beyond. In addition, stated concerns for children's safety—despite decreasing instances of actual crimes reported against children—have also reached fever pitch. These anxieties contribute to the withdrawal of children from the streets, the decline of children's unstructured time spent outside, and the concomitant proliferation of what the Dutch researcher Lia Karsten called "indoor" and "backseat" childhoods.[4]

Of course, childhood has always had different significance in different contexts. More than just a figure fixed by the calendar, age is a number whose meanings vary dramatically; children have what has been called a "social age," with attendant rights and responsibilities that differ depending on local assumptions. Children old enough in some countries to take care of other children, for example, are not old enough in other countries to be left alone without the authorities stepping in.[5]

Even in advanced industrialized nations, however, children are increasingly viewed not just as bundles of need but as people who make choices within constraints, just as adults do. Paradoxically, at the same time as the advance of "concerted cultivation," children in these countries are increasingly recognized as individuals with their own capacities for decision-making, their own rights and responsibilities, and their own legitimate opinions. These expanded child selves occupy not just the consumer realm but also family court, international aid agencies, and politics, especially in the Nordic countries and in the United Kingdom. Enabled by new technologies, children and youth have new social identities, making their own meaning and enacting, in a limited way, their own forms of citizenship.[6]

If children are increasingly perceived as active agents with their own desires and abilities at the same time as mothers' increased paid employment means more mothers are spending more hours at work, then we might reasonably expect mothering expectations to decline commensurately. In other words, if mothers are getting busier with paid work just as children are getting culturally "older," surely understandings of adequate mothering might contract, to match both a decreased demand and supply.

Yet as Sharon Hays has pointed out, the opposite has transpired. Mothering has become *more* intensive, so that merely being an adequate mother involves more self-sacrifice, more altruism, more attention than earlier in the twentieth century. Today, for example, contemporary working mothers actually spend significantly more time per child with their children than did stay-at-home mothers in 1965. Hence we have a mystery—of the intensification of maternal duty coinciding with the expanding capacities of children, with their increasing "social age."[7]

WHAT INSECURITY MEANS FOR MOTHERING

We can perhaps solve this mystery by looking to insecurity culture, the flourishing of precariousness at work coupled with the withdrawal of the state. Women have expanded and intensified motherhood to adapt to the anxieties stemming from risk, to be sure, and mothering fads—the constant stream of new books and articles outlining new right and wrong ways to parent—add to the weighty responsibility that we make mothers bear: the sense that perhaps mothers can save us from ourselves, that good mothering can make up for the ravages in our social fabric. Intensive motherhood also appeals to mothers, however, because insecurity renders newly notable, and newly compelling, those commitments like parenthood that are held to be unshakeable.

Intensive motherhood includes concerted cultivation seeking to develop whatever passions, skills, and talents the child demonstrates, in addition to the increasing surveillance enabled by the nanny cams, GPS locators, online access to school grades, and other technologies. Such "parental hypervigilance," as the geographer Cindi Katz dubs it, in part stems from the profound anxieties stoked by insecurity culture, scholars note. Mothers, particularly advantaged ones, displace their concerns about larger insecurities onto their children, which impels them to intensify their efforts, according to Marianne Cooper, who writes about parenting in "risk climates" that vary by class, in what she calls "the inequality of insecurity." As mothering researcher Ana Villalobos suggests, the "protective, highly involved form of strategic mothering forefronts the mother-child connection as an antidote to the world's ills." While some scholars might study "what women do as mothers," Villalobos contends, "the real story may be what they expect from motherhood—the security they intend to create by mothering the way they do."[8]

Florence Brines is a white divorced mother of three who was married for twenty-eight years before her executive husband started having affairs and refusing to end them. Nonetheless, there were signs of trouble earlier on in the marriage, a commuting relationship for years before it collapsed. For example, Florence decided their children would be better off in private school, but when her husband disagreed, she sent them anyway, paying for it out of her own part-time earnings. When at last they parted ways and finances, Florence was left nearly penniless while her husband and his new childless partner made more than $500,000 annually. Florence declared bankruptcy shortly thereafter and found herself unable to sell the family home for enough money to pay off her mortgage. But when Jennifer, one of her older daughters, wanted to go to a state school in Virginia, Florence left Illinois, where she had lived and raised her children for decades, and moved to Virginia with her youngest, who was the last one left in the home, to ensure Jennifer would have state residency and thus smaller loans to repay.

The move was difficult for Florence, as she did not like her relatively low-paid job as a retail manager (in which she made one-tenth her ex-husband's annual salary) and had no friends and no prospects of a relationship. Florence's divorce and subsequent downscaling have led to some embittered thoughts about the transience of work and love. Still, she said, a parent has no choice.

> I think a parent owes their child a sense of security above just about everything else. To know that they're loved. To know that they're secure in the living arrangements. They're secure in the relationship. That there is unconditional acceptance and love for what they do. And all that to me falls under the umbrella of security. That they can feel like, no matter what they do, no matter what they

say, whether they make mistakes or not, that they have this security of knowing that there are parents that are going to support them. I really believe that. I think that's important for all children.

The duty to provide security was paramount in an insecure world.

Yet insecurity culture seeps into mothering not just by displacing maternal anxiety but also by demanding maternal devotion. By making some commitments seem elective, insecurity lends a certain mystical freight to those that are not. Many women embedded in insecurity share the same inflated understandings of adequate mothering, the notions that frame mothering as naturalized, altruistic, and exceptionally dedicated. For many, it is as if the care work ethic is deeply, powerfully fundamental to their identities, almost pleasurable not just in the performance of it but also in the sheer scope of its demands.

Like Lola, most mothers I spoke to laid claim to an attentive, focused mothering identity central to their personhood. Felicia, a single mother who had been laid off, was an independent soul at work and in intimate life, although she pledged duty to her children. "I feel I owe them, not as much monetarily as I can give them, but as much—I guess I owe them as much as I can. As much as I can do without suffering," she laughed, and then added, "*too* much." She knew that if she married again, her difficult financial situation would likely improve. "I'd like to share my life with someone, but I almost feel like I have to wait until I get through this first, you know. Yeah, I feel like I have so much to worry about with my kids, you know. Just getting them into adulthood," she said.

Intensive mothering takes on its powerful symbolic cargo in part from its contrast to lighter, looser relationships, just as we saw in chapter 6, where duty led to rescuing on the part of those less advantaged workers, particularly women, in insecure work. While the call to duty to children claimed all kinds of parents—up and down the class ladder and within and without insecurity—for the insecurely employed, the very intransigence of intensive motherhood seemed to be part of what made it so compelling.

INTENSIVE MOTHERING: HOW MUCH SACRIFICE IS TOO MUCH?

Intensive mothering generates some of the firmest commitments people can make. Yet scholars argue that such mothering has problematic implications for women and for the people who depend on them, for low-income families, and for men's capacity to care. Intensive mothering

ratchets up standards of what a child needs, and what constitutes adequate care, to levels that are nearly impossible for less-than-affluent
mothers to uphold; it hypersymbolizes the mother, so that she comes to
encapsulate all of the family's care, eliminating any pressure for men or
children to share in that task; it eradicates the space for women to express ambivalence, because it makes their sacrosanct roles as mothers
more important than their complex individual selves; it underscores
a gendered system of domesticity that shores up male privilege and time
demands at work; and it compensates for and thus enables the withdrawal of the state from care needs.[9]

In addition, this ideology occasionally seems to hurt mothers because of
the total self-sacrifice it inspires, leading, paradoxically, to situations that
sometimes harm children. Florence, who had moved to Virginia after her
divorce to give her daughter Jennifer in-state tuition, was now distraught
about the adolescence her youngest was experiencing, rife with insecurity,
poverty, and alienation, and a far cry from the parental teamwork and affluence that characterized her older siblings' upbringing. Florence also
finds herself continually having to beg for money from her ex-husband.
Although she called the conversations "games," they were actually humiliating dramas of power and control, as she recounted them:

> I know, ultimately, he is going to give it to me, so what we have to do is we have
> to go through this little game where he'll say—I'll say, "Can I talk to you for
> a minute," and he'll say, "As long as it's not about money." And I'll say, "Well,
> Paula needs to take driver's ed and it costs x amount of money, and I want her to
> take this and it's happening right now. And I'd like for her to do it now, she's out
> of school as of yesterday." And he'll say, "I'm not paying for it. I don't have the
> money, that's what child support's for." And I'll say, "Well, you know, the child
> support has to be used for rent." And he'll say, "Well I'm not paying for it, this is
> it, I'm not going to do it." And I'll say, "And I also need extra money because my
> rent is due." "I'm not giving you another cent. I told you I'm not giving you an
> other cent. Absolutely not. This is not—no more. I've tried to tell you no more."
> So, and I'll say, "Well, then I don't know what I'm going to do because my rent is
> due and I'm short, let's just say, $200.00." And he'll say, "I can't, you know, we've
> got to stop this. You've got to stop calling me every time you need money."

At this point in the conversation, Florence said, she would ask him again:
"Well, what are we going to do about Paula and her driver's ed?"

> He says, "Well, I can do one or the other." That's what he told me this past week.
> He said, "I'll either give you money or I'll pay driver's ed." So, I said, "Okay. Then

give me money because I cannot have my rent check be late." So then I text him and I say, "I will call and ask one of the girls [meaning Paula's older sisters] to pay for her driver's ed." So see, he's not going to want that to happen, so then he texts me back and says, "Okay, who do I make the check payable to and how much is it?" So that's a game we play.

Florence finds herself at rock bottom, participating in degrading "games" to survive, in part because of choices she made to prioritize her children, in particular her older ones, in service to an ideology of intensive motherhood.

Intensive motherhood is not just the province of women from affluent backgrounds; it even shapes the choices of some low-income mothers. Brianna hesitated to ask for child support because she feared what the commensurate increase in custodial time with their father would do to her kids. She lived with her children and her third husband, a mechanic whose insecure work had led them to move fifteen times in ten years. Her children were starting to exhibit disturbed behavior due to all the moves, she admitted.

> Yeah, Mackenzie's real friendly, she can make friends wherever she goes. I think her heart gets broken because she does get attached to people. . . She gets attached to people very easily and it hurts when she leaves. But she's my most resilient one. Austin, on the other hand, he's [a] recluse. For the most part he's always stayed to himself. But right before we left Woodbridge about two years ago he had made a friend named Stefan. And Stefan and him were the best friends, and moving away from that had a devastating effect on my son. He would not come out of his room for days at a time.

Austin was diagnosed with childhood bipolar disorder, partially the result of some early trauma from Brianna's earlier relationship. His mental health is one reason Brianna does not want to work outside of the home, and she is proud of being a stay-at-home mother and the financial sacrifices she knows they are making.

> When my son was diagnosed, I realized after his first trip to the hospital that the only way he was going to get any better was if I stayed very hands-on involved. And I was seeing the benefits of being hands-on involved with my kids; I've seen a difference. Not to say I'm perfect; I'm far from that. But I've seen the difference in them from me being home and sacrificing the two cars and the trips to Disneyland. Versus the kids that come over whose parents are always working. But his mental health was my main concern.

Yet certainly if Brianna thought it advisable to hold down any kind of employment, the family would not have had to move so often. "I think we finished out two leases the whole ten years we've been together," she marvels.

Brianna sees the price her children pay for this mobility. "It's my daughter looking at me and going, 'Mommy, can we decorate my room this time or is it just going to stay in boxes?'" she said soberly. "It's finally taking the risk of making a few friends here and there then having to turn around and walk away." Austin's mental health problems surely constitute a significant need, but it is not clear that those needs are better served by her intensive stay-at-home motherhood than by greater stability in his overall environment.

While we might contest Brianna's decision, we cannot do so without also recognizing that she faces a devil's choice, made particularly acute in the United States: if she were able to secure stable part-time employment with a living wage, or if the state were more focused on mental health care, caregiving for children, or income support for poor people, she would not have to opt for either appropriate care for Austin or being able to afford to stay in one place. Intensive mothers labor not only for their families but also on behalf of a system of insecure work and a neoliberal state, struggling to provide the care that seems to be receding elsewhere.

Like Brianna, many mothers derive moral purpose from their intensive brand of childrearing, even as it also ensnares them in often-difficult choices. Mothers approached caring for children with an overarching sense of duty, as did the involved fathers we saw in chapter 5. Their own sense of the precariousness of modern work imbues childrearing with a sense of profound importance as commitment's final frontier. Yet if their roles were clear, what about those of their children? What sort of world were they preparing their children to face, and what sort of children were they preparing to face it?

"HOW PERFECT IS THAT?": PREPARING CHILDREN FOR WHAT IS COMING

In their talk about their children, parents reflect their expectations of the future, based on what they know about the past. Recall the example of Fiona, who in chapter 4 was jubilant about her son singing what we might consider a "leaving song" in the back of the car as she drove off from another ill-fated relationship. "Put one foot in front of the other, and soon you'll be walking out . . ." she mimicked. "He just started singing that in the back of the car. He's like four years old." She laughed, adding, "I mean, how perfect is that?" Her question raises another for us here: When it comes to raising children in the tumbleweed society, for parents, what counts as "perfect"?[10]

There is considerable evidence that instability has negative effects on children. In addition to the impact of family transitions, research suggests that job insecurity has important and deleterious effects that extend beyond the insecure worker. Parental job insecurity touches teenaged children and is associated with youth lower self-efficacy, poorer grades, higher risk of illness, more cynicism and less trust, social problems, and lower work motivation. How teenagers perceive these job changes has implications not just for their commitment to work but a host of other concerns fanning out to their health and well-being.[11]

While they may not know this research, parents are concerned about the impact of insecurity on children. But for many, avoiding it is not within their power; few would choose to get laid off, of course. As a result, most parents are instead working on making children able to handle the insecurity they think is inevitable; they try to raise "flexible" children, children exposed to change, ready for change, able to change. Most of the time, this flexibility involves a certain detachment from current relationships stemming from an independent stance.[12]

BRINGING UP FLEXIBLE CHILDREN

Anita is a white married woman who relocated for her husband's career as a military contractor in Europe and throughout the United States, bringing up four children in different places around the world.

> And we wanted . . . for them to grow up with the flexibility of being able to go somewhere, take a look around and say, 'This is what I need to do to fit in here.' With society changing to be a mobile society, we thought that would be useful to them, as opposed to the growing up with roots and living in the same town forever like our generation did.

They made the conscious choice to encourage their children to adapt to change, even after considering the cost: their almost nonexistent relationship to extended family.

> The kids are heading toward teen years and they didn't know their cousins. We deliberately chose a mobile lifestyle to teach them how to fit in on a local situation in the world. But at the same time we sacrificed the fact that they

couldn't name their cousins if their life depended on it—or their aunts and uncles or grandparents.

Anita thinks it was worth it to sacrifice meaningful connections to extended family for the benefit of having her kids grow up flexible. "Ask anybody for their résumé these days. They are going to say, 'Yeah, I lived here, I grew up here, but I work here.' And people don't stay in one place anymore." The alternative was for them to be unable to adapt to new situations, and she considered that a significant problem, one she witnessed when her sister came to visit. "And I saw firsthand, when my sister came to visit us in Brussels. She has lived three miles from where we grew up and she's in her mid-sixties. And she was like a fish out of water, really. And I didn't want—I see that as a disadvantage."

We might expect such language from an independent soul like Fiona, for whom the prospect of moving along is ever alive, even though she is now newly remarried—recall her musings: "If your spouse is being really horrible? That's easy. You just . . . I'm committed as long as it's good. I'm not committed to anything bad." But Anita has been married for thirty years, and she herself adheres to a particularly submissive brand of pragmatism; her extensive efforts to surrender to the overriding priority of keeping her family together led her to make statements like "Sometimes if you act and force it, then you can convince yourself that maybe this isn't so bad after all." While Anita's intimate practices are acutely pragmatic, her childrearing emphasizes mobility, flexibility, and change, all the virtues enshrined in the principle of independence.

Like Anita, most other parents emphasized their children's adaptability and flexibility. They counseled teenagers to maintain light relationships with friends and love interests; they advocated independence; and they tried to steer their children away from troubled peers. When they talked about commitment, most parents focused on their children's commitment to schoolwork, activities, or principles—to swim, soccer, or baseball practice; volunteering at church; trying their best in math; or staying firm in their chastity pledge. Only a few talked about commitment to other people.

These broad brushstrokes paint a fairly monochromatic picture of parental agreement about cooling friendships and the need for flexibility. While most parents living within insecurity converged on the goal of flexibility, however, they diverged dramatically in what that flexibility was for. Some considered *flexibility as opportunity*, the almost gleeful capacity to take advantage of prospects at work and in private life, while others considered *flexibility as armor,* the necessary, preemptive, and sometimes embittered response to expected betrayal.

Relocators, the affluent winners of insecurity culture, make up most of the first kind. Meanwhile, the less advantaged people who had been laid off constitute most of the second group, for whom flexibility is as necessary as a shield. In contrast, while the stably employed may occasionally talk the talk of flexibility as opportunity, they are also among the few to emphasize and actually enforce their teenagers' promises during "commitment crises," those moments when prior obligations come into conflict with other priorities. Neither our experience of insecurity, then, nor our relative advantage generate the priority we make of our children's flexibility, but instead a combination of the two, shaping how we prepare our children for work and for love.[13]

FLEXIBILITY AS THE ROAD TO OPPORTUNITY

Anita preferred her children to be truly "flexible" rather than, for example, deeply connected to their cousins. The point of flexibility, she maintained, was that it was the best preparation for them to be able to take advantage of opportunities in the future.

> You can go anywhere you want, do anything you want. I wanted to give them opportunities to open their minds to not just, "I'm from this town and here I'll stay forever." Not that that is such a bad thing, but I just wanted them to be able to have the opportunity to do what they wanted to do. And I knew that if they saw that they could make friends anywhere or they could learn a different language or learn local customs or learn to eat local foods, that that would be a benefit to them in their own little grownup life.

The alternative was closed-mindedness, which itself could serve to block off new avenues of experience.

Tara relocated with her family overseas, but they had returned stateside when her youngest daughter was very young, so the girl had grown up mostly in the United States. Tara was concerned that the family's move back meant that her daughter would not have the benefit of a flexible mind. After all, she went to a private school with the same people since kindergarten, children whose families all knew each other and vacationed in the same place. "Very American and not even that much traveling. So I'm a little worried about her," she lamented:

> [I worry] that she's going to end up being really closed-minded. That she's not going to be adventurous. That she's going to—she's going to miss opportunities

to meet some great people or to have some great experiences because her friends aren't going to do it, so she's not going to do it kind of thing.

Flexibility enabled children to grab at "great experiences." Said Dorothy, another relocator: "And so it's good for kids to move. As devastating as it is, there is a big wide world out there and you are going to make friends. And different is not bad, it's just different." Dorothy considered it important that kids get a sample of the "big wide world out there," rather than experience the same thing day after day. Similarly, Tara observed approvingly that her son, Gavin, had refused to go to his father's alma mater in Virginia. "He just felt like it was just too close to home, he just felt like he wanted to do something different, and I think part of that is from the overseas experience, that he knew there's a big world out there and this would be another opportunity to see that," Tara said.

Parents did not just advocate flexibility for its own sake, however, but also as a useful set of habits preparing youth for good outcomes. With flexibility, children could take advantage of opportunities both at work and in their relationships with others.

Flexible Work

Vicky had moved with her family six times in nine years, but she thought her son had developed skills as a result of their peripatetic lifestyle that might someday be useful for his work. Even though she was finally refusing to relocate for her husband's job during her son's high school career, she did not regret the moves they had made, she said:

> I think he's trying to get roots, but I also think he's very adaptable. I don't think a lot shakes him—he's very calm and he doesn't get flustered—but I think maybe internally it kind of bothers him. If he's a little stressed inside he doesn't show it, which is actually a pretty good management technique. I think he is eventually going to be able to use that someday.

Rochelle thought moving enabled her son, Bobby, to get over his inherent shyness, which ultimately helped him get a job and "manage on his own."

> I think the kids are much more adaptable. When you have been forced to move and making new friends and going to new schools, you quickly kind of lose that inadaptable piece. They are very social, very unafraid to—I think moving has definitely helped in that category of just making them very outgoing. My son

Bobby went with my husband to Tokyo and traveled before he graduated. Chuck does a lot of work over there, and so he went with him and worked with him. Chuck did not hold his hand, he put him at a table with people who did not speak very good English. I mean he did not hold his hand at all. And he [Bobby] loved it.

Flexibility prepares you to take advantage of the future world of work, where the challenges, and opportunities, are not always predictable.

Flexible Intimacy

In this view, flexibility-as-opportunity applied not just to work but also to personal relationships, with friends, intimate partners, and even parents themselves. Parents believed their children would make new friends, and viewed those friends to some degree interchangeably, certainly just as good as the ones they left behind. These parents downplayed their children's current relationships; they offered tips on how children could make new friends easily; and they viewed the costs of holding on to existing relationships—the opportunity cost, one could say, of prospects unpursued—as seemingly quite high.

Bruce was a teacher, and thus as a stably employed person he was unusual in his language about the opportunity of flexibility, although he was among the few teachers to adopt an independent stance toward work, saying, "I think you just need to be flexible and move on and change. And it's a new experience, life is different every day." He said he was not distressed by some conflicts his children were having with friends in their local schools.

> And in some cases I'm happy those things have come up, because I don't think they're destined for long-term relationships anyway. Those aren't the people they are going to be hanging out with. Those are people that they have sort of bonded with, but it's just not going to last.

Bruce's words convey that he has an idea of who his children should be friends with, people who would be better matches for them. The friends his children "have sort of bonded with" for now, are replaceable with other, better friends who are out there somewhere, Bruce seems to suggest.

Parents also gave their children tips on making new friends, to enable them to take advantage of new prospects. Vicky taught her son the "five-friend rule," in which he needed to make not just one good friend but five (which she then modified to three, because it was too difficult for him to befriend five):

> I've always told him things like, especially when we were moving, like you always need more than one friend, don't latch on to one person. You have to force yourself to make at least three friends so you can circulate with them. When you move to a new place and when you're in your life at that new place. Yeah, because he wanted to have just the one friend and then he would be very disappointed if the person was doing something else—then he would be lonely because he was all by himself as an only child. So I taught him to use that technique.

Parents tried to equip their children to spread out their affections, to minimize their attachment to one person, in case that one should prove fallible.

People who viewed flexibility as opportunity saw clearly the costs of commitment. Bruce believed sticking with a high school sweetheart was limiting, even though he knew his wife would disagree, given that he, at nine years her senior, was her first boyfriend.

> I'm not saying they should bounce around or be promiscuous or any of that, but I don't want them to marry their high school sweetheart. I don't want to see that happen. Well, *God*, there's got to be something else out there in the world. I mean I just think that is just so limiting. That is my point of view. You think you're going to be with this person—fine. Then go to Ireland for three years and come back or something. Go do something, but don't just stay here and settle down. That doesn't mean you can't have a really good long-term relationship either.

Bruce is horrified—"Well, *God*, there's got to be something else out there"—that someone would stick with a girlfriend from high school. That sort of girlfriend is perfectly adequate for having "a really good long-term relationship" but, clearly, one that would end. To do otherwise was "just so limiting."

Rochelle, who followed her husband around the Eastern Seaboard, buying, renovating, and selling their homes, was pleased to predict that none of their children would settle where she and her husband lived now, in Richmond.

> I don't think any of my children will feel compelled to have to stay near me. I think they will want a lot of experiences. I think they are not going to be content to just hang out near home, probably. They are going to want to go, I think, to exciting places. You do get the itch once you start moving. I would predict that my kids will have that itch, because we have it.

Flexible children would prioritize having "experiences" even over re-lationships with their own parents—and for some, that was a good thing.

FLEXIBILITY AS ARMOR

Less advantaged parents with precarious work certainly shared the same general understanding of flexibility as good for their children. Stanley, an actor who had been laid off several times from various day jobs, was proud of his daughter's adaptability.

> I think that basically no matter what life throws at her, it's going to throw some curve balls, it's going to throw some things that she doesn't like, and there are also going to be some things that are great. And, no matter what comes, that she has the ability to look at it and deal with it. She doesn't necessarily have to like it, but that is life.

Yet Stanley's words form a sharp contrast to the beliefs of those who framed flexibility as opportunity: he saw flexibility as an unfortunately necessary element of a child's protection, helping them weather the storms ahead. People who talked this way wanted their children to prepare themselves against the future, rather than letting the future take them by surprise.

Armor against Work Disaster

Flexibility served as a sort of armor that was particularly useful for handling uncertainty at work. Laid off from his job in desktop publishing, Clark managed to make a living of sorts in part by playing in a local band on weekends. He urged his daughter to master the violin, because he saw giving private lessons as a good fallback in the event of losing one's job.

> That's the most important thing. It's something I've always had with my music. And I don't care what it is, you know, but you have to have some kind of a fall-back so that if you do fall on hard times, you've still got something going again.
>
> That's probably the—one of the biggest things I've tried to impart to both my kids. You have to have a fallback of one type of another. And don't put all your [eggs] in one basket.

Flexibility will be what makes his daughter able to jump nimbly when the ground underneath starts to shake, Clark said. She was not quite listening, however, he complained.

> I'm trying to prepare [her] for a very—the very difficult world that she's going to live in. Too few jobs and too many people. I see it coming. Okay. I mean, I'm already seeing it coming. You know. There are part-time jobs out there, precious few full-time jobs. And I think that's going to be the case as we go on. I think it's going to get worse and worse and worse.
>
> As I've explained to her, there's a good possibility by the time she's forty and she has a full-time job, they're going to lay her off and hire somebody much younger for a lot lower salary. And, of course, this doesn't make any sense to her, but it's just—I can see it coming.

Clark felt like Cassandra, warning the unheeding of a coming disaster, when "they're going to lay her off and hire somebody much younger for a lot lower salary"; his prescription of "flexibility" means not putting all your eggs in one basket.

Armor against Intimate Disaster

In the realm of personal relationships, some parents deployed flexibility as a sort of armor against intimate betrayal or other calamitous event. Barbie tried to comfort her son after they moved to a new neighborhood and he lost some old friends. Most people don't keep all their friends, she told him. "I said, 'When you walk away from this and when you get done with high school and you get done with college, if you still have five friends that you can count on one hand, then that's all you need.' I was like, 'Then that's all you need, because most people don't have that.'" Barbie uses flexibility discourse to ready her son for attenuated friendships.

Others sought to encourage their children to do the attenuating. Claudia, whose layoff led her to declare bankruptcy, lauded her daughter's independence from errant peers, those who experimented with sex or drugs, who just seemed to be going down the wrong path. She reported that her daughter had taken a pledge of chastity.

CLAUDIA: She said she's lost a lot of good friends as they've become sexually active.

AJP: You mean girlfriends who have felt constrained by her pledge?

CLAUDIA: Just that they, not that her girlfriends would leave her, but she doesn't accept it. She's, she's—

AJP: So when they do it, she leaves them? Wow.

CLAUDIA: Yeah. She's amazing. She's real strong in her faith.

The daughter's commitment to chastity enabled her independence from "a lot of good friends," Claudia reported approvingly. Likewise, Sarah, who had been laid off from a small family firm, said that her daughter was great at moving on.

> I think as grownups we tend to hold on to things. . . . It's like, oh, we fret and we carry on and we feel bad and we lose sleep over it. And as we move into opportunities it's kind of like you take responsibility for something and then you move on. And, I've noticed with Sonya in particular, and maybe it's because I realize she's leaving, but she does a great job with that. I wish I could encourage her as she gets older to continue with that. It's like she doesn't dwell on things. She doesn't go back over it. She's doesn't beat herself up. She doesn't beat somebody else up.

Within this vision, "beating herself up" was the same as "taking responsibility for something" and "holding on to things"; Sarah respects her daughter for instead pulling back from particular situations and relationships.

Sometimes children were expected to don the armor of flexibility in response to calamity rather than betrayal. Felicia, who had been laid off from a sales job, considered it important that she prepare her children for the possibility of her own death, given they had already lost their father when her ex-husband had died in a car accident. They could develop crucial resilience that way, she thought. "I kind of have to be realistic with them but reassure them at the same time, because, I mean, what if something does happen to me? You know what I mean?" she asked. "They're getting to be teenagers. They have to"—she paused and interrupted herself. "I don't make them adults. That's not what I'm setting out to do, but I want them to be prepared."

Felicia's words suggest some discomfort here, that she is trying to fine-calibrate her parenting, weighing the need to prepare her kids versus scaring them, or even taking away their childhoods (witness her "I don't make them adults"). Still, she considers it important for them to contemplate frightening eventualities, even including her death, in order to encourage their ability to bounce back.

Katherine, another layoff survivor, was also a widow, after the unexpected death of her ex-husband, the father to her two daughters.

I think I would rather they be more adaptable, because you never know what's going to happen in life, where it's going to throw you for a loop. Anything can happen. In the past couple of years, a lot has happened, especially with Jessica [her daughter]. And I think if she was more adaptable to change, I think she would've dealt with certain situations differently.

Life's adversity was certain to come, albeit unpredictably; her daughter needed to be prepared, with flexibility, to handle it. In contrast to those who viewed flexibility as opportunity, then, those who viewed it as armor sometimes considered the stakes high because the potential cost—of failing to instill flexibility as part of childrearing—was not insularity or closed-mindedness but their children's very survival.

NO MORE PRINCESSES: ANTICIPATING BETRAYAL

Some of these moments often had a distinctly gendered feel, as laid-off parents, often women, tried to ready their daughters not to rely on men. Mindy's ex-husband had managed to wrest full custody of their children from her, an act from which she has not fully recovered. Her sense of betrayal is raw, as discussed in chapter 5, and it permeates the lesson she imparts to her daughter:

And the other thing is you buy into the dream. The dream that girls are told, you live happily ever after when you get married. Well, that's not true. And you got to teach your kids to be self-supporting and to be accountable to themselves and of course not blame other people for your problems.

Olivia had been told she could never have children, so she was surprised when, after seven years with a man, she found herself pregnant. The man left the next week. Fourteen years later, when she caught her teenaged daughter, clothing in disarray, with another youth, her disappointment was laced with the expectation of betrayal.

I was so mad. And I said some things to her, I said you shouldn't do that because he'll be here today and he's gone tomorrow. Just because of my experience I had with her father. I said some things about the boy and I probably shouldn't have said it. So yeah, I was mad at her, maybe too mad.

The way Olivia handles the situation of catching her daughter with a boy is not, say, to talk about the other opportunities ahead, opportunities that she is forsaking by getting waylaid by boys, but instead to advise her that most boys will leave. Lena, who had felt herself overly reliant first on her father and then on her husband, only to learn how to stand on her own two feet when she became a single mother, wanted above all independence for her daughters.

> I hope that they all are able to support themselves and able to be independent and . . . so they can not have to depend on anyone else . . . not like I have had it. It's nice to know somebody's there if you need them, but it's better for yourself in your mind and body if you know you can do it on your own.

Independence was a feminist issue, particularly for less advantaged women immersed in insecurity, and the armor that flexibility helped to produce was valuable for girls in particular to take on in advance of men's betrayal.

THE EXCEPTION: STABLE PRAGMATISM

While most parents in this study converged in their hopes for a flexible child, a few adults counseled a different kind of approach, in which they tried to model how youth could stay in a job or a relationship, principally by suppressing their own desires in favor of the imperfect status quo. Most of these were the stably employed, preparing their children for the same kind of pragmatism with which they greeted the world, and that had worked for them.

Sylvia, a social worker, tried to prepare her special-needs son for the emotional control that is understood as professionalism—the suppression of desire and impulse, part of what Eva Illouz dubbed "cold intimacy" at work.

> I've hired him to do lawn work for me and I said, "I'm going to come and I'm going to check the quality before I pay you." And of course I went out there and the quality was not great, so I said, "You need to redo this." And he started mumbling to me and I said, "Leo, remember, we had an understanding that I'm your employer and I will pay you if you do the job." And so I said, "This mumbling to me is not acceptable. So you didn't do a job that was up to par and either you redo it or I don't pay you, but if you mumble to me I will fire you." He kept on mumbling [and] I said, "You're fired now, you don't get paid for anything."

By modeling the harshness of "real world" workplace behavior, parents try to ready their youths to suppress their own frustration, hoping they would instead build the self-control and muted emotional register of work behavior.

Stably employed people thought it was important to teach their children to ignore or downplay their own desires. Melissa was furious, for example, when her brother let his daughter stay home on Christmas night because of a fight with a boyfriend, rather than insisting that she join the extended family that had traveled to be there.

> I said, "You know what? If my kid tried to pull that stuff," I said, [*whispers*] "I don't give a shit about you and your boyfriend, you do this for your family. This isn't about you and your boyfriend. This is about your grandmother and your aunt," and you know. And we have kind of a running joke in our family because my grandmother used to say, "This could be my last Christmas." And, of course, one year it was. So we always joke about how, you know, "This could be their last Christmas. You got to go, you got to show, you got to be there." So I was really annoyed that she was allowed to not go.

To give in to the whimsy of someone's particular wants was to cultivate a dangerous self-indulgence.

While they often adopted the pragmatic approach of surrender and compromise, however, some stably employed parents also demonstrated that they were aware of the cultural ascendance of flexibility, adopting mobility language, rather warily, for their children. Patrick was the police officer we met in chapter 5 as an involved father. He contrasted his own deliberate, cautious lifestyle with that of his risk-taking, itinerant brother, who made choices he would not have made. "And I think to myself, 'I wouldn't do that,'" Patrick said. Yet when talking about his three daughters and their future, he straddled the line between risk-taking and "traditional" values:

> I see them all three being very, what I would say, very traditional. But I see them all three individually being successful in getting to where they want to be. But I don't think that any of them will ever just settle for something like I did. I think they will constantly be looking for new opportunities. And whether they make a big change every time or not, I don't think they will. But I think they'll be pretty smart about productively moving on in life.

His daughters will be "traditional," but that will not inhibit them from reaching for new opportunities. They'll make change, but not every time. Patrick assures us that they will be flexible, but only just enough to be productive and successful. Their own lives standing as bulwarks against change, stably employed parents sometimes used language that valued flexibility, but sometimes only partially, lacing it with words that expressed their ambivalence.

THE DREAM OF THE FLEXIBLE CHILD

Like Marin and Lola, whom we met at the beginning of the chapter, most mothers put children in a separate category, at one remove from the tempestuous churn of work and intimacy. This stance reflected a widespread understanding about the duty that parents, particularly women, owe their children, a conventional wisdom encouraged by the hypersymbolization of motherhood, and generated by the "common sense" of precariousness.

Yet as children are recognized as individuals, rather than simply objects of care and affection; as they are documented as caregivers, rather than simply care receivers; as they are viewed as competent social agents, rather than simply vessels of increasing need, what do these changes mean for mothers? A tension exists between women's cultural power as mothers and children's increasing status as competent individuals. Expanding perceptions of children's capacities dovetail with women's increased participation in the labor force, paradoxically, at the same time as mothers' intensifying obligations to children. Yet this convergence is no coincidence, I argue, but reflects the animating force of insecurity culture, amplifying the symbolic power of motherhood as security practice.

In an age of insecurity, parents choose different paths to navigate the unstable realms of work and family, but even those who vary in their socioeconomic backgrounds converge in their desire to raise flexible children. Nonetheless, the meanings of flexibility—and the reasons why they counsel their children to develop it—differ dramatically depending on their experiences in the new ways of work. Flexibility means the ability and inclination to handle change—of both a voluntary and involuntary nature. More advantaged itinerant workers mostly advocate flexibility as opportunity, as the best way for their children to be able to take advantage of new prospects, while those less advantaged laid-off workers approach flexibility as a kind of armor, and urge it upon their children as the best preparation for inevitable betrayals at work and in their intimate lives. For those who viewed flexibility as an opportunity, it signified a certain choosiness, as if someone would not settle for second best in order to stay in a relationship or job, but would instead move on in search of better choices elsewhere. For those who saw flexibility as armor, it signified a certain resilience, as if even after getting hit by unasked-for change, someone would bounce back, ready for anything.

Amid this debate, stable working-class parents are the most anachronistic of life's victors, akin to a Roman garrison marching down a freeway. Much stable, lifetime employment for people with high school degrees bled out in the industrial hemorrhaging of the last half century. These parents, then, are the rare examples of those for whom the world functioned just as it was "supposed to," where they worked hard and received just rewards. At the same time, they are not ignorant of the massive economic changes facing their children. Thus they give a certain nod to change when they talk about childrearing, but their stories feature the strictest enforcement of prior commitments; when "flexibility" and "dependability" collided, they choose the latter. In this, the stably employed are unusual.

While the insecure take different paths to get there, with one reaching for change and another seeking shelter from it, perhaps the most important observation is not how they vary but how similar they are. Their parenting reflects the same sense of the inevitability of insecurity that, as we saw in chapter 2, generates the one-way honor system at work, the notion that since the tumbleweed society is here to stay, the best we can do is adapt to it. Under this widespread parenting paradigm, children may approach flexibility joyfully or warily. But approach it they must.

CHAPTER 9

༄

The Coral Society

Molly Linwood had been married to Meyer for just a year and a half when she moved out with her baby daughter, Zoe. Theirs is a far from typical story, however, not least because Molly and Meyer have stayed extremely close, in a warm and generous relationship that for more than a decade has blended material and emotional support through years of sickness and health, new jobs and new homes. Meyer even recently suggested that Molly and her current partner temporarily move in with him, while the pair renovated a house they had bought. What's more, they agreed to do so, so Zoe spent six months with her parents under the same roof again, without having to switch from Mom's house to Dad's in the standard midweek shuffle.

They are also unusual because Molly, a white human resources worker, slowly made her way into a lesbian community a few years after she left Meyer, and she is now in the sixth year of a committed relationship with Joan and talking about getting married. "Both of us already feel like we are 100 percent in for this," Molly said. Joan was the first girlfriend Molly had who did not mind that Meyer slept in Molly's game room on Wednesdays when it was his weekday night with Zoe. "She understands our relationship better, I think, because she can see that [Meyer and I] don't belong together," Molly said. "There is no threat there for her." When Joan and Molly contemplated how they would fix up their new house, it was Joan who first talked about setting aside a bedroom for Meyer to stay in. "She was like, 'Well, we'll even make sure we've got enough room for you to have a bedroom when you come to stay the night.' Yeah, it was nice that she said it before I had to," Molly said. "And she told me, 'I didn't think he would take us up on it [which he did], but it's not that bad.'"

We have seen in this book all kinds of families, with myriad configurations of care and varied experiences of insecurity and advantage: single-parent families like Fiona and Jimmy, who sang about "walking out the door"; stepfamilies like Marin and Justin and their "fourteen Christmases"; grandparent families like Abby's parents, who helped to raise Peyton when Abby was in Alaska; and even "fictive kin" families like Nicki and her adoptee, Karma. The diversity of families represents an important step forward, an improvement over the one-size-fits-all family of the mid-twentieth century. Yet the variety comes at some cost, that of constant transitions, the "churn" that sociologist Andrew Cherlin has diagnosed for many American couples.

Molly, Joan, and Meyer show us another way, however; here are three adults, working together to raise their child with care and constancy. Zoe has three parents, in a working vision of family that is an additive model, rather than one that requires parents to substitute for each other. This little family is one solution to a central conundrum of the tumbleweed society: How can we enable both diversity in form and endurance in time in our relationships?

Molly and Meyer's lives twist together like the fibers in thread. Molly still gets Meyer's dry cleaning and mends his pants when they tear. On top of her primary employment as well as two other side jobs—donating her time to a family enterprise and selling jewelry she makes—she also handles the books for his business and completes the paperwork for the slew of rental homes they have come to own together. Meyer, a contractor, still repairs Molly's house when she needs it, tightening the outlet covers, fixing windows. She keeps a record of tasks for him to complete when he comes over, so that her ex-husband still has a proverbial "honey do" list. They all have dinner together periodically; they share holidays such as Thanksgiving and Christmas; they borrow each other's phones, cars, and houses. "We are real close to each other's family," Molly said. "Even now to this day, my mom [a housekeeper] still comes and cleans his house for him. But we just love each other still and we just love each other's family."

They have a split schedule for taking care of Zoe, but when life intrudes—when Molly has to work at her second job, say, and Joan has a surprise rugby game—Meyer will come over to be with Zoe to help out; Molly said she does the same for him. This year, the three are talking about taking a vacation together, so that they can trade off being with Zoe and enjoying some free time.

When Joan and Molly decided to move, Meyer was initially not happy, because their old house was just six minutes from his. "We all sat down together and talked about it. At first he didn't like the idea, then he was talking about, 'Let's get a bigger house with maybe a garage and put an apartment above it.' And he would live in the garage." Joan and Molly ultimately declined his offer: "We were like, 'We really don't want to do that. I'm past that point now.'" But, as is clear from the list of their shared endeavors, Meyer's enthusiastic proposal that these three adults and their child share a common household was not completely outlandish. "We actually did go house shopping together [years ago]," Molly recalled. "We've always been so close."

There are a number of reasons why Molly, Meyer, and Joan have been able to construct this homegrown arrangement, from the longstanding friendship that predated Molly and Meyer's marriage, to their unusually amicable divorce, to their tolerance of each other's differences, to their shared dedication to the child. In addition, however, Molly, who attended college but never ended up graduating, has enjoyed very stable employment with a large public employer, working in the same office since Zoe was a six-month-old infant. Hired as a clerk, she was promoted steadily to positions with more responsibility and pay, which she augmented with her extra jobs. Coupled with Meyer's consistent child support, Molly's stable employment meant she was able to provide a living for Zoe, without being forced to move to another city to get a job or to put up with a new partner chosen, in desperation, by what another mother called her "broken picker-outer."

Molly thought she was able to rise so quickly through the ranks at work because she did not resist assignments, even when she thought they were misguided. What makes a good employee? "Pretty much doing what they ask, even if you don't like it," she said. "I mean just doing it, and that's one good thing I am with them. If I don't agree with it, I just kind of do it, and I've found that you get further a lot quicker if you are that way." She evinced a certain pragmatism at work, then, suppressing her own judgment in service to succeeding at her job. If she disagreed with plans, she might make her reasons known, she said.

> Like Friday I told my boss, "This change you want me to implement is going to cost me a lot of time and a lot of grief if any of it gets done wrong. And there's a good potential for it to get done wrong." I said, "We could potentially lose a lot of money. So I'm happy to do it; I just, you want to know here are the problems that could come up. But I'm working on it." And he's happy with that—my boss's boss was happy with that.

Overall, if her supervisors wanted something, she would do it, masking her own desire unless she could make it theirs as well. "So, you've kind of got to know how to please them, kind of make it their idea basically when you want something," she said. She was getting a little bored by it, however.

> I feel kind of stagnant in the last year, and I've even thought to myself in the last six months, I'd really like to find a new job but I know right now the market is not the time to move, so I kind of feel like I need to stay put but at the same time I don't feel like I'm aggressively working, I just kind of feel like I'm sitting behind a desk.

The problem with a stable job, of course, is that it can get old.

On the other hand, stable employment also comes with some benefits. The presumption that a job will be there next year allows for long-term horizons and planning. It offers workers the basis for dignity, when the relentless striving for employability can feel a bit like scrambling (except, of course, for those at the very top of the heap, constantly being lured by competing offers). It seems to foster the sort of pragmatism, the habits of compromise and surrender, that we have seen enables the practice of settling in intimate life, by dampening the sense that there might be a better relationship or situation out there worth chasing, and by encouraging people to modify their own desires in service to other goods.

Most important, however, particularly for those without a college degree, is the fact that stable employment, at least that which pays a living wage, frees you from worry about whether or not you will be able to make ends meet. As a single white mother with no college degree, Molly shares more than a few characteristics with Fiona and others in chapter 4 who declared their independence from faithless men as they bumped from job to job. But a crucial difference between them, we can see, is that Molly simply has to battle boredom and the sense that she knows better than her boss, instead of having to protect herself from poor mate choices while cobbling together a meager living from low-wage work with high turnover.

THE CORAL SOCIETY

We are unlikely ever to return to the bygone days of the 1950s, when families featuring nuclear, heterosexual, first marriages with male breadwinners and female caregivers were culturally dominant (although not numerically dominant; as the demographer Donald Hernandez has observed, the share of children living in such families never reached 40 percent). Nor, however, should we want to. Those unions depended in part upon stable labor reserved largely for skilled white men, and were rooted in deep inequalities—of gender, of sexualities, of class and race, among others—that are too steep a price to pay for stability. It also offered the same model of intimacy to all, despite the enormous variety of human coupling; we might even dub this family-and-work combination the "AstroTurf society" for its very fixity and homogeneity, resembling the fake grass of sports fields whose owners value uniformity and endurance. The AstroTurf society forces people to either fit themselves into that model—and to stay in it forever—or exclude themselves from sanctioned families.[1]

While these critiques are widely shared, many reasonable people remain uneasy about what the contemporary array of human diversity in intimacy means for the fate of children. They worry, as did the character Abdul Wahid in Helen Simonson's novel *Major Pettigrew's Last Stand*, that "sometimes when we pick and choose among the rules we discover later that we have set aside something precious in the process." Children on average do better in households with their two biological parents (although the vast majority of children of divorced couples are well adjusted).

Important recent research, however, deemphasizes questions like whether children's parents are married or divorced, and instead focuses on instability: the more transitions children have, including those remarriages that gain them new stepfathers, the worse off, on average, they are. It does not matter as much what your family looks like so much as how long it endures. White parents without a college degree—their prospects of good jobs at good wages worsening with the evisceration of the manufacturing sector—experience particularly high rates of coupling and decoupling. While the tumbleweed society may feature expanded diversity in family types, from heterosexual cohabitation to same-sex couples to single mothers and so on, those types are also marked by increased instability for both adults and children.[2]

Yet there is a third option, and Molly, Meyer, Joan, and Zoe show us one path to get there. In what we might call a "coral society," people live in diverse types of families that at the same time manage to endure, like coral reefs in their immense and brilliant variety, and in their rock-like solidity. In the coral society, children and adults benefit from stability and diversity at the same time.

HOW PRAGMATISM WORKS

When Molly talks about Meyer, she echoes the resigned tone of other pragmatic people in long-term partnerships. Meyer stays in Molly and Joan's house every week, for example, which is "like having another child when he is there, somebody else to clean up after and that kind of thing," Molly says. She has even gone forward with choices that she says she knew were wrong, because it was what he wanted. She observed: "I guess I have a lot of patience with him—and I do, I treat him, not with kid gloves, but I treat him sometimes like a child, if I can't get through to him. He is a very smart man and I value his opinion, but sometimes I just kind of have to say, 'Let's try it your way first.' And, knowing it is the wrong way . . ."

How does the magic of pragmatism work? Like other stably employed people, Molly brings home the same pragmatic attitude that at work enables her to go along with misguided ideas from the boss. The stance fosters settling, including the deferral to someone with whom you disagree, for the sake of maintaining the relationship. Molly bends her own notion of the perfect in order to sustain this long-term connection with her daughter's third parent.

Molly also visited a counselor when she and Meyer were arguing during one phase when he had a steady girlfriend. The therapist first advised her to dismantle much of their interdependence, which they have not done. She also advised her to let go of her expectations for Meyer. "And she said, 'What you need to do is don't depend on him for anything at all, and what you get is a bonus.' It took me a couple of weeks and I was like, 'Okay, I think I get it.' So whatever I didn't get from him, to me it didn't matter," Molly said.

Most important, they have backed down from arguing about their radically distinct parenting, one of the major disagreements during their brief marriage.

> Our parenting skills were completely opposite ends of the spectrum. I'm very strict and wanted things to run a certain way. This was back then—I wanted things to run a certain way and everything needed to be done a certain way. And she needed to be disciplined and he didn't want her to have—and he was, [sketching an imaginary scenario] "Oh, she's only in the hospital. She didn't mean to blow up the school, it was an accident." So that is kind of his mentality through the whole—I mean he is just like that with her.

The therapist gave them some help here, counseling that Molly should cede control over the way Meyer runs his own house and the rules Zoe must follow there. "The therapist said, 'So you have to let go of what he does at his house and know that when you get her back she has got to follow your rules. She will eventually learn the difference.' And she has, and boy did it take a long time," Molly recalled.

This compromise became too difficult only when they moved back in together temporarily, because the two sets of rules then had to obtain under one roof. "Living with Meyer was hard," she said. "It was just that he's a slob, he expects people to clean up after him, and it was just tight quarters. I'm used to running my house a certain way, and like the counselor said, 'You can make rules in your house but not in his house.' We combined houses with different sets of rules, and Zoe was confused at what to do." Once again, the adults involved took a careful, thoughtful approach to re- solving the ensuing tensions. "We would have family meetings every week. We would say, 'This is how things need to work. These are the rules and they might be tweaked, but these are the rules.' And so it was kind of hard," Molly remembered, but they made it through.

For his part, it appears that Meyer has also made other compromises in service to this long-term relationship. As one might expect, sometimes there were challenges when Meyer or Molly had significant others (other than Joan) for any length of time, people who did not understand their closeness or felt threatened by it. Meyer prefers not to have a long-term girlfriend, according to Molly. "He is not looking to settle down; he admits it every day. 'I don't want to settle down, I just want to play the field and have fun.'" Nonetheless, if he ever chose to commit to another intimate partner, it would involve major adjustments to this smooth *pas de trois*, since, as Molly says, in the past, "Whenever he got into a serious relation- ship is when our relationship would kind of subside." The absence of a long- term partner for Meyer undoubtedly makes some of the negotiations around housing and caregiving easier.

However challenging, these compromises seem to make for a warm and loving arrangement for Zoe, who, despite Meyer and Molly's divorce, has never lost a parent. Indeed, she gained one instead. "Joan and me and Meyer really parent together, the three of us," Molly said. "The three of us are a family—it's me, Meyer and Joan. And that is how a lot of people view us. A lot of people are like, 'That's pretty cool.' And some people are like, 'That is weird.' But it works—it works for us as a family." They innovate with a new kind of family, supported by stable employment, and glued into constancy with the help of compromise.

BUILDING A CHILD-CENTERED NEW FAMILY

Animated by a shared focus on care, Molly and Meyer look past their con- flicts, because they agree upon an overriding concern: Zoe. It seems so ob- vious, the need to prioritize the child when a marriage falls apart, Molly said. "And I wonder, why isn't the rest of the world like this?"

Why can't they just say, "We don't belong together but we have this child to- gether"? He and I do not agree with the way to raise her, but I think we have both been the type to just say, "Okay." And it was not always this way. It was a little irrational in the beginning, as far as parenting, but we have always said, "Here is my thought, here is your thought, and somewhere we have got to come together, if not going to somebody else's opinion." So that is kind of how we take it.

While Molly refers obliquely to earlier disputes—"It was a little irrational in the beginning"—they have since pulled back from their disagreements.

Molly and Meyer put a considerable amount of work into forging these relationships. From the start, they worked out their own custody and child support issues without going to court, and they update the figure Meyer pays Molly every year, taking into account different incomes and living situations. "And just for the record, he never—and I guess this makes it easier than most relationships, because of this—he has never not given me money for her," Molly said. "Every year we get on the website, the state-issued website, where it calculates it for you. What you should give each other, whoever has custody for whatever you are making. And we get on there and we figure it out ourselves. And he pays me and always has and never late, except when he went on disability [after a motorcycle accident], and even then, we worked it out," meaning they used more of a barter system.

They also consult with each other when problems arise or seem imminent. When Molly decided that she might actually commit to a lesbian lifestyle, and might be ready, therefore, to tell Zoe about it, for example, she consulted first with Meyer. "And I'm thinking, 'Okay, Zoe needs to know. This is me. I'm feeling good about this.' So I call Meyer and I'm like, 'Look, I think I'm ready to tell Zoe.' I said, 'So I don't know how to start.'" Meyer consulted a psychologist made available to him by the large company where he was working, who then gave him advice about how to tell an eight-year-old—don't give her too much information, but let her know, on her level, what it means—and she and Meyer sat down and told Zoe together (she already kind of knew, Molly said).

In addition to stable employment, then, the resources, skills, and shared cultural background that each parent brings to the table help to make these arrangements possible. They both are prepared to visit a therapist for help through the rough spots, are open to different sexualities, own up to responsibilities of support and visitation, and prioritize the child in decisions about moves, schools, and work. Through shared goals, mutual respect, a little counseling, a pragmatic attitude that involves serious compromises, some patience, and some steady employment, Molly and Meyer have constructed a life apart, together.

CHILDREARING WITHOUT MARTYRDOM

It is not that Molly and Meyer are saints. While they make Zoe a mutual priority, for example, Molly stops short of the martyrdom of intensive mothering. They strive to protect her from instability, but some changes feel urgent enough to supersede that rule. Molly is thus willing to care for her child, but not willing to lose herself entirely in Zoe and her needs.

They have tried to maintain continuity for Zoe in their relationship since her disrupted early years, Molly said. "I'm real consistent about her life." Molly recalled how Zoe suffered from selective mutism as a toddler, when she moved three times in the year after she left Meyer. "I was really concerned that I had screwed her up," Molly remembered, and so for over a decade since that period, she refused to move her.

Yet Zoe's life has certainly involved change and transitions, just ones that seem less visible, that go nearly unremarked in Molly's narrative. Meyer's love life underwent considerable turnover; Molly dated a few different people before Joan; and different family members have moved in and out of the home when it was economically necessary. Most important, however, was Molly's three-and-a-half-year relationship with Candace, who installed herself in the household as the stay-at-home mother. "Candace was taking Zoe to school back and forth. Candace was doing the laundry, Candace was giving her a chore list and reading with her every night," Molly remembered. In fact, Candace helped Zoe get through a difficult moment when she was having a problem with reading comprehension. "And Candace was really able to get Zoe back on track with that, and I'm thankful for that, because that's huge and I don't think I would have had the patience for it."

But their intimate partnership did not last, and Molly asked Candace to move out one day while Zoe was away. Molly does not give a good sense of what this was like for Zoe, and maintains that Candace was too strict anyway ("Zoe never asked where she was; she was kind of relieved she wasn't there, and I could sense that Zoe wasn't really liking her") so it is hard to evaluate the impact on the child. Undoubtedly Candace's departure changed Zoe's day-to-day life enormously.

Yet the magnitude of this transition for Zoe seems somehow invisible to Molly. I mention that Candace's departure was a potentially big adjustment, because of the time they spent together, and Molly answers from Candace's perspective, as opposed to Zoe's. "When we broke up Candace missed the family life that we had. We had dinner on the table every night and there was a family consistency to it. So I know that Candace missed it, but like I said, it just wasn't working for me." Molly does not want to maintain Candace and Zoe's relationship, which may have something to do with the absence, in her narrative, of the fact of Zoe's feelings about the termination of Candace's caregiving.

Some change is visible, then, and some change is not. When it is recognized, Zoe's dedicated parenting team is on it, with family meetings, bedtime chats, even consultation with a counselor as warranted. When it is not, it is not even part of the conversation. It might even be less likely to be recognized in those moments when there is a conflict between the meanings of the change for Molly and its meanings for Zoe.

Some transitions seem to get right at the balance between adult and child, revealing the tension between identity (for adults, the fundamental question of who they are) and commitment (for children, the profound question of who is in their caring circle). Intensive motherhood sometimes seems to render the mother invisible, as the all-consuming priority of the child erases all sign of her except as she who serves. In contrast, Molly establishes herself as a whole person, with desires and needs that transcend her caregiving role.

Meyer has never complained about Molly's sexuality, Molly said, which she said was "a great thing." "Meyer has always been real supportive. He's always been like, 'Whatever you want to do,'" she said. Instead, as we might imagine, all his worries involved Zoe. Despite his qualms, however, research shows that children of gay and lesbian parents are not different from those of heterosexual couples on a host of measures—from psychological health to school outcomes to relationships with others. What matters most, scholars report, is the quality of family relationships and the warmth and competent parenting they receive. As the Virginia psychologist Charlotte Patterson writes, these children "may be exposed to prejudice against their parents in some settings, and this may be painful for them, but evidence for the idea that such encounters affect children's overall adjustment is lacking." Still, parents can worry about how their children's friends might react, and Meyer voiced some concern.[3]

"His worst fear was that she was going to get picked on, because she had a mom that was a lesbian—that was his worst fear," Molly remembered. "And still today, he thinks when we moved to this area—she's shy, so she doesn't meet a lot of friends . . ." Meyer worries that Zoe is not asking anybody over for playdates or sleepovers, now that they have moved to a new neighborhood. "And Meyer goes, 'Do you think it's because you're a lesbian?'" Molly recalls. "I was like, 'I don't think so but maybe.'"

> I mean it could be, and I feel horrible about that, but like I told him, "I don't want to change my lifestyle. And I really enjoy what I'm doing." It's like my friend

Katie at work said, "You can choose to be unhappy until she's eighteen and then live your life, or you can live your life now and let her toughen up." And I kind of took a little bit of that and a little bit of what Meyer said. And that is kind of how I'm dealing with it.

If Zoe is shy because of her mother's sexuality, then that would pit Molly's daughter against Molly's identity and force Molly to weigh what she owes her daughter against what she owes herself. Part of Molly's response to this quandary is to reconfigure her parental mandate, so that what might be best for Molly is not to bow to her daughter's shyness but instead to enable her to overcome it. "Letting Zoe toughen up" is the cost of Molly staying true to herself and what she likes about her life now.

A dedicated parent, Molly nonetheless sets boundaries on the priority that she makes of Zoe. "I don't want to live my life for my child only," she said, in a statement that perhaps seems radical only in an era of intensive motherhood. "I want to live it for me and my child."

FORGING A PATH WITHOUT INSTITUTIONAL HELP

Molly and Meyer strive for a predictable life for Zoe, and their warm and cooperative parenting arrangement undoubtedly helps her to thrive. The stability of that arrangement would be easier to achieve, however, with a little more institutional help. Legislatures, courts, and schools are some of the establishments that make it hard to forge an intimate life that differs from the married heterosexual breadwinner/caregiver model, as we have seen with the optional fatherhood that the courts assumed for Clark in chapter 5. Such institutional intransigence forces Molly and Meyer to act as pioneers, educators, and even agitators, like other minorities when they too break boundaries.

Molly and Meyer's homegrown divorce was sometimes difficult for institutions to handle, for example, as they had no court papers delineating their arrangement. When Zoe was younger, a mother from the cheerleading squad turned them in for having her attend a school that was out of district from Molly's home, even though Meyer's was within the allotted zone. "In the fifth grade [the school] calls and says, 'We need to see your court papers, because Zoe shouldn't be going to [a Richmond suburb] schools if you live in [a neighboring town]," Molly remembered. "I said, 'Well she also lives in [the first suburb]. We have both addresses on file.' 'Well, we need to see the court papers.' And I said, 'But there aren't any.'"

And I had a conference with the principal and I said, "We broke up when she was young. We don't have any legal papers." I said, "We've worked this out between the two of us our whole lives." I said, "It is working for us." I said, "She stays with him half the week, she stays with me half the week. Sometimes she stays with him more than me and sometimes she stays with me more than him." I said, "But she legally has a right to go to [the Richmond suburb] schools, he is paying taxes there, there is nothing you can do." I said, "Y'all need to let me know what needs to happen." He goes, "Well, can you get court documents?" I said, "Absolutely not." I said, "I'm not going to pay to go to court. I don't need to pay to go to court."

Meyer, who was present at the conference with the principal, was outraged at the implications, Molly recalled.

And Meyer looked at him like he was stupid. He's like, "Are you kidding?" He said, "Why would you take a couple that doesn't have to do that and make them do that?" He said, "Absolutely not. You let us know if there is something legal we are doing wrong." And he walked out of the meeting.

The institutional environment had some difficulty assessing the legality of a relationship formed outside of the court system.

The legal system exerted influence in other ways as well. In most multiparent families in the United States—including any family with two biological parents and one "social" parent, such as many heterosexual stepfamilies—one biological parent has to renounce their legal rights to a child before a social parent can legally adopt. The US legal system thus generally forces one parent to bow out legally before allowing another one into the picture, in what has been dubbed a "substitutive" model of parenting. The difference is more than an abstract one: many stepparents complain that because they are "legal strangers" to the children in their midst, they lack the capacity even to sign a school fieldtrip form.[4]

There is some evidence that this situation is changing: some courts in Massachusetts and California have recognized three-parent families; the California governor recently signed a law allowing courts to find that a child may have more than two parents; and some legislatures such as Delaware's have passed statutes giving legal benefits to de facto parents like Candace or Joan, the nonbiological parent involved in the child's care. Other countries have found other solutions for this pervasive dilemma, one that affects stepparents, LGBT parents, surrogate parents, adoptive parents, and indeed any family in which reproduction and caregiving extend beyond a biological twosome. In the United Kingdom, for example, more than two parents can legally share "parental responsibility," provided those with preexisting responsibility agree.[5]

This institutional backdrop is shaping the next chapter of this multiparent family: when Molly and Joan considered having their own child—with Molly carrying this one as well—they debated having Meyer act as sperm donor and decided against it, because, while that child would be full sibling to Zoe, nevertheless, as Joan said to Molly, "It's none of me." Instead, Joan's brother volunteered, and the threesome were in the process of trying to get pregnant. Also, knowing Meyer as the active, engaged, enthusiastic father he was, they predicted he would never give up his parenting rights. "[Joan] knows he won't," Molly said, "and that's the only reason she won't do it. She said, 'He won't give up his parental rights and I don't want to have to worry about that.'"

The insecurities of lesbian parenting are acute in a state like Virginia, which (at the time of this writing) does not legally recognize lesbian relationships, and in fact does not even allow for second-parent adoption, giving Joan no legal rights and no prospect of them. The legal environment means that Joan and Molly have to be particularly careful about whom they invite to help make their baby, so as not to create problems if anything were to happen later on to cast doubt on either of the two women's legal claim to the child. For lesbians, insecurity culture means that not just raising a child but bearing one has to involve careful planning for hypothetical disruptions.

THE PATH TO SOCIAL CHANGE

To create a coral society, one in which people are encouraged to forge enduring families of all kinds, institutional reforms are clearly needed, as we have seen. State legislatures and courts could enact and apply statutes that support diverse families and their efforts to construct lasting care arrangements and responsibilities.

While reforming institutions to pave the way for the legal, political, and cultural recognition of varied families that might help them last is important, so too are the economic arrangements that enable caring and providing in myriad ways, to meet the needs of children and adults for care stability in a variety of relationships. While we cannot say stable employment causes commitment, it certainly enables families to endure, with the benefits of financial predictability and the pragmatic approach to relationships. Conversely, job insecurity might not cause decoupling, but, as we have seen, it can heighten the salience of security issues, leading some to eschew obligation altogether after a rational calculus of self-interest, others to construct a moral wall that helps them to see and name betrayal, and still others to sacrifice greatly in service to others, holding their fingers in the dike against overwhelming need and vulnerability.

Widespread notions of the inevitability of insecurity protect US employers from responsibility. Yet other countries, with similarly developed economies, have been more able to plan for both sides of the labor relationship. They act as if their citizenry includes business owners as well as the people in their employ, using a combination of regulations, income support, and other policies to balance the need for flexibility with the need for security. Some attempt to legislate endurance through employment protection legislation, such as mandated severance, rules regarding the provision of notice, or penalties for employers whose firms demonstrate high turnover rates. Some states have tried to loosen up some of these restrictions to allow employers more flexibility, while at the same time offering additional training and social insurance as protection for those employees who have been let go. To be sure, there is no panacea, as states face lower employment rates, labor markets divided between the lucky core and the periphery peering in, or training programs that fail to match employer needs. Still, these efforts, aided by healthy collective bargaining, do try to balance the multiple interests involved, and they have an impact on the citizenry: studies show that people's perceptions of insecurity are directly related to the degree to which their governments work to protect them from its effects.[6]

It is not that we can mandate particular families or force people to stay together—nor would we want to. Yet economic policies and management fads do not just have to happen to us like tsunamis or hurricanes, and the families that arise in response do not have to suffer their consequences, like bent palm trees and broken windows in their wake. Instead, the organization of work helps to contribute to the kind of people we are at home.[7]

At the same time, without a reinvigorated voice for working people—be it economically or politically—it is unclear whether we in the United States will even get to have a conversation about what we owe each other at work. This conversation is not just a matter of how we work, and it is not just for workers; as we have seen, it is a matter of how we care, and is thus for adults and children alike, for women and men, for all who think about and benefit from commitment. This book is one effort to get that conversation started.

∽

Epilogue: The Tumbleweed Society

We live in a tumbleweed society, where job insecurity is both profound personal experience and mundane conventional wisdom, widely seen as inevitable, part of what people consider the inescapable cost of broad social forces that none of us can do anything about, such as the spread of globalization, information technology, privatization, and neoliberalism. These social forces have stripped the economy of all but its most Darwinian aspects, so the story goes, compelling business leaders to adopt tactics like layoffs and outsourcing to succeed in a brutally competitive environment. The best the state can do, in this view, is to get out of the way. But this perspective surrenders as already lost the battle for stable employment—the very thing that, as this book has shown, can be vitally important for how we understand what we owe each other, even for how our society knits together, person by person, family by family.

THE IMPACT OF JOB INSECURITY

Job insecurity is not only hype, however. Through the growth of external labor markets, the rash of mergers and downsizings, and the rise in temporary and contingent employment, companies are transforming the way they organize work, with enormous implications for workers, who have limited avenues for pushing back, particularly in the United States as a result of the decline of unionization. Overall, the new ways of organizing work devolve responsibility to the worker for his or her career success, training, employability, and trajectory. While new working conditions offer gains for some workers, such as greater autonomy and control over their time and money, others lose out, buffeted by greater risk, by work speed-ups, pay cuts, and dislocation.

As we have seen, the sense of inevitability that cloaks the new ways of organizing work leads those workers who are immersed in insecure environments to adopt a "one-way honor system," in which they maintain high standards of what they themselves owe to the job, while limiting their expectations of their employers. This paradox rests on the different moral frames people use to produce and evaluate these obligations: employers are seen as no longer bound by a social contract that social forces dissolved, while workers as individuals adhere to an employee covenant, in which loyal, hard work is a sign of their personal character. A small subset—most often those advantaged relocators—disentangle loyalty from the work ethic, suggesting employees must work hard, yes, but that they are free to look for a better offer and even obliged to leave should they get one.

Those who are stably employed are strikingly, even surprisingly, different. They may have vaguely heard about rising insecurity for other people, but it seems of little relevance to their own lives and has minimal influence on their perspectives. Instead, most hold themselves and their employers to standards of mutual responsibility, often invoking family metaphors that describe how they pragmatically resign themselves to each other's imperfections. They act as if they are from an entirely different world than media accounts of the tumbleweed society portray, a world with a prevailing social contract, which, when violated, is cause for outrage at the unexpected betrayal.

We can hear in these descriptions echoes of the stances that anchor the way people talk about commitment. Independence exalts the responsibility of taking care of oneself, and thus emphasizes shrinking one's obligations to minimize the risk of vulnerability or exploitation; one neither expects constancy nor entertains compromise, and is under very little compulsion to stay should a situation or a relationship go sour. Duty exalts one's responsibility to others, expanding obligations, pledging them fervently and expecting others to fulfill them as well or risk the shame of being a deserter; with duty, we do expect constancy but brook little compromise. Pragmatism does not quite exalt anything, as it is in a more moderate register, one that involves a stance of being "realistic," making compromises, and assuming the constancy of others. One's vantage point on the new economy—born out of the personal experience of insecurity and relative advantage, and the opportunities and constraints that arise therefrom—is linked to the stances one adopts, stances that then serve to generate the expectations, practices, and emotions we bring to bear as we make our way at work.

BEYOND THE CUBICLE

These differences also have repercussions beyond the workplace, for stability in the intimate sphere, family diversity, the meanings of dependence, and the experience of care. We have seen how job insecurity and relative advantage combine to shape the way people talk about commitment in their intimate lives as well. People who maintain different standards for work and home—from advantaged flexible workers like Robin Galbraith to less advantaged laid-off workers like Gary Gilbert—erect a moral wall, fending off the insecurity that they assume prevails there, in the hope of keeping it from infiltrating their intimate lives. For advantaged workers, the moral wall means they adopt a pragmatic stance that enables their long-term relationships at home to last, even as they use the language of "choosing" to describe their ensuing bend and sway.

In contrast, some less advantaged women in insecure jobs, who continue to be responsible for the care of the children, sick, and elderly in their lives, are as trapped by the new precariousness of employment as they are by the withdrawal of caregiving support formerly administered by the state and through marriage. For some, their needs power the "marriage-go-round" for which this group is known, in which they reach again and again for relationships to get them out of their fix. That they sometimes tout their defiance does not make their circumstances, or those of their dependents, any less dire. Indeed, the triumph of independence, their paeans to self-reliance, their impatience with vulnerability—these, I would argue, are not evidence of character flaws nor the signs of a people who have lost the capacity to commit. Rather, they are the distress signals of those caught in an emergency, who face both swelling needs and a withering of the support required to meet them.

One surely rational, albeit sometimes tragic, response to this squeeze—of the expanding need for and diminishing supply of care—is to disparage care and dismiss needs, or, as we have seen, to invoke the moral absolution of detachment brokers, those observers urging us to let go. In Michelle De Kretser's novel *The Lost Dog*, an elderly woman, Audrey, fervently wishes not to be a burden. "It was one of Audrey's mantras: I wouldn't want to be a burden. Love was represented as a load; one saw tiny figures broken-backed under monstrous cargos." Love as a burden is the cost of the insecurity squeeze.[1]

Others who suffered an involuntary departure from a job cling to the notion of duty, erecting the same moral wall as the affluent, but one borne of their dismay rather than their discernment. They maintain high standards in their intimate lives, arguing that at least there, duty should prevail.

For some, many of them men, the displacing of their disappointment lends their relationships a certain fraught quality, with others' betrayal easy to see and name, reflecting their gendered expectations of other people's duty, stemming from a historical trajectory of entitlement.

For others who hearken to duty, many of them women, gendered expectations of their own obligation propel them to unimaginable feats of rescuing. To be sure, they derive some moral power from commitment heroism, which buoys them from within and without in their local communities. At the same time, we cannot forget the problematic social conditions that produce, and reproduce, such rescuing—the gendered distribution of need, of struggle, and of caregiving responsibility, and the institutional failure that produces, invisibly, the gaps that these heroes step in to fill. Ultimately, even they contribute to insecurity, in part by enabling the blithe ignorance, daily practiced by the rest of us, of the social conditions that produce the dire needs, and the struggle to meet them, in the first place. Rescuing acts to furiously bail out a sinking boat, while we all sail on; without it, we would all be forced to face the cold fact of the water gathering around our ankles.[2]

In contrast, the stably employed are settling—at once settling down and settling for—relying on pragmatism at work and at home to bolster their endurance. Molly's steadiness at home involves some of the same tactics she employs at work; as Ed, the firefighter, described it: "[Work] is kind of like a marriage. You kind of give a little and take a little." Despite this variation, many parents converge on the duty they owe their children and the flexible children they hope to raise, flexible enough to seize opportunities or to recover from insecurity. Only the stably employed seemed to think they might be raising a child for a dependable world.

BROADER IMPLICATIONS

The implications of these discoveries are manifold. First and foremost, the tumbleweed society features a wide array of family formations, reflecting the principal change in care and intimacy over the last half century: the move from the dominance of one kind of family to a kind of radical pluralism today. While we may celebrate this variation as the freedom to love and live with whom we choose, we nevertheless seem to have paid for diversity with rampant instability, as some career from family to family. Yet Molly, Meyer, Joan, and Zoe suggest how we might find our way to a different world, one in which stable employment, augmented by institutional changes, could engender the capacities for all kinds of families to endure.

Choosing, defying, displacing, rescuing—these strategies all reflect different configurations of obligation, ones that rely upon a certain kind of individual responsibility but differ in their understanding of commitments to others. The stories of those employed in precarious work show us that the less advantaged diverge into those who prioritize independence like Fiona and those who frame their choices through the lens of duty, which can lead to great feelings of betrayal, such as that felt by angry white men, or to great heights of self-sacrifice, such as that performed by Nicki. Of this panoply, some commentators—swayed by their language of choice and independence—seem to visualize only Fiona. Far from there being only one kind of an autonomous, risk-taking, neoliberal self, however, people demonstrate varied identities that seem to share a certain agentic self-efficacy, even as they differ in exactly what they claim responsibility for.

These configurations seem to rely upon a combination of gender and history; the difference between defying and displacing lies in gendered trajectories of entitlement. Fiona defies the old expectations triumphantly because for her ilk they are a trap, while the less advantaged men displace their expectations angrily because they are for them a prerogative.

In contrast to the travails of the laid-off, the long-term relationships of the relocators and the stably employed hum with pragmatism, sharing remarkable resemblance across significant class divides. Relocators are usually quite privileged, with elite educations and substantial incomes in the mid six figures; the stably employed that we have seen here include teachers and lower-middle-class clerks, or working-class firefighters and police officers, many of them without college degrees. Prior scholarship would lead us to expect that the divergent education levels of these two groups would put them on different trajectories for divorce and breakups. When we dive deep into their accounts of intimate relationships, however, their similarities stand out: both use pragmatism to reject the quest for perfection that insecurity culture urges them to pursue. Given these accounts, we must ask ourselves: Does stable employment enable less advantaged people to create long-term partnerships, despite the fragile relationship destinies that analysts have read into their comparative disadvantage? If relative privilege acts to buffer the impact of insecurity, does relative stability act to buffer the impact of disadvantage?

Finally, job insecurity clearly matters deeply for the emotional landscape. People perceive flexibility and adaptability as ascendant cultural values, and many of them worry about the discrepancy when their feelings do not comply with the new rules. This book has documented the anguish that bubbles up through the gaps between how they feel and how they are supposed to feel, their emotional dissonance. The laid-off often feel not only left behind but, perhaps even worse, that they have little right to that feeling—in essence, they feel abandoned to their abandonment. Relocators feel compelled to explain, justify, or mask their anachronistic willingness to settle at home. This is the emotional impact of the tumbleweed society, the power of its perceived feeling rules to shape people's sense of what is valid for them to feel, to expect, and even to hope.

The stories of the stably employed show us that job security matters for how people approach compromise and constancy, and it suggests that when thinking about intimacy, care, and identities we need to consider not just class differences but also exposure to job insecurity. With some analysts focusing on family structure and character issues and others focusing on economic inequality, we have missed how insecurity and inequality can intertwine to create different intimacy patterns; in our assessment of the roots of family disruption, employers, as supported by the state, are worth another glance.

THE PROBLEM OF DEPENDENCE

Many different kinds of families, and diverse arrangements of family caregiving, have been shown to meet the needs of dependents well, just like Molly, Meyer, and Joan in the last chapter. Nevertheless, relentless insecurity strains our capacities to take on caregiving responsibilities. In so doing, insecurity makes the old problem of dependence new again.

Through its external labor market, emphasis on constant employability, and the separation of workers into groups of those who are owed stability and those who are not, the tumbleweed society offers the starkest of incentives for people to be on call for unpredictable work demands, to stay late at the office, or even to move. By imposing what Joan Williams has called the "ideal worker norm," it spurs on those who decline to take on obligations to others, makes it difficult for people to step up to care, and masks gender discrimination as caregiver discrimination. But some people need more active care to sustain and nurture life, such as the sick, disabled, elderly, and very young, and these groups pose an existential challenge to the notion of autonomy that undergirds our national mythology. At the same time, these are populations that all of us will move in and out of throughout the course of our lives.[3]

In addition, many moments of dependence are particularly stressful and challenging. The Alzheimer's-afflicted parent, the child with the attachment disorder, the bedridden husband whose back was broken when he was thrown from a crane at work—these are extreme cases of need.

How long can or should we rely on rescuing by the few, who use commitment to anchor their identities amid insecurity? Even more mundane caregiving situations test fairly deep stores of patience, humor, and even altruism. In a society that expects and rewards mobility, at what point will these tests act as their own tripwires propelling family caregivers out of connections and obligations that are too difficult?

Insecurity magnifies the view of dependence—the sort of local, static, demanding connections that drag on someone's mobility, such as Molly's desire not to move Zoe during her selective mutism phase—as a problem. The demand for mobility serves to dislodge people from the opportunities —and the predilection—to care, not only within families but also with communities, friends, and extended kin. And while feminists have long shown the costs of caring work, in part to recognize the penalties women pay for taking on the lion's share of it, more recent work also documents some of the interpersonal and identity gains caregivers can earn. The existing social organization of care, in which women are often "forced to care" by moral pressures and socioeconomic inequalities, serves to obscure or eliminate these benefits, of course. Nonetheless, people experience their own humanity in the practice of caring for others. We might say, then, that the impediments to dependency posed by insecurity culture bear their own costs, for "dependents" who need care, to be sure, but, just as important, for the rest of us who need to give it.[4]

THE DEATH OF COMMITMENT?

Is commitment dead or dying? Not at all, not even in the tumbleweed society. People are still connected, still facing needs and meeting them, still striving to do what is honorable. Yet prior understandings of commitment— where it has been and where it is going—have been too one-sided; we hear stories of decline—mostly men's—or celebrate new freedoms—mostly those of women and gay men. We are better off including more voices when we consider how we adapt to insecurity culture, and how these adaptations themselves affect what we expect from each other.

The different stories here about how people respond to precariousness at work should help to drive home one central point: insecurity is not some undifferentiated cultural sea in which we all swim. It is instead tied to the particular experiences and contexts of precariousness, which produce specific kinds of adaptations, stances toward obligation that we adopt and that help to shape the kind of selves we find honorable, the dilemmas that worry us, the very choices that we can even see. While anxiety about insecurity might be widespread for some, certainly contributing to the sense of inevitability that animates the one-way honor system for many, it is but a distant echo for the stably employed. Some of their ranks help us keep the outlines of an alternative—the coral society, vibrant, varied, and enduring—in our sights.

In a globalized, outsourcing world, different countries have adopted different approaches to the matter of how much employers and workers owe each other. In contrast, American policies, in obeisance to the drive to maximize profits, sacrifice the worker citizen to the shareholder. It is almost as if the United States were a company town, with work, school, and general store beholden to the same employer and politics largely silent about its own complicity. Yet this raises the question: What is an economy for? Does it have its own logic, its own dictates to which we must merely yield, as if it were some force of nature? Or is it our own creation, and thus there to serve us? What is the kind of "us," then, we want it to serve? What kind of "us" do we want to be?[5]

In the United States, it seems, we answer the question by negating the very concept of "us" at work. Yet as this book has shown, our experiences of insecurity shape the way we talk about obligations, how we interpret them as commitments we will or will not shoulder, how we conceive of what we owe each other—indeed, how we are able to weave the fabric of our connected lives. If we are not an "us" at work, then, we are hardly likely to be one at home.

ACKNOWLEDGMENTS

The midwives for this book span the globe; many have read this book from beginning to end in its many different iterations, some people more than once. These are gifts given without recompense, and I am humbled by the support. Christine Williams and Denise Walsh share the same keen sense for injustice, reminding me to watch out for what really matters: the inequalities that give people few choices. Jennifer Cyd Rubenstein helps me find the threads of analytic logic, drawing a two-by-two table on a napkin, while Jennifer Petersen and Marianne Cooper sift through the detritus to find what I really want to say, or what is worth saying. Sarah Corse is often there to listen once again to a reworking of what she's encountered already many times, her incisive gifts for framing proving invaluable. These six women, from Texas to Virginia to California, have given of themselves time and again to help improve this manuscript, and I am profoundly grateful. I hope they can see their influence as clearly as I can (and are not too exasperated by where it did not take).

My deepest thanks also go to the people who opened their lives to us in these lengthy, personal conversations all over Virginia and Washington, DC. My primary motivation, as I wrote and rewrote drafts, was to honor the gift of their stories with the book that emerged from them.

James Cook, my editor, has been hearing about these ideas for a long time, reading the manuscript more than once, sending chapters back repeatedly in a flurry of emails, offering sound editorial advice and a useful scythe; I'm grateful for his support, feedback, and acute judgment. Thanks also go to Tristan Bridges, Andrew Cherlin, Arlie Hochschild, Eva Illouz, Maria Klutey, Ilse Lenz, Cameron MacDonald, Jim Pugh, Rosemary Pugh, Jeremy Schulz, Stephen Sellers, Rachel Sherman, Vicki Smith, Martina Verba, and one anonymous reviewer for influential and timely counsel that shaped the book in important ways. I am also grateful to Barrie Thorne, Viviana Zelizer, Kathleen Gerson, Karen Hansen, and Bob Zussman, fellow interpretive travelers, for their advice and support on this project over the years.

Early on, Vicki Smith and Ofer Sharone gave important feedback on sampling issues, while Stephen Sweet has been a kind supporter from the start, brave enough to comment upon the first deluge of data as a discussant at a panel at the 2010 Eastern Sociological Society meetings. A sabbatical year spent in Australia in 2010–2011, under the auspices of the United States Study Centre, was a wonderful opportunity to analyze interviews and write up some of my ideas. Margaret Levy made some excellent suggestions, while Felicity Turner and Blake Gilpin helped to make the Centre a great place to work. I thank Margaret, Sean Gallagher, and Geoffrey Garret for the opportunity.

Audiences provided helpful critical feedback at Boston University, Georgetown University, the University of California, Berkeley, the University of Chicago, the University of Maryland, the University of Massachusetts, Amherst, the University of Missouri, and the University of Sydney. A summer spent as the Marie Jahoda Visiting Professor for International Gender Studies in Bochum, Germany, meant that I could present material from the book to eleven different audiences; I am grateful to Ilse Lenz for the opportunity. Particularly helpful sessions were at the lecture to the Faculty of Social Science at the Ruhr University Bochum, as well as at the Hans Böckler Foundation in Dusseldorf, the Faculty of Gender and Work at Bielefeld University, the University of Duisburg-Essen, and the Rhein-Waal University of Applied Sciences in Kleve. That summer offered a powerful illustration of the similar challenges that face the United States and Europe, and the striking differences in how societies strive to meet them.

I also presented material on the "moral wall" and the "one-way honor system" at the outstanding "Redefining Work" Working Group at Stanford's Clayman Institute for Gender Research, where Shelley Correll, Joan Williams, Erin Kelly, Julie Kmec, KT Albiston, and Mary Blair-Loy, among others, pushed my thinking. Steven Lukes, Russ Muirhead, and Matthew Crawford challenged my ideas—and came up with some intriguing titles—at the UVa Work and Worth Conference in 2012. The Work and Family Researchers Network's 2012 conference heard about "commitment heroes," and Kathleen Gerson and Jennifer Silva contributed to a stimulating discussion there. I presented material at the Social Trends Institute in Barcelona, and also at the Young Lives, Changing Times: Perspectives on Social Reproduction Symposium at the Department of Anthropology, the University of Sydney, where Ute Eickelkamp, Gillian Cowlishaw, Rose Butler, and Cindi Katz helped me rethink the project. Helpful feedback also came from Christine Williams, Yiannis Gabriel, and the audience at the Postindustrial Culture and the Flexible Self panel at the 2011 American Sociological Association, as well as at the Eastern Sociological Society meetings in 2010,

2012, and 2014, with special thanks to Steve Vallas for his useful commentary there.

At Virginia, colleagues have been very influential at various points; in particular, Sarah Corse, Jeff Olick, Andrea Press, and Josipa Roksa have offered crucial advice at different moments in the book's life cycle. An early presentation to the interdisciplinary Socio-Cultural Workshop elicited important commentary from Ira Bashkow and Susan McKinnon. An entire team of graduate students at Virginia has been a part of this project at one time or another, for which I am very grateful. Roscoe Scarborough conducted many interviews and read the entire manuscript, offering insightful feedback; his indefatigable efforts made him an excellent research partner. Michele Darling ran a focus group of some of the teenaged children of interviewees, while Katrina Van Blaircum chased down some elusive secondary data. Matthew Morrison and Jennifer Silva went from orthodontists' offices to libraries to community centers posting recruiting flyers. Andrew Lynn sent an impassioned and ruminative critique after hearing me talk about the book, while Ben Snyder proposed a thoughtful title. Tonie Gordon helped with proofreading, and Candace Miller was outstanding with some last-minute bibliographic assistance. Thanks are also due to Anne Neison and her team for the voluminous transcribing and to Jennifer Carlson for taking careful notes for an entire day of feedback in a manuscript workshop at Berkeley.

Research was supported by an Alfred P. Sloan Foundation Work-Family Career Development Grant. Analysis and writing were supported by a postdoctoral fellowship at the United States Study Centre at the University of Sydney, a Sesquicentennial Research Grant and a Faculty Summer Research Award in Humanities and Social Sciences from UVa's College of Arts and Sciences, a Professors-as-Writers Book Manuscript Conference Grant from UVa's Teaching Resource Center, and a Bankard Fund for Political Economy Research Award. I am grateful for this assistance, which was indispensable at each stage. Material from the book has also been published in the inaugural issue of the *American Journal of Cultural Sociology* in a piece entitled "What Good Are Interviews for Thinking About Culture? Demystifying Interpretive Analysis," and in the *Hedgehog Review*, in an essay entitled "The Social Meanings of Dignity at Work."

Thanks are due to my family and friends for support, ideas, comments, contacts, and advice, especially Roger Pugh, Joanne Pugh, Jim Pugh, Robin Pugh, Andy Pugh, Rosemary Pugh, Maria Klutey, Betsy Pugh, Ann Pugh, Mark Cancian, Nora Brookfield, Ann Lucas, and Tina Verba. As with my first book, Andy Pugh stepped up again with some crucial last-minute work to preserve the confidentiality of the participants. Taryn and Ray La Raja,

Janet and Jeff Legro, and Beth and Tom Lorey have all been hearing and talking about this book for a long while; more importantly, watching and listening to them over the years has shaped my understanding of how we know commitment when we see it. Finally, Sophie, Lucy, and Hallie have cheered and inspired me every step of the way, but words can only understate how much I rely on Steve.

APPENDIX A

———— ⌒⌒ ————

Commitment Talk

This is a study of the emotional cultures through which people adapt to job insecurity and the meanings they impute to commitment and obligation, meanings that then take on a life of their own, by making some actions honorable and others less so. Using what Kristen Luker has called the "logic of discovery," I relied upon in-depth interviewing with eighty people whose experiences varied, in order to explore the ways in which women and men with different histories of job insecurity and relative advantage interpret the contemporary challenges of working and caring.[1]

THE PEOPLE IN THE STUDY: WHO WERE THEY?

In this study, a graduate student researcher and I interviewed eighty mothers and fathers from three groups: thirty-three who experienced layoffs plus thirteen who moved to get work they did not have already, who were thus on the more anxious end of the spectrum of job insecurity; thirty-two employed in relatively stable positions, such as police, firefighters, or public school teachers; and twenty who had been relocated for jobs, sometimes for their spouse's job and sometimes for their own. These numbers add up to more than eighty because eighteen people overlapped these groups, such as those who had relocated but then been laid off, like Beth in chapter 2.[2]

I purposely varied the experience that study participants have had in the labor market—whether as people with firsthand knowledge of the newly precarious position of many workers (people laid off or so desperate for a job they moved without any certainty of getting one), those who have experienced a long-term stable career with the same employer, or those who, as relocators, were often so prized by their employers that they were grooming them for advancement. Most of the laid-off had experienced their job dislocation within the past three years, although the dislocations ranged from a few months to eight years prior to our interview. Similarly, most of the relocators had moved in the last few years, although a few had moved as long as ten years beforehand.

For the people in this study, their relative advantage—what we might call their socioeconomic status, as ascertained by their occupation, income, and education—overlapped with their experience of insecurity. The bulk of the relocators had either elite/affluent or professional/managerial backgrounds. All but three relocators had a college degree, with many having completed postgraduate educations as well, and their average income was just under $200,000, with some couples earning many times that. In addition, seventeen of them (85 percent) were in long-term relationships (either their first marriages or second marriages/partnerships that had lasted ten years or more), with an average duration of twenty-four years. For this research, I spoke to either the relocated employee or to his or her spouse, who was more often employed in a less demanding job.

Most of the stably employed were lower middle class or working class, in that they had average incomes of $54,000, and they were largely employed as teachers, in office jobs such as paralegals or accounting clerks, or in jobs conventionally understood as working-class occupations, such as firefighting or law enforcement. There is a small subset (five people) that has higher degrees and higher incomes, who work in social work, accounting, and the like in small family firms or other stable employment. Overall, this group had wide differences in education, ranging from the GED of someone who worked in a sheriff's department to a teacher's graduate degree. The bulk of them were married or cohabiting; twenty-five of them (about 78 percent) were in long-term partnerships (either in their first marriages or a second marriage/partnership that had lasted ten years or more), with an average duration of twenty years.

I combined the laid-off and movers into the same group, because analysis revealed that they generally adopted the same stances to obligation; I called them both "laid-off" for simplicity's sake. The bulk of this group and the stably employed shared many characteristics, except, of course, their stable employment. Most of the laid-off were also lower middle class or working class, with most of them moderately educated and employed in such jobs as welding, retail, or personal care services. Like the stably employed, this group also had a small subset (six people) from professional/managerial backgrounds, with college degrees, and working in such fields as human resources or information technology. The group's average individual income (including several who reported "0" because they were currently looking for work) was $29,870. They were less likely to be partnered; thirteen (28 percent) were in long-term partnerships, with an average length of nineteen years.

The study thus straddles insecurity culture, with two out of three groups immersed in it (the relocators and the laid-off) and one apart, at the same time as it straddles inequality—with two groups at some disadvantage (the laid-off and the stably employed) and one apart. While there are groups missing—stably employed advantaged people (such as tenured college professors), elite professionals who have been laid off enough that they have become discouraged workers, many LGBT workers, etc.—the existing variation allows me to address the intersections of insecurity and inequality. Claims would have been more difficult to make, or the research period would have been much longer, if I had included these other groups in big enough numbers to be able to say something useful about them.

Most of the interviews were with white women with some college attendance, like the majority of employed women in the United States. I included men and people of color in order to be able to generate some ideas about how gender and race/ethnicity shape adaptations to insecurity culture. Thus this study was able to document the optional quality of many men's caregiving and the gender innovations of some individual men, as well as the interplay of race, poverty, and gender that produces particular kinds of rescuing, for example, and African-American women's broad understanding of which children count as "kin." Future research will have to delve more deeply into how people of color experience the twin pillars of job insecurity and inequality, however, as of the eighty people in this study, ten (12.5 percent) were nonwhite, including eight African-Americans and two Latinos.[3]

I solicited study participants mostly through venues for parents of teenagers, such as parent-teacher organizations at area high schools, homeschooling websites, and social networking sites such as RichmondMom.com. We also posted flyers in orthodontist's offices, community recreation centers, public libraries, bookstores, and local churches. All participants received $30 in the form of a gift card. Finally, all interviews were transcribed by a professional service; I retained the original tapes, however, and listened to them while analyzing the material, to enable me to capture emotional and other oral cues.

THE STUDY LOCATION

Interviewees came from four areas: Washington, DC, and environs, as well as two large coastal cities and a smaller city in central Virginia; the majority of interviewees lived in the Richmond area. The capitol of Virginia, Richmond is a midsized city of about two hundred thousand people, about half of them African-American, somewhat similar in size and racial/ethnic makeup to Rochester, NY (which has more people of Latino descent) or Shreveport, LA. Richmond and its suburbs constituted the nation's forty-fifth largest metro area in 2011. The twenty largest private employers together employ 81,700 people; only five cities in the nation have more corporate offices. Besides state and local governments, major employers include the Capital One Financial Corporation (with almost ten thousand employees in the greater Richmond area), three area hospitals, Wal-Mart, the utility Dominion Resources, and the cigarette maker Philip Morris USA.[4]

Most people lived at the time of their interview in Virginia and Washington, DC, but the intentional composition of the sample entailed they were recounting lives spent all over the United States, although predominantly in the Northeast, and in some cases overseas, although mostly limited to Europe. Twenty-four people had relocated to get or keep employment, and talked about their lives in Maryland, Connecticut, Ohio, and even Switzerland or Poland; twenty-one of those who had been laid off came from other states, such as Colorado, New Hampshire, and Michigan; even fifteen of those employed in stable jobs had moved from places such as New York, Florida, and North Carolina. Thus sixty people, or 75 percent of the sample, and the majority in each job category, had originated in other parts of the country or had lived extensively elsewhere. For this reason we can surmise that interviewees for this project represent a more geographically diverse set of experiences than just the Virginia–Washington, DC, area.

The study location did shape the profile of one group in particular: the stably employed. In other areas of the United States, teaching, firefighting, and the like are unionized occupations, with collective bargaining rights that shape the experience and meaning of obligations and security in the workplace. As a "right-to-work" state, however, Virginia prohibited collective bargaining by public employees in 1993, codifying in law a decision reached by the Virginia Supreme Court in 1977. Unionization in the Virginia public sector stands at about 10 percent, in contrast to almost 40 percent of public sector employees nationwide.[5]

Certainly, unionization is an important part of the story of how most lower-middle-class and working-class jobs became stable in the first place, as the fight for job security has been a fundamental battle for most unions. Unions are also in all likelihood one of the crucial components of change, in that we are unlikely to get more stable employment without a collective voice for workers clamoring for it. Nonetheless, it is unclear how (or whether) Virginia's special antipathy to unions altered the results of this study of adaptations to insecurity culture; probably those who are stably employed—unionized or not—would expect job security and espouse a certain pragmatism at work and at home, as opposed to ceding the workplace to the insecurity of the "new economy." Unions matter in shaping employment relations, to be sure, but perhaps not in shaping the need, predilection, or capacities of *workers* to commit.

THE INTERVIEWS

Interviews lasted from one to three hours, averaging about 2.5 hours, and took place in cafés, offices, homes, and libraries. They involved the taking of what we might call a "commitment history," including narratives of change and stability at home and at work. We explored how people interpret change, what counts as betrayal at work or in intimate relationships, how their experiences align with or confound their expectations, and what sort of cultural work they do to resolve any contradictions. We asked for specific examples to illustrate their notions of what we owe each other, for moments when they had decided it was time to no longer see someone or when someone left them, for recollections of when they tried to get their child to quit or stay with a friend or activity, and for memories of troubled times in their important relationships and how they handled them.

The interviews were often intense, powerful experiences, and required a concentrated, empathetic attention that was ultimately quite draining, making it difficult to do more than one in a day. Many people wept as they recounted the disloyalty of others or shameful moments that haunted them still; interviews that asked about commitment often ended up being about betrayal. Generally, they reported that the experience was meaningful, even powerful, and sometimes unsettling. "Yeah, I could sit here for hours," Molly said, but added: "It makes me remember too much, though." "Yeah, I'm really glad we're having this conversation, because I'm kind of working it out in my head," said James, a white married father of two. "I've done more thinking about myself in the last two hours than I have in years," Bruce, a white teacher, told me. "It feels really good to talk," said Lena, a white divorced mother of three. "I feel better getting it all out."

ANALYZING OBLIGATION

Qualitative research refers to more than just the way in which the data are collected; in addition, a crucial component is the analysis to which they are treated. Data analysis can span radically different versions, from a surface-level gleaning of "answers" to "questions" to a profound excavation of semiconscious meaning. What I term interpretive analysis involves strategies to unearth what Luker calls the "mental maps" of "some aspect of social life."[6]

Interpretive analysis scrutinizes language use. The analytic process involves several steps, in which the researcher turns to the interviewee's words again and again, coding them for persistent ideas, gleaning relevant themes from this data, repeatedly returning to the texts to check and recheck themes, and linking codes and themes into analytic memos. In analyzing the interviews for this project, for example, I kept several different logs simultaneously while reading my interviews again and again, including lists of jokes, turns of phrase, and metaphors about issues of persistence and adaptability. By attending to such rich uses of language, I could engage more deeply with how people were experiencing their lives, rather than simply how they reported that experience.

Like other relatively small-scale studies, this project is particularly apt for studying culture—how it works, how people perceive it, how people use it in their daily lives. My findings are not numerically generalizable, meaning you cannot extrapolate from them how widespread a particular trend is—such as how many people in the general population might be rescuing, for example, or how many enduring multiparent families exist, or even how many among us construct a "moral wall" cordoning off insecurity at work. Instead, close-in, interpretive studies like this are best for revealing processes (such as how people use pragmatism to avoid the quest for something better), meanings (such as how people shrink or expand the definition of obligation), and emotions (including not just how they feel but how they feel about how they feel). Furthermore, by focusing on and comparing particular kinds of people who vary in particular ways, my findings become theoretically generalizable, revealing the impact of job insecurity, filtered through inequality, on the processes and meanings at stake.

Reports about what counts as honorable behavior act as a window onto prevailing culture, the kind that presses in on people, the kind that constrains and enables certain kinds of practices and ideas and not others. When almost everybody talks about how hard they work, for example, giving 100 percent, 150 percent, or 200 percent on the job, we do not have to verify these claims so much as take note of them as a statement of the good. Experienced interviewers also know ways to counter people's tendency to speak in general belief statements that may or may not correspond to practice.

Sometimes, however, we are granted an even closer view. Occasionally, in-depth interviews bring out contradictions between how people want to present themselves and how they actually feel, where one notion seems to bubble up despite the efforts of the reasonable, honorable self to suppress it. What makes these contradictions particularly valuable is their vertical character—that they animate different levels of feeling. The surface level often acts, I think, as a kind of cultural barometer, a reading of what is admirable behavior for the interviewee in his/her social setting, particularly useful for understanding social pressures and the cultural ascendancy of particular ideas and practices. What bubbles up, on the other hand, is rarely trotted out simply to solve a new problem—rather, it can often be an admission of contrary yet powerfully held emotional conviction. That these admissions are often painful is testimony to the arduousness, and the profoundly personal nature, of the reconciliation work interviewees must undertake to resolve the contradictions that they face.

Finally, through interviewing, we sometimes glean not just what people perceive is honorable, and not just their inner feelings, but also the intersection of these two pieces, the metafeelings–that is what it feels like, given what counts as honorable, to feel these feelings, to hold these ideas. In so doing, we are able to bring the larger cultural environment to bear on what initially might seem like purely individual stories of personal notions of commitment and obligation.

NOTES

1. See Pugh (2009).
2. For a compelling account of work-family configurations as a series of phases, see Gerson, 2010.
3. See Terkel (1972:xxii).

CHAPTER 1
1. All names of my interviewees, and some identifying details, but none of their words, were changed to protect confidentiality.
2. I use the term "flexibility" not in the sense that predominates in research on work-family conflict, in terms of control over the timing or the place of work, but rather in terms of adaptability and resilience; when I use it with regard to work, this definition is more in keeping with how work scholars use it, to capture employers' ability to expand or contract their labor force in response to changing markets. Commitment is mostly defined by duration, but the word has many other dimensions, such as intensity, periodicity, effort, etc. I attended to how the people in this study defined the term, as evidence for how they thought about obligations.
3. GE executive "Neutron" Jack Welch is perhaps the most well-known persona trumpeting the benefits of layoffs and downsizing, of which his "20-70-10" system (a "rank and yank" system in which the bottom 10 percent of employees are fired every year) is a prime example (Welch and Byrne 2001).
4. Some analysts argue the changing organization of work is but one crucial part of a larger array of transformations contributing to the rise of the flexible, autonomous individual, one who claims "personal responsibility" for what is actually shaped by neoliberal social forces. While Giddens (1991) offers a more positive view of these developments, he joins Zygmunt Bauman, Ulrich Beck, and Elisabeth Beck-Gernsheim in arguing that contemporary intimacy has become individualized, disenchanted, and contractual. While trenchant, however, these analyses often lack empirical grounding, sometimes sound nostalgic for days that were actually beset by significant inequalities, and most important, tell an overly totalizing story, in which people develop neoliberal subjectivity simply by virtue of swimming in the same cultural sea, instead of due to their particular experiences, trajectories, or social contexts (Kingfisher and Maskovsky 2008). See Beck and Beck-Gernsheim (1995), Beck-Gernsheim (2002), Bauman (2003), and Giddens (1991).

5. Smart and Shipman (2004) argue against the "individualization thesis" for a more variegated account of contemporary family-making.

6. The college-educated are more likely to stay married than those with less education, and this association has strengthened since divorce rates peaked in the early 1980s (Stevenson and Wolfers 2007, Martin 2004).

7. I use the term "insecurity culture" as a more accessible synonym for neoliberalism, to capture the combination of "deregulation, privatization, and withdrawal of the state from many areas of social provision" and the emphasis upon agency and personal responsibility that accompany these institutional shifts. See Harvey (2005:3) and Gershon (2011).

8. The theme has been taken up by parodies as well: in one sendup by the satirical newspaper the *Onion*, the headline read "Media Company Looking for Ways to Get Rid of Veteran 24-Year-Old Employee." Schmidt (2000) argues that whatever the actual change in insecurity may be, what matters is that more workers were convinced their jobs were insecure, and that insecurity would come at greater cost to their incomes. Andrew Fullerton and Michael Wallace (2007) analyzed survey data about workers' perceptions of job insecurity over twenty-five years to report that the "flexible turn" in the labor market has led workers to have a heightened sense of vulnerability. Aside from these perceptions, scholars debate whether work is actually more insecure. Some remind us of both the brief stint in time of the twenty-year career and the narrowly defined worker (mostly male, skilled) who got to enjoy it (Cappelli 1999), or they argue that job tenure numbers have not changed appreciably (Stevens 2005). Most scholars agree, however, that job security is declining, with more of the debate centering on questions of degree and timing (Neumark 2000). "By virtually any measure, more recent cohorts of workers have been with their current employers for less time at specific ages," reports Henry Farber (2007:2), who has worked extensively on this topic. Greenhalgh and Rosenblatt defined job insecurity as a "perceived powerlessness to maintain desired continuity in a threatened job situation" (1984:438).

9. Changes in work create the need for a self that "must be carried like a snail carries a shell," one "coherent yet mutable, fixed yet multiple and flexible," writes Walkerdine (2006:38).

10. For job turnover, see Reuters (2013) and Horovitz (2014). For worker concern, see Schmidt (2000). For the dual-career couple data, see Sweet, Moen, and Meiksins (2007).

11. For "contingent workers," see the 2006 GAO report (US Government Accounting Office 2006); I subtracted part-time workers from the total, as they are often in more stable arrangements. For union membership, see Bureau of Labor Statistics (2014a). See also Kalleberg (2009). The Silicon Valley figure is from Reichheld (2001). The private research firm CareerXroads surveyed a cross section of large firms in several different industries, employing 1.3 million US employees. See Kalleberg (2009,2011), Reichheld (2001), and Crispin and Mehler (2011).

12. Data on the decline in job tenure and long-term employment come from Farber (2009:1). For sanguine economists, see Blinder (2006).

13. These trends are not limited to the United States, of course. In Australia, the cellphone provider Vodafone played with anxieties about newly fleeting intimacy in an advertising campaign in spring 2011 that took on the themes of short, uncertain relationships and blurry obligations. Selling a short-term mobile phone contract, the company promised "a definite maybe for commitment phobes." They asked: "Why buy the cow when you can get the milk for free?" People are still

marrying, of course, and in this they are not totally reinventing new ways of intimacy (Gross 2005). For cohabitation data, see Cherlin (2009); Goodwin, Mosher, and Chandra (2010); and Kreider (2010).

14. Some writers conflate family structure, or the particular form—heterosexual marriage, nuclear arrangements, two-parent families—with family commitment, or particular duration. People are not simply choosing insecurity, however, but also responding to it, and not simply in the domestic sphere but also in their work lives. Many scholars seem to make the same mistake as Sleeping Beauty's father: assuming that job insecurity is like an unwelcome fairy whom you can just not invite to the party. Yet this unwelcome fairy is coming to the party anyway, I argue, whether we invite her or not. See Cherlin (2009); for anniversary data, see US Census (2012c) and US Census (2012b). For "churn" at work, see Smith (2010).

15. For workers, precarious work is linked to negative financial outcomes as people struggle to find jobs with comparable pay; job insecurity also reduces psychological well-being and job satisfaction (see De Witte 1999 for a review). At the organizational level, scholars have found that job insecurity can have negative consequences for employee morale, the intent to stay on the job, and performance (Sverke, Hellgren, and Naswall 2002). Furthermore, outsourcing and other management practices linked to job insecurity do not lead to higher productivity nor to higher stock values over the longer term, but instead to depressed wages and higher profits (Baumol, Blinder, and Wolff 2003). Greenhalgh and Rosenblatt (2010) recently conducted a review of twenty-five years of research, arguing that the "nonwork consequences of job insecurity" is an "under-researched" area. For a review of the costs to family life of job insecurity, see Burchell (2005). For poverty and the lack of marriage, see Gibson-Davis (2009); for the deinstitutionalization of marriage, see Cherlin (2004); for expressive individualism, see Cherlin (2009).

16. Schmidt (1999) documents rising anxiety among college graduates in the 1990s, so that their rates of job insecurity converged with workers without a college degree. For data about the "divorce divide" between the college-educated and others, see Martin (2004) and Aughinbaugh, Robles, and Sun (2013). See also McCall (2004).

17. Some of the scholarship that generated this knowledge includes Burawoy (1979), Willis (1977), Thistle (2006), and N. Lee (2001).

18. This "common sense" reigns even though evidence suggests that "the flexibilization of labor" does not yield productivity growth; see Baumol et al. (2003), and for an example of this evidence Lucidi and Kleinknecht (2010). Thanks to Mari Franklin for the phrase "employee covenant."

19. The most influential proponent of the "character" argument is Richard Sennett's book *The Corrosion of Character* (1998). In it, he offers the powerful insight that while we may have criticized the old ways of working—and they deserved it, he says, as he tries to argue against the nostalgic view—they were nonetheless anchored in stable institutions that created habits in workers that led to good character, habits such as delayed gratification, the work ethic, reliability. Now, Sennett contends, we have none of these—and are left instead with a weak attachment to work and a thin superficiality of relationships. Sennett's treatise is a grand effort to see beyond the cubicle, to the "personal consequences" of insecure work; in doing so, he has influenced my own book project. Nonetheless, the book sometimes misreads its own philosophical musings as social fact. Most

important, Sennett offers an argument suggesting that the home life is (still) a haven in a heartless world; people will flee the insecure workforce and communities to focus entirely on the home, he contends. Sennett therefore misses the significant ways in which insecurity at work and at home might be related, relying instead on an outmoded compensatory model that ignores the "churn" at home and instead assumes/hopes the domestic sphere will serve as a container for all the unrealized connections foresworn at work. Would that there was such a container, many might maintain. Scholars have also criticized the home-as-a-haven model for ignoring women's perspective on the home as a site of significant (although unpaid) work (Cowan 1983). As Gary's story begins to make clear, the home-as-container serves as an ideology that paradoxically, and woefully, makes home life more fraught, more fragile, even more unable to fend off the culture of insecurity. A more recent salvo about character has come from Charles Murray, whose recent book (2012) suggests that with increasing class segregation among whites, the disadvantaged lead ever more dissolute lives; he refuses to consider economic causes for this, since the years in question included economic boom times, he writes. While profits and productivity may have been soaring, however, wages and security were not.

20. When you break down the numbers, particularly in the private sector, women's job tenure has risen, reflecting their increasing attachment to work, while men's job tenure has declined, reflecting the changing structure of work (Farber 1998, 2008; Hollister 2011, Hollister and Smith 2014). Gender is inescapable when we talk about postindustrial changes, as women's partial gains have come about in part through the breakdown of distinctions between a male "core" and the female "periphery." Men were able to uphold their side of the social contract primarily because of the unpaid caring labor of women in the home. Women were excluded from participating in these social contracts themselves, by explicit company policies and by cultural convention, and that exclusion penalized them directly economically, even as it supported their unpaid care work through marriage. This system served, through state policies, to act as a disciplinary force against working-class women, women of color, single mothers, and others. Meanwhile, studies repeatedly find that "women do not differ appreciably from men in job involvement" (Highhouse, Zickar, and Yankelevich 2010:354, Hyde and Plant 1995). For a gendered analysis of Atkinson's "core-periphery" arguments about firm flexibility, see Walby (1997). See also Thistle (2006). Cappelli, of the Wharton School, offered the choice metaphor of the downward escalator during a talk at the Work-Family Researchers Network conference in New York City, June 2012.

21. Although labor flexibility relies on individuals to get their ontological security from elsewhere—broad and deep connections to others outside of work—it penalizes those who actually carry the load of those connections (Buzzanelli 2000). Even today, despite the greater involvement of some men, women retain primary responsibility for paid and unpaid care. In households with married parents, mothers spend an estimated 50 hours a week with children, as opposed to an estimated 31 hours a week for fathers (Raley, Bianchi, and Wang 2012). Single mothers still comprise the overwhelming majority of single-parent families, at 85 percent. Women comprise about 70 percent of informal caregivers for the elderly, including care given as spouses and as adult children (Bianchi, Folbre, and Wolf 2012). Of paid home care workers, women make up 90 percent of labor force (Glenn 2010). Nancy Folbre's *For Love and Money* is a thorough discussion of

patterns of caregiving in the United States. For the motherhood penalty, see Correll, Benard, and Paik (2007). See also Fineman (2005).

22. Of course, it is not that dependence was once lauded, only to be castigated now. Rather, my argument is that dependence is newly visible as it is newly recognized as being restricted to ever more limited pockets of humanity. When women were viewed as dependents, their partial claims to adulthood served to complicate its moral status (N. Lee 2001). As corporate capitalism, the state, and liberal feminism ally in support of the market, however, dependence and the care work that addresses it become further stigmatized. Zygmunt Bauman once said the poor were newly castigated as "flawed consumers"; so too, then, we might argue that insecurity culture makes of the immobile "flawed independents." For the continuity of dependence as a problem, see Fraser and Gordon's fascinating article (1994), in which they argue that dependence has always signified inferiority (albeit with varying degrees of moral opprobrium), but that its meanings have changed radically, with implications for the new economy.

23. Bauman (2000:58).

24. The majority of American adults are neither highly disadvantaged nor economically privileged, falling instead somewhere in the middle; the "moderately educated" is Cherlin's term for those who have a high school degree or some college but no bachelor's degree. As Sassler (2013:259) puts it, "Because the moderately educated account for more than half of all women of reproductive age, those studying family change must pay closer attention to them."

25. I was ably assisted in interviewing by Roscoe Scarborough, a PhD candidate in the University of Virginia's Department of Sociology; I interviewed the majority of the respondents myself, and interviewers are identified in the text where need be by initials.

26. Of course, other stances exist—in particular, a few seem to use "authenticity" as a measure of the good, which seems to limit one's obligations, and posit being true to one's self as a central goal, as opposed to being hypocritical. This notion overlaps with independence in the crucial dimensions, however, in that it expects little constancy and engenders little compromise; thus I do not elaborate upon it here. The three I outline were the most important among my interviewees.

CHAPTER 2

1. In Kletzer's (2001) careful study of jobs lost in sectors subject to foreign competition (such the one in which Beth's husband worked), 69 percent of those who lose their jobs (excluding in manufacturing) found full-time employment, 55 percent of the reemployed took lower-paying jobs, and as many as a quarter of them took jobs that involved pay cuts of 30 percent or more. In about one-third to one-half of all families with working wives, women make as much or more than their husbands (except in the lowest-income families, where almost 70 percent of wives do), according to a study of census data conducted by the Center for American Progress, a Washington think tank. Women are the breadwinners (or "co-breadwinners," making more than 25 percent of household income) in 63.9 percent of families, they report. See Glynn (2012).

2. Lane (2011) offers a powerful account of how unemployed workers expect insecurity and manage their own readiness for it.

3. See Kalleberg (2009) for a persuasive marshaling of the evidence of increasing job insecurity.

4. Those in this study who thought employers owed workers very little were most of those employed in the insecure economy; the stably employed felt differently, which I discuss further in chapter 7. The one-way honor system may be gendered: Erickson and Pierce (2005) found that women and men service workers diverged in loyalty, with women reporting much more; using a sample of paralegals and restaurant workers, they report women talked about personal loyalty to their bosses, while the men portrayed themselves as "occupational transients" on their way to better jobs or, in the case of waiters, eschewed loyalty in defiance of the poor jobs available to working-class men. Generational cohorts may also differ in their propensity to take part in the "one-way honor system": compared to the Baby Boom and Millennial generations, young workers of Generation X (aged eighteen to twenty-seven in 1992) were most likely to report working hard (Rubin 2012). As parents of teenagers at the time of their interview, most people in this study were in this cohort, now aged forty to sixty.

5. Some researchers have explored similar questions under the rubric of the "psychological contract," the "beliefs, values, expectations and aspirations of the employer and employee" (Smithson and Lewis 2000:682). I contend the cultural material that makes up the "contract" is itself something to investigate; in the United States, this cultural material helps to benefit employers through the one-way honor system. The "psychological contract," then, is embedded in a cultural and economic system that offers us a limited set of such "contracts" that we might strike with one another; indeed, the very notion of "contract" assumes a quid-pro-quo approach to obligation, a cultural framework that is apt for some people but utterly inapplicable to others, such as the commitment heroes I chronicle in chapter 6. This book aims to chart these cultural frameworks and how they act to bridge insecurity culture at work and at home.

6. Psychology and organizational behavior studies have parsed "work ethic" into multiple measures, including such dimensions as job involvement, occupational commitment, organizational commitment, work engagement, and the like. Scholars have generally found that these measures are correlated but not redundant (Cooper-Hakim and Viswesvaran 2005). My own research considers "work ethic" to be closest to the "job involvement" measure, in which people attest to finding their identity in working hard at a particular job (Lawler and Hall 1970). Later, I distinguish between the overall work ethic and a group of respondents who promulgated a "high-performance, low-loyalty" approach; these informants' work ethic was closest to an occupational commitment measure. For an analysis of gender and "discretionary work effort," see Kmec and Gorman (2010:3); for an influential piece on job involvement, see Lawler and Hall (1970). For a review and meta-analysis of job involvement research, see S. P. Brown (1996). For the correlations of different measures of "work commitment," see Cooper-Hakim and Viswesvaran (2005). For work tracking the "lottery question" over time, see Highhouse, Zickar, and Yankelevich (2010) and Weaver (1997). See also Blair-Loy (2003).

7. Every year MetLife does an annual study of employee benefits; its release is often an occasion for hand-wringing in the business press. The 10th Annual MetLife Study of Employee Benefits Trends, released in March 2012, reported employee loyalty had reached a seven-year low, with 42 percent of employees reporting that they felt a strong sense of loyalty to their employers. Generally, however, and perhaps not coincidentally, research has moved away from questions of loyalty or work commitment to measures of "work engagement." Prevailing measures of work engagement seem almost oddly personal—Gallup has a standard

assessment that features statements like "My supervisor or someone at work seems to care about me as a person." One cannot help but wonder about these kinds of measures, which do not ask about expectations of job security or anything that might obligate the employer. Why are we looking at how workers are bound to their jobs on an emotional and personal level but leaving questions of what employers owe their employees unasked? As it turns out, this scholarship matches how many workers themselves feel: bound to their work on a personal level, one that goes beyond simple calculations of effort, and no longer asking much of anything from employers. The widely reported 83 percent figure is from Right Management, a research arm of ManpowerGroup, which surveyed people who happened upon their online instrument; the national survey reporting that the number was actually 21 percent comes from Harris Interactive. See Right Management (2013) and CareerBuilder (2014). See also TNS Research (n.d.).

8. For workers of every race, gender, wage, see Mishel (2013). For the parity in hours worked in the United States and Europe in the 1970s and the subsequent diverging trend, see Alesina, Glaeser, and Sacerdote (2006). For US and OECD work hours, see OECD StatExtracts (n.d.). See also Hochschild (1997).

9. Survey research suggests that the higher the socioeconomic status, the more likely a person is to consider that employer loyalty has waned. In one 2006 report, almost 70 percent of college graduates said employers showed less loyalty today than 20 or 30 years ago. The 2006 report found that the more money people made, the more education they had, if they were employed, or if they were white—all indicators of greater privilege—the more likely they were to find that employer loyalty had declined. See Pew Research Center (2006). For the reversal of wages and hours worked, see Kuhn and Lozano (2008). See also Ferris (2009).

10. Mercer reported the figures for employees' "going beyond" and having a "strong sense of commitment," based on a random survey of 2,400 US workers. The report of US employee satisfaction was based on a random survey of 600 sampled from the American Community Survey, analyzed by the Society for Human Resources Management. See Mercer (2011) and Society for Human Resource Management (2011). See also Lincoln and Kalleberg (1985); Luthans, McCaul, and Dodd (1985); Glazer, Daniel, and Short (2004); and Near (1989). For "work devotion," see Blair-Loy (2003) For low-income people who do not want to support "those who don't want to work," see Sherman (2009).

11. Robin Leidner notes that "for most women, the decline in traditional limitations has meant a dramatic increase in the importance of paid work for self-identity" (Leidner 2006:430). For work on young adults, see Rosenfeld (2007) and Silva (2013).

12. Only a handful of people took exception to these intense proclamations of dedication to the job: those who were explicit about making their family needs a priority, promulgating what I came to consider a "care work ethic" explored in later chapters. In addition, the only significant exceptions to the prevailing low expectations for loyalty from employers were those men and women who worked in putatively stable jobs, either for family firms or in stable working-class jobs protected by strong community norms and contracts; we hear more about them in chapter 7.

13. Karen Ho's book (2009; quotation from p. 122) offers a fascinating anthropology of Wall Street deconstructing the inevitability of insecurity culture. In *A Company of One*, Carrie Lane (2011:161–162) reports the prevalence of the notion of the inevitability of insecurity in her study of laid-off white-collar workers, and makes

note of its cultural and political costs: "Even as they and their families stagger under the heavy burden of those costs [of insecure white-collar employment], job seekers continue to conceptualize the system as inevitable, looking for ways to manage it, rather than change it. . . . Their adherence to the principles of career management renders other ways of explaining and reacting to the situation invisible."

14. For the firm-level economic consequences of layoffs, see Baumol, Blinder, and Wolff (2003); see also McCall (2004).

15. The Dutch also have a longstanding norm of job security that endures today, researchers maintain (Pruijt and Derogee 2010). After sampling more than eleven thousand people across eighteen European countries, Salladarré, Hlaimi, and Wolff (2011:555) reported: "Job security is viewed as at least important by more than 85 percent of European wage-earners." (But see Smithson and Lewis [2000:684] for a study of young people in the United Kingdom finding that "job security, though desired by most, is not expected.") For unionized Denmark, see Wilthagen, Tros, and van Lieshout (2003). See also Wilthagen and Tros (2004), Viebrock and Clasen (2009),and European Commission (2007).

16. *Heroes of Their Own Lives* is the title of Linda Gordon's excellent history of family violence in Boston (1988).

17. Among the thirty-three who had been laid off, twenty-two did not blame their employers (and of the eleven who did, five blamed multiple people, from mothers to coworkers to friends—these were angry people generally). Those who declined to blame their employers included single mothers, people who had received no severance, and others who were in particularly strapped situations thanks to their job dislocation. What people tell interviewers is often what they think is valid or reasonable; we have to do a little more digging, analyzing their words for metaphor, omissions, and buried emotion to get at ideas or feelings they might try to hide. See the appendix for more details about what we can take from interviewing. See also Pugh (2013).

18. Most studies of layoffs and their aftermath focus on the impact on downsizing "survivors," or those who remain with the firm, rather than victims (or, for that matter, those who implement the downsizing). Of course, responses to involuntary job loss can vary; there is also some evidence that they vary over time, resembling a grieving process. In my research, most interviewees had been laid off within the year prior to our conversation, with a handful recalling a job loss from several years ago; according to existing research, this kind of sample (with more recent layoff victims) would tend to overestimate the extent of anger. In an influential qualitative study, Kets de Vries (Kets de Vries and Balazs 1997) found four types of layoff victims: the adaptable, or those who move on to new jobs and see themselves as better off; those who make major life changes; the depressed, as the laid-off "quite regularly" become stuck in the mourning process; and those who get angry. The first three of these map loosely onto the types I outline here, adopting stances of anticipation, self-blame, resignation, and defiance. De Vries is less interested in worker attribution of blame, however, and thus he includes in the latter "angry" category those who aim their antagonism at their families. I think we should make careful note of where people direct their anger; I find few are angry at work, and I explore their anger at home in chapter 5. For studies of layoff victims, see Devine et al. (2003) and Makawatsakul and Kleiner (2003); see McKee-Ryan et al. (2005) for a review of the literature on the unemployed.

19. We might dub them "meta-feelings," those feelings we have about our feelings. Arlie Hochschild coined the term "feeling rules" in a 1979 article, and explored them further in *The Managed Heart* (1983); in a 1990 essay, she similarly considers the differences between "what we think we should feel, what we try to feel, and what we actually feel." Thanks to Rose Butler for the 1990 reference.

20. See Clark (1997).

21. I do not imply that there is some sort of precultural emotion residing deep within that then conflicts with "feeling rules." Instead, meta-feelings capture the felt collision between two levels of culturally shaped emotions—a deep, primal level often forged earlier and another generated by the cultural frameworks of the social contexts in which we find ourselves today. Meta-feelings thus document the distance (in time or in space) between cultural codes and the emotional culture that accompanies them. See also Pugh (2013).

22. For deskilled work, see Braverman (1974).

23. Stegner (1987:135).

CHAPTER 3

1. Relocated people come in various kinds, of course—some are forced to move or risk losing their jobs, while others are lured to move, promised advancement as they learn more about different branches of the company; those who move on their own to get somewhere without a job beforehand are in a separate, more desperate, category that resembles the laid-off enough for me to combine them in my analysis. Most of the relocators in this study are of the more privileged kind, enticed to move by employers who are grooming them for higher positions. As Kilborn (2009:5) writes, "A record of periodic relocation—climbing the ranks of one company or bounding from company to company—can grease the way to chief executive." About a third of recently appointed CEOs of Fortune 1000 companies had worked in three or more locations, at their own companies or other ones, Kilborn reports.

2. The "Divorce Divide" is a term Martin (2004) uses to describe the divergence of divorce rates by education, as college-educated people are more likely to stay married than those with less education (Stevenson and Wolfers 2007). See also chapter 1, fn 6.

3. Fligstein and Shin (2004).

4. See Damaske (2011).

5. Industrial psychologists use the concept "organizational commitment" to include the idea of commitment-as-longevity. Those who promulgate a "high-performance, low-loyalty" approach are closest to an "occupational commitment" measure.

6. In addition to these workers, another group appeared more likely to profess high work commitment but low organizational loyalty: men employed as teachers. I talked to three who revealed this approach to work. Said Barry, for example: "I haven't set down a lot of roots; I've just gone in and fixed big problems. [Working at my current school] was the first time I really felt connected. So not only did I come in and sweep out the problem, but now I've even decorated my office." While this group is too small for us to say so definitively, it is possible that the men teachers used the high-performance, low-loyalty narrative in order to perform masculinity in a feminized profession. This cultural frame allows them to sound like active, flexible, risk-takers, with all the dynamism of hegemonic masculinity, as opposed to the safe, sedentary, predictability of a tenured jobholder. Other men employed in masculine-typed stable occupations such as police work and firefighting did not feel compelled to adopt this language.

7. The figures on what is important to employees come from Society for Human Resource Management (2011). Lane's thought-provoking book *A Company of One* (2011) reported that laid-off workers in Texas espoused ideologies that seemed to embody the neoliberal privatization of risk and responsibility, so that they almost seem to be cheerleaders for "managing their own career," even as it trapped them in what Lane identifies as "wrenching moments" of joblessness, depression, and poverty. Smith (2001:148) also found that job club staff encouraged clients to "reinvent themselves" to suit the new economy, furnishing "tips about how the hidden job market works [that] put the responsibility for success or failure soundly on the shoulders of each unemployed individual."

8. See N. Lee (2001) for an interesting discussion of how conventional understandings of adulthood and childhood as opposites are predicated on a particular Fordist organization of stable, secure work, and how the new economy, hand in hand with new concepts of the evolving self, are upending these old oppositions.

9. Of course, these career aptitude tests have been around since the birth of vocational psychology, when after World War I they were used to place immigrants into industrial jobs. See Savickas and Baker (2005).

10. For the "portfolio career," see Handy (1989); for the "boundaryless" one, see Arthur and Rousseau (1996).

11. The moral wall also separates work and home even when the distinctions between these domains are blurry, as they are for many, since paid work actually permeates intimate life in many ways, and vice versa. Mary and Peter, for example, had incorporated Peter's boss into their family lives as a godfather. Yet recall from the last chapter that after he sold the company, left with his winnings, and stopped seeing them socially, Mary said she wouldn't expect anything more, because it was just "what you would do" in the business world. At the same time, Mary and Peter practiced such an extreme form of loyalty in their family life that they were paradigmatic examples of the "rescuing" profiled in chapter 6. Even as their work and family lives were knit together so as to make unclear where one ended and the other began, Mary thus imposed and patrolled a border to sharply distinguish them as two worlds, with distinct rules and expectations about what we owe each other. The moral wall divided symbolically what was actually, for Mary and Peter, as for many people, a more integrated whole.

12. Still, a majority of all categories said they believe in soul mates, including 65 percent of college graduates, 70 percent of people with greater than $50,000 in income, and 68 percent of white people. See Marist Poll (2011). A 2001 Gallup survey of adults in their twenties found an even higher percentage, reporting that 88 percent believed that there was a "soul mate waiting for you somewhere out there," and 94 percent agreed that "when you marry, you want your spouse to be a soul mate, first and foremost." See Maybury (2002).

13. These more contemporary phrases join others with longer histories, such as "Jewish mother" or "mama's boy," both images involving mothers who are too controlling, too involved. Conversely, we have perhaps fewer that portray leaving in a negative light, as, say, negligence or abandonment, such as "deadbeat dad" or "slacker." See Antler (2007).

14. In general, the jokes were a way to dwell in what we might call, following the psychoanalytic theorist D. W. Winnicott, a "transitional" space, or what the anthropologist Victor Turner termed "liminality," an in-between area not of either/or but rather both/and, where meanings are fluid, contested and blurry, where people can actually innovate with preexisting cultural frames in what the

anthropologist Sherry Ortner (1996) called "serious games." The jokes were also lighthearted ways of addressing the frighteningly high stakes of the issues involved: How much can I count on you? How long will she be around? If everyone else is leaving whenever they want to, why won't you? These are profoundly important, even threatening questions that strike at the heart of what matters most to people, and because of insecurity culture, these questions are also ever present. Jokes skirt the issues while simultaneously raising them.

15. Stearns (1994). Stearns, an emotional historian, has argued that Americans' detached emotional style dates to the early twentieth century. He contends that consumerism, bureaucratization, and homogenization were among the factors repressing emotional intensity. Yet in the realm of intimate life, he noted (Stearns 1999:29) that "despite strict injunctions to keep their emotions under control, twentieth-century Americans value emotional ties to the family and have even invented a demanding category of intimacy—which, ironically in many cases, makes family a less comfortable refuge." This book documents that if Americans are indeed learning to become more detached in their intimate lives, urged by broad cultural patterns to practice a "cold intimacy" of the sort Illouz (2007) suggested, it is for some a painful process, made more visible by its very difficulty. See chapter 5, for example.

16. Of course, the analysis that follows necessarily sets aside the whole question of how good a match these partnerships actually are, as we had no way of knowing just how much compromise or how much surrender each entailed, not to mention how much is too much; we can rely only on their own statements about this.

17. Women with more education are more likely to be employed, and reports of an "opting out" trend have been much exaggerated (Stone 2007). Nonetheless, over the last fifteen years, there has been a steady trickle of highly educated married women pulling out of the labor force as their husbands have benefited more from an increasing skills premium. Two Columbia University economists found that the labor force participation of college-educated women married to men with college degrees who are top earners in their profession had dropped by 20 percent from 1995 to 2005. These are women who are making the same gamble as Rochelle and Lawrence. See Albanesi and Prados (2011) and Barghini (2012).

18. Hackstaff (1999).

19. Of course perfect does not exist, and so on one level the pragmatism of these strategies was assuredly right. Without evaluating their relationships, however, we cannot say how significant those disappointments they tucked away as "realistic" are, but we can nonetheless analyze the means by which they stay in these relationships despite them.

20. Many (but not all) of our relocator interviews were with the spouse of the main jobholder whose employer had moved them, although most of these spouses also worked, albeit in jobs that made less money and involved fewer hours.

21. Most of the people I spoke to in this study were in heterosexual relationships. While Stevenson and Wolfers (2007) report that the college-educated are more likely to stay married (see note 2 of this chapter), there is less information about the comparative divorce rates of working-class couples with stable employment, partly because there are fewer and fewer of these couples as a result of the decimation of American manufacturing and because some of the stable working-class jobs include police and firefighting, jobs whose workers have been shown to bring their stress home with them, creating marital discord (Rogers and May 2003). In addition, job insecurity differs from unemployment, and while there is plenty of

work on the relationship stressors of the latter, the former presents some challenges for scholars to measure, as we have seen. Most important for this omis-
sion, however, research reporting the divorce divide has focused primarily on the
correlation of education levels and divorce, reflecting in part data availability
issues, but potentially (albeit unintentionally) conflating high school graduate
education level with unstable employment, for example. See Charles and Stephens (2004).

CHAPTER 4

1. Fiona's stance toward commitment recalls the "bounded authenticity" on offer
   among the sex workers Elizabeth Bernstein studied in her book *Temporarily Yours*
   (2007). Bernstein argues that not just prostitution but also intimacy in the general population is increasingly characterized by this trend, in part because it
   dovetails with the fluid, flexible, amorphous relations of the postindustrial
   economy.
2. Fligstein and Shin (2004)
3. The prisoners' dilemma refers to a famous hypothetical case that formed the
   basis of game theory, created by mathematicians in the 1950s to measure the
   likelihood of cooperation and defection. Briefly, it involves two people who stand
   to gain if they cooperate and lose if they do not, but, because they do not know of
   the other's choice, are predicted to act in their own rational self-interest and thus
   to incur a penalty. By analogy, both employer and employee stand to gain within
   the confines of stable employment, especially with training and other invest-
   ments in the long-term employee; conversely, each loses the most if the other
   leaves first, and both lose a bit within the context of assumed insecurity, in which
   neither commits to the other. Only a handful of my respondents talked like
   Fiona, but we cannot know from the limited, nonrandom sample that forms the
   basis of this book how prevalent her approach is. Still, conventional notions of
   gender generally call on women to demonstrate more loyalty at home, as we see
   in chapter 6. When it comes to work, researchers find that when we control for
   the kind of jobs men and women hold, there is no appreciable gender difference
   in their organizational commitment (Marsden, Kalleberg, and Cook 1993); see
   also chapter 2, note 6. Pockets of evidence thus suggest "defying" is rare.
4. See Utrata (forthcoming).
5. Arlie Hochschild captured the appeal of work compared to the messy conflict of
   home in her book *The Time Bind* (1997:37). "I walk in the door and the minute I
   turn the key in the lock my older daughter is there. . . . The baby is up. She should
   have been in bed two hours ago and that upsets me. The dishes are still in the
   sink. . . . My husband is in the other room hollering to my daughter, 'Tracy I
   don't ever get any time to talk to your mother because you're always monopoliz-
   ing her time before I even get a chance!' They all come at me at once. . . . I usually
   come to work early just to get away from the house."
6. Illouz (2012:246) offers a trenchant sociological analysis of "commitment
   phobia," invoking an ecology and architecture of romantic choice that favors
   those who create scarcity, and thus value, amid sexual abundance. She cautions
   against the drive for invulnerability. "The goal of gender equality is not equal detachment, but an equal capacity to experience strong and passionate emotions,"
   she writes. "It is now time we re-examine the state of estrangement and alienation created by the interaction and intersection of emotions, sexual freedom and
   economics . . . which has interfered with the capacity of men and women to forge

intense, all-involving meaningful bonds." Illouz calls upon us to rearticulate passionate models of love in a world that she sees as entirely too detached, dislodged from passion by the commodification of sexual freedom.

7. Fiona's story is unique, to be sure. The number of jobs and intimate partners Fiona has had since Jimmy was born makes her atypical. But while 19 percent of my sample (fifteen out of eighty) had had at least three serious relationships since their first child was born, there is evidence to suggest this fraction is not far off of their occurrence in the US population. Survey data have found that 10 percent of American women had three or more husbands or live-in partners by age thirty-five (Cherlin 2009); people in this study, whose teenaged child (the question by which they were screened) was sometimes their last child rather than their first, were generally older than that, with an average age of forty-five, and thus with more chance of losing and acquiring new partners. Cherlin's report was based on unpublished tabulations by Jeffrey Timberlake and Patrick Heuveline, and can be found in his book *The Marriage-Go-Round* (2009). For the deinstitutionalization of the working class, see Murray (2012).

8. There is some evidence that those who subscribe to the notion of "romantic destiny," as embodied in the "soul mate" idea, as opposed to the idea that a relationship grows over time, are more likely to disengage from a relationship when conflict arises (see Knee et al. 2004). But Swidler (2001) found that Americans tend to hold both ideas in their heads at any given time, and use explanations to justify practices instead of to motivate them; I argue that while both notions are available, they each ally with different collections of belief and practices that comprise the stances toward obligation, and while people can avail themselves of different stances, switching from one to the other can be painful, suggesting that cultural ideas can be anchored to our identities by powerful emotions.

9. Behind the independent talk lie the difficult economic straits of these women, as Susan Thistle's book (2006) documents. She writes of how women's household work changed in the postwar era to dislodge the support of the men, employers, and the state, *before* the much-analyzed disappearance of working-class men's jobs; the marketization of care work, and its continued devaluation as women's work, produced great gains for employers and the state. The "new economy of the twenty-first century . . . has taken too much of women's time while paying too little for it," she writes (140). She contends that "the turn from marriage to the market has been more abrupt, the loss of support from men and the state more complete, and the consequences of that loss much harsher for the less-educated, and for black women overall" (173). Thus we can see why working-class women at once "value" marriage so highly and yet declare their own independence.

10. Rosalind Gill (2008:443) makes note of the parallels between the neoliberal self and that which is summoned by postfeminism. "The autonomous, calculating, self-regulating subject of neoliberalism bears a strong resemblance to the active, freely choosing, self-reinventing subject of postfeminism . . . suggest[ing], then, that postfeminism is not simply a response to feminism but also a sensibility that is at least partly constituted through the pervasiveness of neoliberal ideas," she writes.

11. Corse and Silva (in press) similarly find a grim independence among the working-class women they interviewed, for whom intimacy threatens their self-sufficiency. One woman declares: "I'd rather be alone and fierce than in a relationship and be milquetoast."

12. Judith Stacey writes: "We cannot will our desires or funnel them into a single, culturally prescribed domestic norm. . . . No family system is ideal, and no family form can be best for everyone" (2011:203–207). See also Burgess, Propper, and Aassve (2003).

13. Fiona's philosophy echoes that of the "pure relationship" sketched out by Anthony Giddens, the quintessence of two "free-floating" souls sharing intimacy "for whatever rewards that relationship as such can deliver" (1991:6). In this vision of intimacy unfettered by the baggage of kinship, community, and economic and other kinds of dependence, Giddens outlines what happens when people come together entirely of their own free will, and for only as long as they choose. Interestingly, Giddens argues that these relationships involve true commitment, because there is nothing else keeping them together. "Commitment, within the pure relationship, is essentially what replaces the external anchors that close personal connections used to have in pre-modern situations" (92). Zygmunt Bauman (2003) and Ulrich Beck and Elisabeth Beck-Gernsheim (1995) also argued that contemporary intimacy has become individualized, disenchanted, and contractual.

14. See Fischer (2012).

15. See Coontz (2005:306). The trends for cohabitation breakups are harder to discern; a careful review of data for Great Britain found that couples who started cohabiting in the 1980s had about the same likelihood of breaking up as couples who started cohabiting in the 1960s. See Murphy (2000).

16. Scholars have long noted the sex-segregated social and working lives of the working class, in which connections to extended kin prove as or more important than the marital dyad, especially for women (Bott 1957, Young and Willmott 1962, Stack 1974). Some scholars (e.g., Roschelle 1997) suggest that extended family ties have since attenuated among low-income people, particularly people of color, arguing that we can no longer assume they make up for resource constraints and the withdrawal of state support; Desmond (2012) explores how extended kin support is augmented and in some cases supplanted by the "disposable ties" of near strangers upon whom the poor quickly and substantially rely. Still, as Sarkisian (2006: 810) observes, some scholars (e.g., Bengtson 2001) argue that "rather than poor African American families becoming 'more nuclear,' White poor and middle-class families are becoming 'more extended.'" Extended kin relationships, especially to maternal relatives, are often crucial sources of all kinds of support for working-class women, in part explaining why Fiona maintains them so assiduously.

17. See Hochschild (2012).

18. Hochschild (1997) identifies "needs reduction" as a core strategy of those two-income families who struggle to accommodate the intense time demands of the job and the care needs of their families. They thus make cultural adaptations in their family lives to submit to increased demands from work. Defying seems to involve a similar process, in which people continually shrink potential emotional needs in service to their own independence: if need is diminished, then their obligation is as well.

19. Most children of divorce demonstrate no significant difference in outcomes from children of parents who stay married. See, for example, Kelly and Emery (2003) and Cherlin et al. (1991).

20. A few mothers used children as metaphorical detachment brokers when they talked about dissolving their own marriages. "They actually were the ones who

finally told me to have him [her first husband] leave," recalled Amelia, who had refused to merge money with her second husband. "Because I would have put up with anything for them, until like 'Please, can you make him go away?' So that's all it took. I said, 'Okay, it's going to be a tough road but we'll do it.'"

21. Given the differences we have seen between "independence" or "pragmatism" and who invokes which ones when, however, one might be forgiven for thinking that these principles simply stem from economic realities. Among those with insecure work, class inequality shapes the differences between the elite professionals— whose backgrounds, resources, and skills allow them to both pick and choose at work and to commit at home—and the less advantaged. Yet the principles are more than filmy rationalizations draped over material causes, since the less advantaged avail themselves of two options—independence or, as we shall see in the next chapter, a gendered interpretation of duty—to lend deeper meaning to the paucity of their choices.

CHAPTER 5

1. Freud (1966:214) used the term "displacement" to describe, among other phenomena, when one moved feelings that were threatening or difficult to feel from one person or situation to another, as when "the psychical accent is shifted from an important element on to another which is unimportant."
2. In this study, laid-off people were much more likely to talk about betrayal at home, participating in the displacing that Gary typifies. While disadvantaged laid-off men were the most likely to sound like Gary, disadvantaged laid-off women appeared to have two choices: duty or independence. I argue in this chapter that their choice—and men's seeming lack of one—stems from the gendered trajectory of entitlement, which dampens women's expectations of the other, even as it heightens men's.
3. Among others, Susan Faludi's *Stiffed* (1999) is in this ilk. Kimmel (2013:23) also writes: "Even before the anger is pain, the injury of losing something valuable, precious, something that your father may have entrusted to you, or more likely, that you felt your father was supposed to entrust you before he lost your birthright."
4. Fine et al. (1997) studied white working-class boys displacing their rage about postindustrial changes onto racial and gendered others in the 1990s.
5. Townsend (2002).
6. Figures are from Blau and Kahn (2006). They write (61): "Trends in inequality among women [demonstrate] a deterioration in the relative economic status of less educated women that is strikingly parallel to similar trends in the labor market for men."
7. See Hochschild (1989).
8. In contrast to the unmoored self theorized by Giddens, Bauman, and Beck, Illouz (2007) argues that people are not just disengaging; they are channeling their emotional engagement in very particular ways, under increasing pressure to rationalize their emotional life, to fit their emotions into a modular world that enables them to transition smoothly across work teams and worksites.
9. In this they echo what Kathleen Gerson (2010) documented in her study of young adults and their hopes for coupling: while most people wanted to share the burdens of work and caring, where the genders diverged was in their backup plans, when men would settle for traditional families and women settle for going it alone.

10. Ronnie Dunn, recording of Dunn and Coleman (2011).
11. My language here borrows from Pugh (2013).
12. Russo (2001:275).
13. For the costs of masculinity, see Messner (2000:6). For men's work devotion, see Townsend (2002) and Loscocco and Spitze (2007).
14. Nicholas Townsend documents how heterosexual men connect to their families through provisioning, and often to their children through their wives (Townsend 2002).
15. One *Boston Globe* article on "Gen X dads" opened with the claim that "luxury vacations, fast-track careers, and bigger houses used to be a priority for family men, but no longer. Today's young fathers are taking paternity leaves, rejecting overtime, and rushing home after work to do all the things many of their own fathers didn't" (Wen 2005). For the bifurcating trends of fatherhood, see Coltrane (2004) and Pew Research Center (2011). Thanks to Tristan Bridges for the reference.
16. The US Census reports that 15 percent of single parents are men, who in 2011 numbered 1.7 million (US Census 2011).
17. Arlie Hochschild (2003:16) talks about "magnified moments" as "episodes of heightened importance, either epiphanies, moments of intense glee or unusual insight, or moments in which things go intensely but meaningfully wrong." They perform an important symbolic function, coming to represent something crucial for us in our narratives.
18. For an account of how children act as a tether or witness for working-class young parents, see Silva and Pugh (2010).
19. Burchell (2005) reviews the literature on how insecurity shapes family functioning, noting that those families who can shift roles are less likely to experience marital disruption. See also Hochschild (1989) and Gerson (2010).
20. For the night-shift nurses study, see Garey (1995).
21. Can men as individuals undo the structural knots of gender? Christine Williams's work on the "glass escalator" and other benefits accrued to male nurses and other men who work in nontraditional occupations (1995) forces us to be careful when we make claims about gender innovation. The very way in which some of the caregiving men in my study are still held accountable for "doing gender," still called to order by those well-meaning outsiders who commend them for not walking away, for example, suggests that "undoing gender" on a broad cultural level will take more than these individuals charting their own path. In addition, Bridges and Pascoe (2014) argue that new "hybrid masculinities" often reinscribe privilege. Yet the men in this chapter, while heterosexual and white, are not the young, middle-class men that populate much other scholarship on new masculinities; instead, as the laid-off middle-aged, they are struggling with what feels like failures in their other domains. Furthermore, each of these men was trying to redefine care so that it did not reconstruct a gender binary; they undertook to establish good care as part of what it means to be a good parent, rather than a good mother, and to value traditionally feminine ideals of nurture and support. As such I argue it is a form of gender innovation, a personal undoing of gender that is surely at least one step forward, albeit short of the institutional change we would need in order to undo gender on a social scale. For the original piece introducing "doing gender," see West and Zimmerman (1987).
22. As Barbara Risman (2009:82) put it: "We need to be able to differentiate when husbands and wives are doing gender traditionally and when they are undoing it—or at least trying to undo it." West and Zimmerman (2009) argue that

because we can never be free of our accountability to others for our performance of gender, we are able only to "redo gender." This phrase does not quite seem to capture what Clark and others are doing, however, because his actions—meeting his daughter on the bus, making sure she has a hot breakfast—do wrest duties of parenting out of the gender binary, albeit in his limited milieu. See also Connell (2010).

CHAPTER 6

1. To some degree, insecurity appears to be segregated—some of the stably employed in this study, living in small towns or cities with people they have known all their lives, did not seem to run across job insecurity very often. Theresa had to rack her brain to think of people who changed jobs frequently. "I don't know who they are. I don't know, they're not people I know. Yeah, like I'm thinking, I very rarely even have to change an e-mail address." Perhaps it was this segregation of insecurity that meant many relocated and stably employed people in my sample did not seem to see dire needs as often as laid-off people did.
2. How did I decide what counted as rescuing? I let them tell me: if their stories involved lengthy hardship in order to care for someone in need, at what they perceived as substantial sacrifice, they were counted here. This definition means I perhaps missed people who declined to spell out how hard they had it, for example, but I would argue that over the course of a long, emotional conversation, those details are going to emerge, regardless of your predilection for noting them. As part of a qualitative study, these numbers can tell us little about the prevalence of rescuing—extreme or otherwise—in the general population. We can surmise only that they exist, and that they are rare. Rather, in-depth studies show us how they understand the world and justify their actions, such as the meanings that make their acts comprehensible.
3. Linda Blum (2007) has written about the "invisible disabilities" of children's social/emotional/behavioral disorders and the challenges they pose, mostly for mothers, in navigating institutions in an "era of public stinginess."
4. Patchett (2011:233).
5. Cheadle, Amato, and King (2010) found 32 percent of fathers see their children once a year or less, while Ward (2008) reported that nearly one out of seven seniors had not seen at least one of their living adult children in over a year.
6. Scholars have found that men are much more likely to divorce a seriously ill spouse than are women (Glantz et al. 2009; thanks to Cameron MacDonald for the reference). Of the seventeen cases of commitment heroism in the study, fourteen are women (more than the study sample's 3:1 gender ratio would predict).
7. The Census Bureau reports that in 2012 there were 10.3 million single mothers and 1.9 million single fathers living with children younger than eighteen. See US Census (2012a).
8. The Urban Institute reports that even in the difficult financial climate of 2008–2010, the federal welfare program Temporary Assistance for Needy Families did not step up to the plate. During these years, the unemployment rate increased 88 percent, while the national caseload increased by only 14 percent, they report. See Zedlewski and Loprest (2011).
9. Orloff writes that a state is woman-friendly to the extent that it makes her survival less dependent on marriage. "The capacity to form and maintain an autonomous household relieves women of the compulsion to enter or stay in a marriage

because of economic vulnerability," she says. "The right of exit—in this case, to be able to choose not to enter or stay in a marriage—alters the power relations within marriages," with implications for gender-based violence (Orloff 1993:321).

10. Stepfathers have more mixed effects on children: interestingly, recent research takes issue with the notion that as one father steps in, another must back off; scholars have argued that of three options for children's experience in mother-stepfather families—father accumulation, substitution, or loss—the accumulation model is rarer, but can produce the best outcomes (White and Gilbreth 2001, Pryor 2008). See also chapter 1, note 7, as well as McLanahan and Sandefur (1994), Popenoe (1996), and S. L. Brown (2006).

11. Chabon (2012:133). The "othermothers" Patricia Hill Collins describes are an African-American icon, those women who, like Mrs. Wiggins from Chabon's novel, take on all the need that they can carry, patching together communities rent by poverty and incarceration, and bringing their people to safety. See Collins (2000).

12. Mary is cynical as she talks about the school's rising to help Eric during this period. "We couldn't get any support until he was a senior in high school, and all of a sudden because he would go in and tell them, 'Oh my parents kicked me out.' You know these horrendous stories. So now he's a victim so the school is, like, working to help him. I'm like, 'We would have done this years ago if we knew this is how you get them to help you.'"

13. See Silverstein (1964).

CHAPTER 7

1. People who perceive their jobs are secure have more job satisfaction and job involvement, sleep better, and experience less anxiety, researchers have found. For a meta-analysis and review, see Sverke, Hellgren, and Näswall (2002); for sleep and anxiety, see Burchell (2009).

2. Most of the stably employed in this study are teachers, police officers, or firefighters, but there are also accountants and paraprofessionals in other private-sector settings, including small family firms. Of course, small firms have a much higher failure rate than large firms; among those that survive, however, there is evidence that family firms offer more stable employment than large firms. While they are not protected by collective bargaining—Virginia features low private-sector unionization (just 5 percent in 2013), and a longstanding ban on such action by public employees—some of these work settings resemble those of unionized employees in other states, particularly in the longevity of their jobs. The Virginia State Supreme Court outlawed collective bargaining for public sector employees in 1977, however, and these occupations are now represented by "voluntary associations" that offer "input" that the state's governor has called "helpful." For family firms, see J. Lee (2006). See also Mora (2011). Virginia's private-sector unionization is less than half of the US average of 11.3 percent. See Bureau of Labor Statistics (2014b). See the appendix to this volume for a discussion of how Virginia's antiunion laws established the setting for the stably employed in this study.

3. For a discussion of how advertising raises and then puts to rest particular anxieties, see Pugh (2005).

4. While 23 percent of first marriages of women with just high school degrees end in divorce or separation after five years, 26 percent of those of women with some

college do, twice the rate of those marriages of women with college degrees. See Cherlin (2009:168) and Martin (2004). See also chapter 3, notes 2 and 19.

5. There are a number of alternative explanations, however. Many of the stably employed I spoke with had been married for decades; perhaps there was some selection effect here, and if I had spoken to more stably employed who were divorced, then I would hear more about their independence or their duty betrayed. This "selection" critique assumes that one's experience of enduring marriage is what produces the pragmatism, rather than one's experience of job security. Or perhaps one's experiences of relationship longevity and a stable job are themselves caused by an unrelated factor that happens to coincide with pragmatism. Of course, I did include divorced people among the stably employed with whom I spoke, and almost all of them had been remarried or repartnered for more than ten years, and most of these also adopted a pragmatic stance to discuss their intimate lives. There were also divorced stably employed people who had not been repartnered who spoke with a pragmatic emphasis. But ultimately, we can only suggest what these stances "cause," and what "causes" them, given the scope of this study. In-depth, interpretive, cross-sectional (conducted at any one given time) analyses such as this one with small, nonrandom samples are best at pointing out deep meanings, such as of duty or pragmatism, that arise under certain circumstances—such as when a person enjoys job security and a long intimate partnership—and suggesting where further research is needed. Longitudinal research could help to confirm the causal arrows of particular stances, the practices of commitment they engender, and longevity in either domain.

6. Almost half of the people in this study were still in their first marriage or serious partnership, and the median length of these relationships was twenty-four years; when we include those who were currently in any enduring partnership lasting ten years or more (some of which might be a cohabiting union), then it includes 58 percent of the people in the study. Most of these (about two-thirds of them) were on the more educated end of the group, in keeping with the trend of lower divorce rates for those with college education. About 60 percent of those in such enduring relationships who did not have college degrees, however, were drawn from the ranks of the stably employed (twice as many as from any other group).

CHAPTER 8

1. These notions call on women to care for children, but do so in racially distinct ways; race, and the way it shapes public and private experiences, influences how mothers talked about commitment and what they owed to which children. More African-American women, born in, and historically charged with taking care of, communities under siege, seem to have a more fluid sense of to whom children "belonged," as we saw with Nicki in chapter 6. In contrast, white people speak about being devastated if they "lost" children to other relatives. While white mothers invoked possession of their "own" children, they also sometimes talked about informally adopting neighborhood children without strong family bonds to whom they were not related. "We pick up strays," said Ellie, a white remarried mother of four. Race informed both the mandate some women of color perceived for them to defend their racial communities, expanding the definition of what children counted as kin, and the notion that some white women seemed to maintain of family as a zone of privacy and possession, into which they could invite needy others who were not kin.

2. There are many fine accounts of women's moral authority arising from their roles as mothers and its impact on politics; although the cult of domesticity was thought to be waning in the early part of the twentieth century, middle-class women in particular benefited from symbolic power stemming from maternal righteousness. "Government is only housekeeping on the broadest scale," the head of the Women's Christian Temperance Union once wrote to Susan B. Anthony (quoted in Gittell and Shtob 1980:S69). For father's property, see Mason (1994). For the cult of domesticity, see Cott (1982). For mothers' moral authority see, for example, Matthews (1987) and Gittell and Shtob (1980).

3. For children as economically priceless, see Zelizer (1985). For the individuation of children through consumption, see Cook (2004).

4. For "concerted cultivation," see Lareau (2003). For anxiety about children, see Best (1993). Karsten (2005) found three kinds of childhoods among her Dutch respondents: "outdoor," those childhoods spent outside playing without adult supervision; "indoor," those childhoods driven indoors by concerns about safety and supervision; and "backseat," those childhoods spent being transported from one activity to the next.

5. Scholars have chronicled these new rights of children, including the way in which they vary by context. Solberg (1997) argues that children have a "social age," reflecting their greater or lesser responsibilities. See also Valentin and Meinert (2009).

6. See Roche (1999), Jans (2004), and Hill et al. (2004).

7. Hays (1996) suggests that motherhood has intensified as women have joined the workforce, as their care work stands in symbolic refutation of the values of economic rationality that pervade the business world. Similarly, Hochschild (2003) argues that motherhood is hypersymbolized as a bulwark against growing commercialization of intimate life. My argument relies upon and expands these ideas, by tying trends of motherhood to the particular trends that have beset economic life, in this case insecurity. See also Bianchi (2000:404).

8. Villalobos (2010). See also Katz (2005). For the quote "what women do as mothers," as well as the argument that mothers displace their anxieties about insecurity onto their fears about children's lives, see Villalobos (2014). See also Cooper (2014).

9. For maternal ambivalence, see Almond (2010). See also Hays (1996). For the gendered system of domesticity, see J. Williams (2001); for the ratcheting up of standards of adequate mothering, see Ruddick (1998); for the hypersymbolization of the mother, see Hochschild (2003).

10. We cannot say definitively here how parents are actually raising their children, but instead merely offer a window into how they hope they are raising their children, itself an occasion for them to convey what they think is best for facing the brave new world.

11. See Barling, Zacharatos, and Hepburn (1999), Lim and Leng Loo (2003), Margolis and Farran (1984), Barling and Sorensen (1997), Stewart and Barling (1996), Flanagan and Eccles (1993), and Barling, Dupre, and Hepburn (1998).

12. Nelson (2010:31) describes how elite parents aim for flexibility in their children. "In the absence of a clear understanding of what the future might bring, elite parents seek to create adaptable children with multifaceted skills and abilities," she writes.

13. Adrie Kusserow (2004) found that parents tried to instill in their children two kinds of individualism, "hard" and "soft," mapping onto their advantage, with working-class parents focusing on their children's tough resilience, for example.

CHAPTER 9

1. Hernandez calls these "idealized breadwinner-homemaker families." When we remove the stipulation that the children be born within their parents' only marriage, or what Hernandez calls an "intact family," then the proportion of children increases, to 57 percent in 1960, although he notes that "the proportion of children living in such families never reached 60 percent" (Hernandez 1993:102).

2. This research suggests we should care about insecurity, less because of its impact on family structure than its impact on family transitions. See Amato (2010), Cherlin et al. (1991), Deleire and Kalil (2002), Wu and Thomson (2001), and S. L. Brown (2006). See also Simonson (2010:181).

3. For "may be exposed," see Patterson (2006:243). Stacey and Biblarz (2001) critique the persistent reports of "no differences," arguing instead that there are differences in children's openness to homosexuality, and that these differences are positive ones we should not downplay.

4. See Cherlin (1978), Afifi and Schrodt (2003), and Skinner and Kohler (2002).

5. The inability of the US legal system to recognize more than two parents—dubbed the doctrine of exclusive parenthood—applies not only to gay and lesbian families but also to heterosexual blended families. Because stepfamilies are more likely to divorce (Sweeney 2010, Bumpass and Raley 2007), children in these cases are then more likely to be left with only a single parent, having lost their other biological parent as well their social parent (Mason and Mauldon 1996, Skinner and Kohler 2002). The argument is being taken up by feminist legal scholars, such as Nancy Polikoff at American University's Washington College of Law. See Bartlett (2001). See also Bennett (2010) and Polikoff's blog, *Beyond (Straight and Gay) Marriage,* at http://beyondstraightandgaymarriage. blogspot.com/. For shared "parental responsibility" in the United Kingdom, see https://www.gov.uk/parental-rights-responsibilities/what-is-parental-responsibility. Accessed January 11, 2013.

6. In 2007, the European Commission issued a report defining and advocating flexicurity, in which countries were supposed to protect workers rather than particular jobs. Denmark and the Netherlands are two primary state leaders in these policies, with the latter emphasizing nonstandard workers. Critics argue the policies have ushered in more flexibility than security, especially as unemployment soars in recessionary periods. These problems are particularly acute in southern European nations like Spain, Portugal, and Italy, which have less developed social safety nets. Those social safety nets matter, as government expenditures are directly tied to the insecurity people perceive. As Mau, Mewes, and Schöneck (2012:671) conclude, "Those living in countries with higher levels of welfare state spending are considerably less concerned about their future socioeconomic standing than individuals living in countries with lower welfare state effort." An in-depth review of policy alternatives is beyond the scope of this book; see Louis Uchitelle's *The Disposable American* (2007) for an excellent discussion of other options. For an influential piece on flexicurity, see Wilthagen and Tros (2004). See also European Commission (2007), Tangian (2011), and Vermeylen (2008).

7. Kittay (2011: 56) writes: "It is the obligation and responsibility of the larger society to enable and support relations of dependency work that takes place in the more intimate settings, for that is the point and purpose of social organization—or at least a major one." See also Cooper (2014).

EPILOGUE

1. The quote comes from De Kretser's novel *The Lost Dog* (2007:197), set in Australia, where they value independence similarly. In the novel, the elderly character immigrates from India and contrasts, unsentimentally, the personalized care she would have gotten there with what was on offer in the Anglo world to which she moved. "In India, finding herself in need, she would have had recourse to a web of human relationships. Here goodwill, or at least obligation, was impersonal and administrative, though no less grudged. She was grateful for sickness benefits; later for the pension. A savings account hoarded every spare cent."

2. As we have seen, women's continued primary responsibility for caregiving, combined with the gendered social organization of poverty, means they are more likely to step forward to care for someone who needs it and, for working-class women, more likely to have to struggle to do so—the primary components of rescuing. Such women, as Annette Baier (1995 cited in Kittay 2011: 54) wrote, are the "moral proletariat."

3. On the norm of the ideal worker as one who can move, see J. Williams (2000) and Bailyn (1993). On various family forms and caregiving, see, for example, Patterson (2006); Baca Zinn (1982–1983), cited in Segura and Pierce (1993); and Rankin (2002).

4. Kittay (2011:54) argues for a public ethic of care that incorporates dependency. As she argues, "Finally if we see ourselves as always selves-in-relation, we understand that our own sense of well-being is tied to the adequate care and well-being of another. Caregiving work is the realization of this conception of self, both when we give care generously and when we receive it graciously." Yet such benefits are elusive when care is coerced. In her powerful book *Forced to Care*, Evelyn Nakano Glenn (2010) outlines the social organization of care under neoliberalism, as shaped by historical assumptions about gender, race, and class, which coerces women, particularly low-income women of color, to care for others and ensures that such care is underpaid. See also Fineman (2005). For a review on the costs and benefits of family care, see Silva and Pugh (2010).

5. Activists John de Graaf and David Batker ask this very question in their 2011 book *What's the Economy For, Anyway?*, which advocates for what they term a "solidarity economy, one that recognizes we're all in this together."

APPENDIX 1

1. Luker (2008:167).
2. The graduate student researcher was Roscoe Scarborough, a PhD student at the University of Virginia.
3. See US Census (2004).
4. For data on the population of the Richmond area and other cities, see US Census Bureau: State and County QuickFacts, Richmond City, Virginia, URL: http://quickfacts.census.gov/qfd/states/51/51760.html, accessed on January 22, 2013. For data on the top private employers, see Taylor (2012). For the data on corporate headquarters and twenty largest employers, see Zimmerman/Volk Associates (2007).
5. For estimates of Virginia union participation in the public sector, and a review of the legal and policy history around collective bargaining, see Hodges (2009).
6. Luker (2008:167).

BIBLIOGRAPHY

Afifi, Tamara D., and Paul Schrodt. 2003. "Uncertainty and the Avoidance of the State of One's Family in Stepfamilies, Postdivorce Single-Parent Families, and First-Marriage Families." *Human Communication Research* 29(4):516–532.

Albanesi, Stefania, and María José Prados. 2011. "Inequality and Household Labor Supply." Paper presented at the Society for Economic Dynamics Annual Meeting. Retrieved December 23, 2012 (http://www.columbia.edu/~mp2558/research/SED_07092011_slides.pdf).

Alesina, Alberto F., Edward L. Glaeser, and Bruce Sacerdote. 2006. "Work and Leisure in the United States and Europe: Why So Different?" pp. 1–99 in *NBER Macroeconomics Annual 2005*, edited by Mark Gertler and Kenneth Rogoff. Cambridge, MA: MIT Press. Retrieved October 29, 2013 (http://www.nber.org/chapters/c0073.pdf).

Almond, Barbara. 2010. *The Monster Within: The Hidden Side of Motherhood*. Berkeley: University of California Press.

Amato, Paul R. 2010. "Research on Divorce: Continuing Trends and New Developments." *Journal of Marriage and Family* 72(3):650–666.

Antler, Joyce. 2007. *You Never Call! You Never Write!: A History of the Jewish Mother*. New York: Oxford University Press.

Arthur, M. B., and D. M. Rousseau, eds. 1996. *The Boundaryless Career: A New Employment Principle for a New Organizational Era*. Oxford: Oxford University Press.

Aughinbaugh, Alison, Omar Robles, and Hugette Sun. 2013. "Marriage and Divorce: Patterns by Gender, Race, and Educational Attainment." *Monthly Labor Review*. October. Retrieved March 25, 2014 (http://www.bls.gov/opub/mlr/2013/article/marriage-and-divorce-patterns-by-gender-race-and-educational-attainment.htm).

Baca Zinn, Maxine. 1982–1983. "Familism among Chicanos: A Theoretical Review." *Humboldt Journal of Social Relations* 10:224–238.

Baier, Annette C. 1995. "The Need for More than Justice." In Virginia Held, ed., *Justice and Care*. Boulder, CO: Westview. As cited in Kittay 2011: 54.

Bailyn, Lotte. 1993. *Breaking the Mold: Women, Men, and Time in the New Corporate World*. New York: Free Press.

Barghini, Tiziana. 2012. "Educated Women Quit Work as Spouses Earn More." *Reuters*. Retrieved December 23, 2012 (http://www.reuters.com/article/2012/03/08/us-economy-women-idUSBRE8270AC20120308).

Barling, Julian, Kathryne E. Dupre, and Gail C. Hepburn. 1998. "Effects of Parents' Job Insecurity on Children's Work Beliefs and Attitudes." *Journal of Applied Psychology* 83(1):112–118.

Barling, Julian, and Danny Sorensen. 1997. "Work and Family: In Search of a Relevant Research Agenda." pp. 157–169 in *Creating Tomorrow's Organizations*, edited by C. L. Cooper and S. E. Jackson. New York: Barry Wiley.

Barling, Julian, Anthea Zacharatos, and Gail C. Hepburn. 1999. "Parents' Job Insecurity Affects Children's Academic Performance through Cognitive Difficulties." *Journal of Applied Psychology* 84(3):437–444.

Bartlett, Katharine T. 2001. "Principles of the Law of Family Dissolution: Analysis and Recommendations." *Duke Journal of Gender Law and Policy* 8:1–85.

Bauman, Zygmunt. 2000. *Liquid Modernity*. Oxford: Polity.

Bauman, Zygmunt. 2003. *Liquid Love: On the Frailty of Human Bonds*. Cambridge, UK: Polity.

Baumol, William J., Alan Blinder, and Edward N. Wolff. 2003. *Downsizing in America: Reality, Causes, and Consequences*. New York: Russell Sage.

Beck, Ulrich, and Elisabeth Beck-Gernsheim. 1995. *The Normal Chaos of Love*. Translated by Mark Ritter and Jane Wiebel. Cambridge, UK: Polity.

Beck-Gernsheim, Elisabeth. 2002. *Reinventing the Family: In Search of New Lifestyles*. Translated by Patrick Camiller. Cambridge, UK: Polity.

Bengtson, Vern L. 2001. "Beyond the Nuclear Family: The Increasing Importance of Multigenerational Bonds." *Journal of Marriage and Family* 63:1–16.

Bennett, Drake. 2010. "Johnny Has Two Mommies—and Four Dads." *Boston Globe*, October 24.

Bernstein, Elizabeth. 2007. *Temporarily Yours: Intimacy, Authenticity, and the Commerce of Sex*. Chicago: University of Chicago Press.

Best, Joel. 1993. *Threatened Children: Rhetoric and Concern and Child Victims*. Chicago: University of Chicago Press.

Bianchi, Suzanne. 2000. "Maternal Employment and Time with Children: Dramatic Change or Surprising Continuity?" *Demography* 37(4):401–414.

Bianchi, Suzanne M., Nancy Folbre, and Douglas Wolf. 2012. "Unpaid Care Work." pp. 40–64 in *For Love and Money: Care Provision in the United States*, edited by Nancy Folbre. New York: Russell Sage.

Blair-Loy, Mary. 2003. *Competing Devotions: Career and Family among Women Executives*. Cambridge, MA: Harvard University Press.

Blau, Francesca, and Lawrence M. Kahn. 2006. "The Gender Pay Gap: Going, Going… but Not Gone." pp. 37–66 in *The Declining Significance of Gender?*, edited by Francine D. Blau, Mary C. Brinton, and David B. Grusky. New York: Russell Sage.

Blinder, Alan. 2006. "Offshoring: The Next Industrial Revolution?" *Foreign Affairs* 85(2):113–128.

Blum, Linda. 2007. "Mother-Blame in the Prozac Nation: Raising Kids with Invisible Disabilities." *Gender and Society* 21(2):202–226.

Bott, Elizabeth. 1957. *Family and Social Networks*. London: Tavistock.

Braverman, Harry. 1974. *Labor and Monopoly Capital: The Degradation of Work in the Twentieth Century*. New York: Monthly Review Press.

Bridges, Tristan, and C. J. Pascoe. 2014. "Hybrid Masculinities: New Directions in the Sociology of Men and Masculinities." *Sociology Compass* 8(3):246–258.

Brown, Steven P. 1996. "A Meta-Analysis and Review of Organizational Research on Job Involvement." *Psychological Bulletin* 120(2):235–255.

Brown, Susan L. 2006. "Family Structure Transitions and Adolescent Well-Being." *Demography* 43(3):447–461.

Bumpass, Larry, and Kelly Raley. 2007. "Measuring Separation and Divorce." pp. 125–143 in *Handbook of Measurement Issues in Family Research*, edited by S. L. Hofferth and L. M. Casper. Mahwah, NJ: Erlbaum.

Burawoy, Michael. 1979. *Manufacturing Consent: Changes in the Labor Process under Monopoly Capitalism*. Chicago: University of Chicago.

Burchell, Brendan J. 2005. "The Welfare Costs of Job Insecurity: Psychological Wellbeing and Family Life." *Trends in Social Cohesion*, Special Issue: *Reconciling Labour Flexibility with Social Cohesion: Facing the Challenge* 15:71–108.

Burchell, Brendan J. 2009. "Flexicurity as a Moderator of the Relationship between Job Insecurity and Psychological Well-Being." *Cambridge Journal of Regions, Economy and Society* 2(3):365–378.

Bureau of Labor Statistics. 2014a. "Percent of Employed, Members of Unions, Years 2003–2013." Union Affiliation Data from the Current Population Survey. Retrieved March 26, 2014 (http://www.bls.gov/data/).

Bureau of Labor Statistics. 2014b. "Table 5. Union Affiliation of Employed Wage and Salary Workers by State, 2012–2013 Annual Averages," in "Union Members—2013." January 24. Retrieved February 16, 2014 (http://www.bls.gov/news.release/pdf/union2.pdf).

Burgess, Simon, Carol Propper, and Arnstein Aassve. 2003. "The Role of Income in Marriage and Divorce Transitions among Young Americans." *Journal of Population Economics* 16:455–475.

Buzzanelli, Patrice M. 2000. "The Promise and Practice of the New Career and Social Contract: Illusions Exposed and Suggestions for Reform." pp. 209–235 in *Rethinking Organizational and Managerial Communication from Feminist Perspectives*, edited by P. M. Buzzanelli. Thousand Oaks, CA: Sage.

Cappelli, Peter. 1999. "Career Jobs Are Dead." *California Management Review* 42(1):146–167.

Chabon, Michael. 2012. *Telegraph Avenue*. New York: Harper Collins.

Charles, Kerwin K., and Melvin Stephens. 2004. "Disability, Job Displacement and Divorce." *Journal of Labor Economics* 22(2):489–522.

Cheadle, Jacob E., Paul R. Amato, and Valarie King. 2010. "Patterns of Nonresident Father Contact." *Demography* 47:205–225.

Cherlin, Andrew. 1978. "Remarriage as an Incomplete Institution." *American Journal of Sociology* 84:634–649.

Cherlin, Andrew J. 2004. "The Deinstitutionalization of American Marriage." *Journal of Marriage and Family* 66:848–861.

Cherlin, Andrew J. 2009. *The Marriage-Go-Round*. New York: Knopf.

Cherlin, Andrew J., Frank F. Furstenberg, Lindsay Chase-Linsdale, Kathleen E. Kiernan, Philip K. Robins, Donna Ruane Morrison, and Julien O. Teitler. 1991. "Longitudinal Studies of Effects of Divorce on Children in Great Britain and the United States." *Science* 252(5011):1386–1389.

Clark, Candace. 1997. *Misery and Company: Sympathy in Everyday Life*. Chicago: University of Chicago Press.

Collins, Patricia Hill. 2000. *Black Feminist Thought: Knowledge, Consciousness, and the Politics of Empowerment*. New York: Routledge.

Coltrane, Scott. 2004. "Fathering: Paradoxes, Contradictions, and Dilemmas." pp. 394–410 in *Handbook of Contemporary Families*, edited by M. Coleman and L. Ganong. Thousand Oaks, CA: Sage.

Connell, Catherine. 2010. "Doing, Undoing, or Redoing Gender?: Learning from the Workplace Experiences of Transpeople." *Gender and Society* 24(1):31–55.

Cook, Daniel. 2004. *The Commodification of Childhood: The Children's Clothing Industry and the Rise of the Child Consumer*. Durham, NC: Duke University Press.

Coontz, Stephanie. 2005. *Marriage: A History—How Love Conquered Marriage*. New York: Penguin.

Cooper, Marianne. 2014. *Cut Adrift: Families in Insecure Times*. Berkeley: University of California Press.

Cooper-Hakim, Amy, and Chockalingam Viswesvaran. 2005. "The Construct of Work Commitment: Testing an Integrative Framework." *Psychological Bulletin* 131(2):241–259.

Correll, Shelley, Stephen Benard, and In Paik. 2007. "Getting a Job: Is There a Motherhood Penalty?" *American Journal of Sociology* 112:1297–1338.

Corse, Sarah M., and Jennifer M. Silva. In press. "Intimate Inequalities: Love and Work in the 21st Century." In *Beyond the Cubicle: Insecurity Culture and the Flexible Self*, edited by Allison J. Pugh. New York: Oxford University Press.

Cott, Nancy F. 1982. *The Bonds of Womanhood*. New Haven, CT: Yale University Press.

Cowan, Ruth Schwartz. 1983. *More Work for Mother: The Ironies of Household Technology from the Open Hearth to the Microwave*. New York: Basic Books.

Crispin, Gerry, and Mark Mehler. 2011. "10th Annual CareerXroads Source of Hire Report." Retrieved January 19, 2013 (http://www.careerxroads.com/news/SourcesOfHire11.pdf).

Damaske, Sarah. 2011. *For the Family: How Class and Gender Shape Women's Work*. New York: Oxford University Press.

De Graaf, John, and David K. Batker. 2011. *What's the Economy For, Anyway?: Why It's Time to Stop Chasing Growth and Start Pursuing Happiness*. New York: Bloomsbury.

De Kretser, Michelle. 2007. *The Lost Dog*. Crows Nest, Australia: Allen & Unwin.

Deleire, Thomas, and Ariel Kalil. 2002. "Good Things Come in Threes: Single-Parent Multigenerational Family Structure and Adolescent Adjustment." *Demography* 39(2):393–413.

Desmond, Matthew. 2012. "Disposable Ties and the Urban Poor." *American Journal of Sociology* 117(5):1295–1335.

Devine, Kay, Trish Reay, Linda Stainton, and Ruth Collins-Nakai. 2003. "Downsizing Outcomes: Better a Victim than a Survivor?" *Human Resource Manager* 42:109–124.

De Witte, Hans. 1999. "Job Insecurity and Psychological Well-Being: Review of the Literature and Exploration of Some Unresolved Issues." *European Journal of Work and Organizational Psychology* 8(2):155–177.

Dunn, Ronnie, and Philip Coleman. 2011. "Cost of Livin'," on Ronnie Dunn, *Ronnie Dunn*. CD. Arista Nashville.

Erickson, Karla, and Jennifer L. Pierce. 2005. "Farewell to the Organization Man: The Feminization of Loyalty in High-End and Low-End Service Jobs." *Ethnography* 6(3):283–313.

European Commission. 2007. "Towards Common Principles of Flexicurity: More and Better Jobs Through Flexibility and Security." COM 359. Retrieved March 3, 2014 (http://www.europa.eu).

Faludi, Susan. 1999. *Stiffed: The Betrayal of the American Man*. New York: William Morrow.

Farber, Henry S. 1998. "Are Lifetime Jobs Disappearing? Job Duration in the United States, 1973–1993." pp. 157–206 in *Labor Statistics Measurement Issues*, edited by John Haltiwanger, Marilyn E. Manser, and Robert Topel. Chicago: University of Chicago Press.

Farber, Henry S. 2007. "Is the Company Man an Anachronism? Trends in Long-Term Employment in the U.S., 1973–2006." pp. 56–83 in *The Price of Independence: The Economics of Adulthood*, edited by S. Danziger and E. Rouse. New York: Russell Sage.

Farber, Henry S. 2008. "Short(er) Shrift: The Decline in Worker-Firm Attachment in the United States." pp. 10–37 in *Laid Off, Laid Low: Political and Economic Consequences of Employment Insecurity*, edited by K. S. Newman. New York: Columbia University Press

Farber, Henry. 2009. "Job Loss and the Decline in Job Security in the United States." Princeton University Industrial Relations Section Working Paper 520. Retrieved September 5, 2012 (http://dataspace.princeton.edu/jspui/bitstream/88435/dsp01xk81jk38d/1/520revision2.pdf).

Ferris, Timothy. 2009. *The Four-Hour Workweek: Escape 9–5, Live Anywhere, and Join the New Rich*. New York: Crown.

Fine, Michelle, Lois Weis, Judi Addleston, and Julia Marusza. 1997. "(In)secure Times: Constructing White Working-Class Masculinities in the Late Twentieth Century." *Gender and Society* 11(1):52–68.

Fineman, Martha Albertson. 2005. *The Autonomy Myth: A Theory of Dependency*. New York: New Press.

Fischer, Claude. 2012. *Still Connected: Family and Friends in America since 1970*. New York: Russell Sage.

Flanagan, Constance A., and Jacquelynne Eccles. 1993. "Changes in Parents' Work Status and Adolescents' Adjustment at School." *Child Development* 64(1):246–257.

Fligstein, Neil, and Taek-Jin Shin. 2004. "The Shareholder Value Society: A Review of Changes in Working Conditions and Inequality in the United States, 1976–2000." pp. 402–432 in *Social Inequality*, edited by K. M. Neckerman. New York: Russell Sage.

Fraser, Nancy, and Linda Gordon. 1994. "A Genealogy of Dependency: Tracing a Keyword of the U.S. Welfare State." *Signs* 19(2):309–336.

Freud, Sigmund. 1966. *Introductory Lectures on Psycho-analysis*. Translated by J. Strachey. New York: W.W. Norton.

Fullerton, Andrew, and Michael Wallace. 2007. "Traversing the Flexible Turn: US Workers Perceptions of Job Insecurity." *Social Science Research* 36(1):201–221.

Garey, Anita I. 1995. "Constructing Motherhood on the Night Shift: 'Working Mothers' as 'Stay-at-Home Moms.'" *Qualitative Sociology* 18(4):415–437.

Gershon, Ilana. 2011. "Neoliberal Agency." *Current Anthropology* 52(4):537–555.

Gerson, Kathleen. 2010. *The Unfinished Revolution: Coming of Age in a New Era of Gender, Work, and Family*. New York: Oxford University Press.

Gibson-Davis, Christina M. 2009. "Money, Marriage, and Children: Testing the Financial Expectations and Family Formation Theory." *Journal of Marriage and Family* 71:146–160.

Giddens, Anthony. 1991. *Modernity and Self-Identity: Self and Society in the Late Modern Age*. Cambridge, UK: Polity.

Gill, Rosalind. 2008. "Culture and Subjectivity in Neoliberal and Postfeminist Times." *Subjectivity* 25:432–445.

Gittell, Marilyn, and Teresa Shtob. 1980. "Changing Women's Roles in Political Volunteerism and Reform of the City." *Signs* 5(3):S67–78.

Glantz, Michael J., Marc C. Chamberlain, Qin Liu, Chung-Cheng Hsieh, Keith R. Edwards, Alixis Van Horn, and Lawrence Recht. 2009. "Gender Disparity in the

Rate of Partner Abandonment in Patients with Serious Medical Illness." *Cancer* 115(22):5237–5242.

Glazer, Sharon, Sophie C. Daniel, and Kenneth M. Short. 2004. "A Study of the Relationship between Organizational Commitment and Human Values in Four Countries." *Human Relations* 57:323–345.

Glenn, Evelyn Nakano. 2010. *Forced to Care: Coercion and Caregiving in America*. Cambridge, MA: Harvard University Press.

Glynn, Sara Jane. 2012. "The New Breadwinners: 2010 Update." Washington, DC: Center for American Progress. Retrieved January 25, 2013 (http://www.americanprogress.org/wp-content/uploads/issues/2012/04/pdf/breadwinners.pdf).

Goodwin, Paula Y., William D. Mosher, and Anjani Chandra. 2010. "Marriage and Cohabitation in the United States: A Statistical Portrait Based on Cycle 6 (2002) of the National Survey of Family Growth." *Vital and Health Statistics* 23(28). Retrieved January 21, 2013 (http://www.cdc.gov/nchs/data/series/sr_23/sr23_028.pdf).

Gordon, Linda. 1988. *Heroes of Their Own Lives: The Politics and History of Family Violence—Boston, 1880–1960*. New York: Viking.

Greenhalgh, Leonard, and Zehava Rosenblatt. 1984. "Job Insecurity: Toward Conceptual Clarity." *Academy of Management Review* 3:438–448.

Greenhalgh, Leonard, and Zehava Rosenblatt. 2010. "Evolution of Research on Job Insecurity." *International Studies of Management and Organization* 40(1):6–19.

Gross, Neil. 2005. "The Detraditionalization of Intimacy Reconsidered." *Sociological Theory* 23(3):286–311.

Hackstaff, Karla B. 1999. *Marriage in a Culture of Divorce*. Philadelphia: Temple University Press.

Handy, Charles. 1989. *The Age of Unreason*. Boston: Harvard Business School Press.

Harvey, David. 2005. *A Brief History of Neoliberalism*. Oxford: Oxford University Press.

Hays, Sharon. 1996. *The Cultural Contradictions of Motherhood*. New Haven, CT: Yale University Press.

Hernandez, Donald J. 1993. *America's Children: Resources from Family, Government and the Economy*. New York: Russell Sage Foundation.

Highhouse, Scott, Michael J. Zickar, and Maya Yankelevich. 2010. "Would You Work If You Won the Lottery? Tracking Changes in the American Work Ethic." *Journal of Applied Psychology* 95(2):349–357.

Hill, Malcolm, John Davis, Alan Prout, and Ka Tisdall. 2004. "Moving the Participation Agenda Forward." *Children and Society* 18(2):77–96.

Ho, Karen. 2009. *Liquidated: An Ethnography of Wall Street*. Durham, NC: Duke University Press.

Hochschild, Arlie R. 1979. "Emotion Work, Feeling Rules and Social Structure." *American Journal of Sociology* 85:551–575.

Hochschild, Arlie R. 1983. *The Managed Heart*. Berkeley: University of California Press.

Hochschild, Arlie R. 1989. *The Second Shift*. New York: Viking.

Hochschild, Arlie R. 1990. "Ideology and Emotion Management: A Perspective and Path for Future Research." pp. 117–142 in *Research Agenda in the Sociology of Emotions*, edited by T. D. Kemper. Albany: State University of New York Press.

Hochschild, Arlie R. 1997. *The Time Bind*. New York: Metropolitan Books.

Hochschild, Arlie R. 2003. *The Commercialization of Intimate Life*. Berkeley: University of California Press.

Hochschild, Arlie. 2012. *The Outsourced Self: Intimate Life in Market Times*. New York: Metropolitan Books.

Hodges, Ann C. 2009. "Lessons from the Laboratory: The Polar Opposites on the Public Sector Labor Law Spectrum." *Cornell Journal of Law and Public Policy* 18:735–774.

Hollister, Matissa N. 2011. "Employment Stability in the U.S. Labor Market: Rhetoric vs. Reality." *Annual Review of Sociology* 37(1):305–324.

Hollister, Matissa N., and Kristin E. Smith. 2014. "Unmasking the Conflicting Trends in Job Tenure by Gender in the United States, 1983-2008." *American Sociological Review* 79(1)159-181.

Horovitz, Bruce. 2014. "JPMorgan to Cut 8,000 Jobs." *USA Today*, February 25. Retrieved March 12, 2014 (http://www.usatoday.com/story/money/business/2014/02/25/jpmorgan-chase-job-cuts/5803057/).

Hyde, Janet S., and Elizabeth A. Plant. 1995. "Magnitude of Psychological Gender Differences." *American Psychologist* 50:159–161.

Illouz, Eva. 2007. *Cold Intimacies*. Cambridge, UK: Polity.

Illouz, Eva. 2012. *Why Love Hurts*. Cambridge, UK: Polity.

Jans, Marc. 2004. "Children as Citizens: Towards a Contemporary Notion of Child Participation." *Childhood* 11(1):27–44.

Kalleberg, Arne L. 2009. "Precarious Work, Insecure Workers: Employment Relations in Transition." *American Sociological Review* 74(1):1–22.

Kalleberg, Arne L. 2011. *Good Jobs, Bad Jobs: The Rise of Polarized and Precarious Employment Systems in the United States, 1970s to 2000s*. New York: Russell Sage.

Karsten, Lia. 2005. "It All Used to Be Better? Different Generations on Continuity and Change in Urban Children's Daily Use of Space." *Children's Geographies* 3(3):275–290.

Katz, Cindi. 2005. "The Terrors of Hypervigilance: Security and the Compromised Spaces of Contemporary Childhood." pp. 99–114 in *Studies in Modern Childhood*, edited by J. Qvortrup. Houndmills, UK: Palgrave Macmillan.

Kelly, Joan B., and Robert E. Emery. 2003. "Children's Adjustment Following Divorce: Risk and Resiliency Perspectives." *Family Relations* 52:352–362.

Kets de Vries, Manfred F. R., and Katharina Balazs. 1997. "The Downside of Downsizing." *Human Relations* 50(1):11–50.

Kilborn, Peter T. 2009. *Next Stop, Reloville: Life inside America's Rootless Professional Class*. New York: Times Books.

Kimmell, Michael. 2013. *Angry White Men: American Masculinity at the End of an Era*. New York: Nation.

Kingfisher, Catherine, and Jeff Maskovsky. 2008. "Introduction: The Limits of Neoliberalism." *Critique of Anthropology*, Special Issue: *The Limits of Neoliberalism* 28(2):115–26.

Kittay, Eve F. 2011. "The Ethics of Care, Dependence, and Disability." *Ratio Juris* 24:49–58.

Kletzer, Lori. 2001. *Job Loss from Imports: Measuring the Costs*. Washington, DC: Institute for International Economics.

Kmec, Julie A., and Elizabeth H. Gorman. 2010. "Gender and Discretionary Work Effort: Evidence from the United States and Britain." *Work and Occupations* 37(1):3–36.

Knee, C. R., H. Patrick, N. A. Vietor, and C. Neighbors. 2004. "Implicit Theories of Relationships: Moderators of the Link between Conflict and Commitment." *Personality and Social Psychology Bulletin* 30:617–628.

Kreider, Rose. 2010. "Increase in Opposite-Sex Cohabiting Couples from 2009–2010 in the Annual Social and Economic Supplement (ASEC) to the Current Population Survey (CPS). Washington, DC: US Census Bureau. Retrieved

January 21, 2013 (http://www.census.gov/hhes/families/files/Inc-Opp-sex-2009-to-2010.pdf).

Kuhn, Peter, and Fernando Lozano. 2008. "The Expanding Workweek? Understanding Trends in Long Work Hours among U.S. Men, 1979–2006." *Journal of Labor Economics* 26(2):311–343.

Kusserow, Adrie. 2004. *American Individualisms: Child Rearing and Social Class in Three Neighborhoods.* New York: Palgrave MacMillan.

Lane, Carrie M. 2011. *A Company of One: Insecurity, Independence, and the New World of White-Collar Unemployment.* Ithaca, NY: Cornell University Press.

Lareau, Annette. 2003. *Unequal Childhoods.* Berkeley: University of California Press.

Lawler, Edward E., and Douglas T. Hall. 1970. "Relationship of Job Characteristics to Job Involvement, Satisfaction, and Intrinsic Motivation." *Journal of Applied Psychology* 54:305–312.

Lee, Jim. 2006. "Family Firm Performance: Further Evidence." *Family Business Review* 19(2):103–114.

Lee, Nick. 2001. *Childhood and Society: Growing Up in an Age of Uncertainty.* Philadelphia: Open University Press.

Leidner, Robin. 2006. "Identity and Work." pp. 424–463 in *Social Theory at Work*, edited by Marek Korczynski, Randy Hodson, and Paul K. Edwards. Oxford: Oxford University Press.

Lim, Vivien K. G., and Geok Leng Loo. 2003. "Effects of Parental Job Insecurity and Parenting Behaviors on Youth's Self-Efficacy and Work Attitudes." *Journal of Vocational Behavior* 63(1):86–98.

Lincoln, James R., and Arne Kalleberg. 1985. "Work Organization and Workforce Commitment: A Study of Plants and Employees in the US and Japan." *American Sociological Review* 50:738–760.

Loscocco, Karen, and Glenna Spitze. 2007. "Gender Patterns in Provider Role Attitudes and Behavior." *Journal of Family Issues* 28(7):934–954.

Lucidi, Federico, and Alfred Kleinknecht. 2010. "Little Innovation, Many Jobs: An Econometric Analysis of the Italian Labour Productivity Crisis." *Cambridge Journal of Economics* 34:525–546.

Luker, Kristen. 2008. *Salsa-Dancing into Social Sciences: Research in an Age of Info-Glut.* Cambridge, MA: Harvard University Press.

Luthans, Fred, Harriette S. McCaul, and Nancy G. Dodd. 1985. "Organizational Commitment: A Comparison of American, Japanese, and Korean Employees." *Academy of Management Journal* 28(1):213–219.

Makawatsakul, Nantaporn, and Brian H. Kleiner. 2003. "The Effect of Downsizing on Morale and Attrition." *Management Research News* 26(4):52–62.

Margolis, Lewis H., and Dale C. Farran. 1984. "Unemployment and Children." *International Journal of Mental Health* 13(1–2):107–124.

Marist. 2011. "2/10: 'It's Destiny!' Most Americans Believe in Soul Mates." *Pebbles and Pundits.* February 10. Retrieved March 8, 2014 (http://maristpoll.marist.edu/index.php?s=soul+mate).

Marsden, Peter, Arne Kalleberg, and Cynthia Cook. 1993. "Gender Differences in Organizational Commitment: Influences of Work Positions and Family Roles." *Work and Occupations* 20(3):368–391.

Martin, Steven P. 2004. "Growing Evidence for a 'Divorce Divide'? Education and Marital Dissolution Rates in the U.S. since the 1970s." Russell Sage Foundation Working Papers. Retrieved February 21, 2012 (http://www.russellsage.org/research/reports/steve-martin).

Mason, Mary A. 1994. *From Father's Property to Children's Rights*. New York: Columbia University Press.

Mason, Mary A., and Jane Mauldon. 1996. "The New Stepfamily Requires a New Public Policy." *Journal of Social Issues* 52(3):11–27.

Matthews, Glenna. 1987. *"Just a Housewife": The Rise and Fall of Domesticity in America*. New York: Oxford University Press.

Mau, Steffen, Jan Mewes, and Nadine M. Schöneck. 2012. "What Determines Subjective Socio-economic Insecurity? Context and Class in Comparative Perspective." *Socioeconomic Review* 10(4):655–682.

Maybury, Kelly. 2002. "I Do? Marriage in Uncertain Times." *Gallup*, January 22. Retrieved March 8, 2014 (http://www.gallup.com/poll/5206/do-marriage-uncertain-times.aspx).

McCall, Leslie. 2004. "The Inequality Economy: How New Corporate Practices Redistribute Income to the Top." Demos Working Paper. Retrieved September 7, 2012 (http://www.demos.org/sites/default/files/publications/the_inequality_economy_final.pdf).

McKee-Ryan, Frances, Zhaoli Song, Connie R. Wanberg, and Angelo J. Kinicki. 2005. "Psychological and Physical Well-Being during Unemployment: A Meta-Analytic Study." *Journal of Applied Psychology* 90(1):53–76.

McLanahan, Sara, and Gary Sandefur. 1994. *Growing Up With a Single Parent*. Cambridge, MA: Harvard University Press.

Mercer. 2011. "Inside Employees' Minds: Navigating the New Rules of Engagement: U.S. Survey Summary 2011." New York: Mercer. Retrieved January 25, 2013 (http://new-rules-of-engagement.mercer.com/New%20Rules%20US/Inside%20Employees'%20Minds%20-%20US).

Messner, Michael A. 2000. *The Politics of Masculinity*. Lanham, MD: AltaMira.

Mishel, Lawrence. 2013. "Vast Majority of US Workers Are Working Harder, and for Not Much More." Economic Policy Institute Issue Brief, no. 348. Retrieved October 21, 2013 (http://www.epi.org/publication/ib348-trends-us-work-hours-wages-1979-2007/).

Mora, Edward. 2011. "Virginia's Education System Has 'Managed Well' Without Teacher's Unions, Governor Says." *CNSNews.com*, March 23. Retrieved January 10, 2013 (http://cnsnews.com/news/article/virginia-s-education-system-has-managed-well-without-teacher-unions-governor-says).

Murphy, Michael. 2000. "The Evolution of Cohabitation in Britain, 1960–95." *Population Studies* 54(1):43–56.

Murray, Charles. 2012. *Coming Apart: The State of White America, 1960–2010*. New York: Crown Forum.

Near, Janet P. 1989. "Organizational Commitment among Japanese and US Workers." *Organization Studies* 10:281–300.

Nelson, Margaret. 2010. *Parenting Out of Control: Anxious Parents in Uncertain Times*. New York: New York University Press.

Neumark, David, ed. 2000. *On the Job: Is Long-Term Employment a Thing of the Past?* New York: Russell Sage Foundation.

OECD StatExtracts. "Average Annual Hours Worked per Worker." Retrieved October 21, 2013 (http://stats.oecd.org/Index.aspx?DatasetCode=ANHRS).

Orloff, Ann S. 1993. "Gender and the Social Rights of Citizenship: The Comparative Analysis of Gender Relations." *American Sociological Review* 58(3):303–328.

Ortner, Sherry. 1996. *Making Gender: The Politics and Erotics of Culture*. Boston: Beacon.

Patchett, Ann. 2011. *State of Wonder*. New York: Harper.

Patterson, Charlotte. 2006. "Children of Gay and Lesbian Parents." *Current Directions in Psychological Science* 15(5):241–244.

Pew Research Center. 2006. "Public Says American Work Life Is Worsening, but Most Workers Remain Satisfied with Their Jobs." Pew Research Center Social Trends Report. Retrieved December 10, 2011 (http://pewsocialtrends.org/files/2010/10/Jobs.pdf).

Pew Research Center. 2011. "A Tale of Two Fathers: More Are Active, But More Are Absent." Pew Research Center Social Trends Report. Retrieved March 19, 2014 (http://www.pewsocialtrends.org/files/2011/06/fathers-FINAL-report.pdf).

Popenoe, David. 1996. *Life without Father*. New York: Free Press.

Pruijt, Hans, and Pascal Derogee. 2010. "Employability and Job Security, Friends or Foes? The Paradoxical Reception of Employacurity in the Netherlands." *Socio-Economic Review* 8:437–460.

Pryor, Jan. 2008. "Children in Stepfamilies: Children's Relationships with Nonresident Parents." pp. 345–368 in *The International Handbook of Stepfamilies: Policy and Practice in Legal, Research, and Clinical Environments*, edited by J. Pryor. Hoboken, NJ: John Wiley & Sons.

Pugh, Allison J. 2005. "Selling Compromise: Toys, Motherhood and the Cultural Deal." *Gender and Society* 19(6):729–749.

Pugh, Allison J. 2009. *Longing and Belonging: Parents, Children, and Consumer Culture*. Berkeley: University of California Press.

Pugh, Allison J. 2013. "What Good Are Interviews for Thinking about Culture? Demystifying Interpretive Analysis." *American Journal of Cultural Sociology* 1(1):42–68.

Raley, Sara, Suzanne M. Bianchi, and Wendy Wang. 2012. "When Do Fathers Care? Mothers' Economic Contribution and Fathers' Involvement in Child Care." *American Journal of Sociology* 117(5):1422–1459.

Rankin, Sonia G. 2002. "Why They Won't Take the Money: Black Grandparents and the Success of Informal Kinship Care." *Elder Law Journal* 10:153–186.

Reichheld, Frederick. 2001. *Loyalty Rules! How Today's Leaders Build Lasting Relationships*. Cambridge, MA: Harvard Business School Press.

Reuters. 2013. "Hewlett-Packard to Cut 5,000 More Jobs." *Reuters*, December 31. Retrieved March 12, 2014 (http://www.reuters.com/article/2013/12/31/us-hewlettpackard-layoffs-idUSBRE9BU0EA20131231).

Right Management. 2013. "Most Employees Plan to Pursue New Job Opportunities in 2014 Reveals Right Management Poll." Right Management, November 19. Retrieved March 22, 2014 (http://www.right.com/news-and-events/press-releases/2013-press-releases/item25643.aspx?x=25643).

Risman, Barbara J. 2009. "From Doing to Undoing: Gender As We Know It." *Gender and Society* 23:81–84.

Roche, Jeremy. 1999. "Children: Rights, Participation and Citizenship." *Childhood* 6(4):475–493.

Rogers, Stacy J., and Dee C. May. 2003. "Spillover between Marital Quality and Job Satisfaction: Long-Term Patterns and Gender Differences." *Journal of Marriage and Family* 65(2):482–495.

Roschelle, Anne. 1997. *No More Kin: Exploring Race, Class, and Gender in Family Networks*. Thousand Oaks, CA: Sage.

Rosenfeld, Michael J. 2007. *The Age of Independence: Interracial Unions, Same-Sex Unions and the Changing American Family*. Cambridge, MA: Harvard University Press.

Rubin, Beth. 2012. "Shifting Social Contracts and the Sociological Imagination." *Social Forces* 91(2):327–346.

Ruddick, Sara. 1998. "Care as Labor and Relationship." pp. 3–25 in *Norms and Values: Essays on the Work of Virginia Held*, edited by J. G. Haber and M. S. Halfon. Lanham, MD: Rowman & Littlefield.

Russo, Richard. 2001. *Empire Falls*. New York: Vintage Books.

Salladarré, Frédéric, Boubaker Hlaimi, and François-Charles Wolff. 2011. "How Important Is Security in the Choice of Employment? Evidence from European Countries." *Economic and Industrial Democracy* 32:549–567.

Sarkisian, N. 2006. "'Doing Family Ambivalence': Nuclear and Extended Families in Single Mothers' Lives." *Journal of Marriage and Family* 68:804–811.

Sassler, Sharon. 2013. "Book Review: Social Class and Changing Families in America." *Gender and Society* 27(2):259.

Savickas, Mark L., and David B. Baker. 2005. "The History of Vocational Psychology: Antecedents, Origin and Early Development." pp. 15–49 in *Handbook of Vocational Psychology*, 3rd ed., edited by W. B. Walsh and M. L. Savickas. Mahwah, NJ: Lawrence Erlbaum.

Schmidt, Stefanie R. 1999. "Long-Run Trends in Workers' Beliefs about Their Own Job Security: Evidence from the General Social Survey." *Journal of Labor Economics* 17(4):S127–141.

Schmidt, Stefanie R. 2000. "Job Security Beliefs in the General Social Survey: Evidence on Long-Run Trends and Comparability with Other Surveys." pp. 300–334 in *On the Job: Is Long-Term Employment a Thing of the Past?*, edited by David Neumark. New York: Russell Sage.

Segura, Denise A., and Jennifer L. Pierce. 1993. "Chicana/o Family Structure and Gender Personality: Chodorow, Familism, and Psychoanalytic Sociology Revisited." *Signs* 19(1):62–91.

Sennett, Richard. 1998. *The Corrosion of Character*. New York: W.W. Norton.

Sherman, Jennifer. 2009. *Those Who Work and Those Who Don't: Poverty, Morality, and Family in Rural America*. Minneapolis: University of Minnesota Press.

Silva, Jennifer. 2013. *Coming Up Short: Working-Class Adulthood in an Age of Uncertainty*. New York: Oxford University Press.

Silva, Jennifer, and Allison J. Pugh. 2010. "What Does Caregiving Do for Young Parents? Beyond the Depleting Model of Care." *Sociological Inquiry* 80(4):605–627.

Silverstein, Shel. 1964. *The Giving Tree*. New York: Harper & Row.

Simonson, Helen. 2010. *Major Pettigrew's Last Stand*. New York: Random House.

Skinner, Denise A., and Julie K. Kohler. 2002. "Parental Rights in Diverse Family Contexts: Current Legal Developments." *Family Relations* 51(4):293–300.

Smart, Carol, and Beccy Shipman. 2004. "Visions in Monochrome: Families, Marriage, and the Individualization Thesis." *British Journal of Sociology* 55:491–509.

Smith, Vicki. 2001. *Crossing the Great Divide: Worker Risk and Opportunity in the New Economy*. Ithaca, NY: Cornell University Press.

Smith, Vicki. 2010. "Enhancing Employability: Human, Cultural, and Social Capital in an Era of Turbulent Unpredictability." *Human Relations* 63(2):279–300.

Smithson, Janet, and Suzan Lewis. 2000. "Is Job Insecurity Changing the Psychological Contract?" *Personnel Review* 29(6):680–702.

Society for Human Resource Management. 2011. "2011 Employee Job Satisfaction and Engagement." Alexandria, VA: Society for Human Resource Management. Retrieved January 25, 2013 (http://www.shrm.org/research/surveyfindings/articles/documents/11-0618%20job_satisfaction_fnl.pdf).

Solberg, Anne. 1997. "Negotiating Childhood: Changing Constructions of Age for Norwegian Children." pp. 126–144 in *Constructing and Reconstructing Childhood: Contemporary Issues in the Sociological Study of Childhood*, edited by J. A. Prout. London: Routledge Falmer.

Stacey, Judith. 2011. *Unhitched: Love, Marriage and Family Values from West Hollywood to Western China*. New York: New York University Press.

Stacey, Judith, and Timothy J. Biblarz. 2001. "(How) Does Sexual Orientation of Parents Matter?" *American Sociological Review* 65(2):159–183.

Stack, Carol. 1974. *All Our Kin: Strategies for Survival in a Black Community*. New York: Harper.

Stearns, Peter. 1994. *American Cool: Constructing a Twentieth-Century Emotional Style*. New York: New York University Press.

Stearns, Peter. 1999. *Battleground of Desire: The Struggle for Self-Control in Modern America*. New York: New York University Press.

Stegner, Wallace. 1987. *Crossing to Safety*. New York: Penguin.

Stevens, Ann Huff. 2005. "The More Things Change the More They Stay the Same: Trends in Long-term Employment in the United States, 1969–2002." NBER Working Paper 11878, December.

Stevenson, Betsey, and Justin Wolfers. 2007. "Marriage and Divorce: Changes and their Driving Forces." *Journal of Economic Perspectives* 21(2):27–52.

Stewart, Wendy, and Julian Barling. 1996. "Fathers' Work Experiences Affect Children's Behaviors Via Job-Related Affect and Parenting Behaviors." *Journal of Organizational Behavior* 17:221–232.

Stone, Pamela. 2007. *Opting Out? Why Women Really Quit Careers and Stay Home*. Berkeley: University of California Press

Sverke, Magnus, Johnny Helgren, and Katharina Naswall. 2002. "No Security: A Meta-Analysis and Review of Job Insecurity and Its Consequences." *Journal of Occupational Health Psychology* 7(3):242–264.

Sweeney, Megan M. 2010. "Remarriage and Stepfamilies: Strategic Sites for Family Scholarship in the 21st Century." *Journal of Marriage and Family* 72:667–684.

Sweet, Stephen, Phyllis Moen, and Peter Meiksins. 2007. "Dual Earners in Double Jeopardy: Preparing for Job Loss in the New Risk Economy." pp. 437–461 in *Workplace Temporalities*, edited by Beth Rubin. Research in the Sociology of Work 17. New York: Elsevier.

Swidler, Ann. 2001. *Talk of Love: How Culture Matters*. Chicago: University of Chicago Press.

Tangian, Andranik. 2011. *Flexicurity and Political Philosophy*. New York: Nova Science Publishers.

Taylor, Andy. 2012. "Top 50 Area Employers." *Richmond Times-Dispatch*. April 23. Retrieved January 22, 2013 (http://www.timesdispatch.com/business/top-area-employers/article_2d2458f5-75e1-5085-b906-a1d46784884b.html.) .

Terkel, Studs. 1972. *Working*. New York: Ballantine.

Thistle, Susan. 2006. *From Marriage to the Market: The Transformation of Women's Lives and Work*. Berkeley: University of California Press.

TNS Research. n.d. "Employee Commitment Links to Bottom Line Success." Retrieved December 10, 2011 (http://www.worklifeonline.com/pdfs/tns_score.pdf).

Townsend, Nicholas. 2002. *The Package Deal: Marriage, Work, and Fatherhood in Men's Lives*. Philadelphia: Temple University Press.

Uchitelle, Louis. 2007. *The Disposable American*. New York: Vintage Books.

US Census. 2004. "Educational Attainment in the United States: 2003." *Current Population Reports*, Document P20–550. Retrieved November 3, 2010 (http://www.census.gov/prod/2004pubs/p20-550.pdf).

US Census. 2011. "One-Parent Unmarried Family Groups with Own Children/1 Under 18, by Marital Status of the Reference Person: 2011." *Current Population Survey, 2011 Annual Social and Economic Supplement*. Retrieved December 16, 2011 (http://www.census.gov/population/www/socdemo/hh-fam/cps2011.html).

US Census. 2012a. "One-Parent Unmarried Family Groups with Own Children/1 Under 18, by Marital Status of the Reference Person: 2012." *Current Population Survey, 2012 Annual Social and Economic Supplement*. Retrieved December 17, 2012 (http://www.census.gov/hhes/families/data/cps2012.html).

US Census. 2012b. "Table A1. Marital Status of People 15 Years and Over, by Age, Sex, Personal Earnings, Race, and Hispanic Origin/1, 2012." *America's Families and Living Arrangements: 2012*. Retrieved January 21, 2013 (http://www.census.gov/hhes/families/data/cps2012.html).

US Census. 2012c. "Table 131. Percent of First Marriages Reaching Stated Anniversary by Sex and Year of Marriage: 2009." *Statistical Abstract of the United States*. Washington, DC. Retrieved January 20, 2013 (http://www.census.gov/prod/2011pubs/12statab/vitstat.pdf).

US Government Accounting Office. 2006. "Employment Arrangements: Improved Outreach Could Help Ensure Proper Worker Classification." GAO-06–656. Retrieved March 26, 2014 (http://www.gao.gov/assets/260/250806.pdf) .

Utrata, Jennifer. Forthcoming. *Women without Men: Single Mothers and Gender Crisis in the New Russia*. Ithaca, NY: Cornell University Press.

Valentin, Karen, and Lotte Meinert. 2009. "The Adult North and the Young South: Reflections on the Civilizing Mission of Children's Rights." *Anthropology Today* 25(3):23–28.

Vermeylen, Greet. 2008. "Mapping Flexicurity in the EU." pp. 191–214 in *Innovating European Labour Markets: Dynamics and Perspectives*, edited by P. Ester, R. Muffels, J. Schippers, and T. Wilthagen. Cheltenham, UK: Edward Elgar.

Viebrock, Elke, and Jochen Clasen. 2009. "Flexicurity and Welfare Reform: A Review." *Socio-Economic Review* 7:305–331.

Villalobos, Ana. 2010. "Mothering in Fear: How Living in an Insecure-Feeling World Affects Parenting." pp. 57–71 in *21st Century Motherhood: Experience, Identity, Policy, Agency*, edited by A. O'Reilly. New York: Columbia University Press.

Villalobos, Ana. 2014. *Motherload: "Making it All Better" in Insecure Times*. Berkeley: University of California Press.

Walby, Sylvia. 1997. *Gender Transformations*. New York: Routledge.

Walkerdine, Valerie. 2006. "Workers in the New Economy: Transformation as Border Crossing." *Ethos* 34(1):10–41.

Ward, Russell A. 2008. "Multiple Parent–Adult Child Relations and Well-Being in Middle and Later Life." *Journal of Gerontology: Social Sciences* 63(4):S239–247.

Weaver, Charles. 1997. "Has the Work Ethic in the USA Declined? Evidence from Nationwide Surveys." *Psychological Reports* 81:491–495.

Welch, Jack, with John A. Byrne. 2001. *Jack: Straight from the Gut*. New York: Warner Business.

Wen, Patricia. 2005. "Gen X Dad." *Boston Globe*, January 16. Retrieved March 19, 2014 (http://www.boston.com/news/globe/magazine/articles/2005/01/16/gen_x_dad/).

West, Candace, and Don H. Zimmerman. 1987. "Doing Gender." *Gender and Society* 1:125–151.

West, Candace, and Don H. Zimmerman. 2009. "Accounting for Doing Gender." *Gender and Society* 23(1):111–122.

White, Lynn, and Joan G. Gilbreth. 2001. "When Children Have Two Fathers: Effects of Relationships With Stepfathers and Noncustodial Fathers on Adolescent Outcomes." *Journal of Marriage and Family* 63(1):155–167.

Williams, Christine. 1995. *Still a Man's World: Men Who Do Women's Work*. Berkeley: University of California Press.

Williams, Joan C. 2001. *Unbending Gender: Why Family and Work Conflict and What to Do about It*. New York: Oxford University Press.

Willis, Paul. 1977. *Learning to Labor: How Working Class Kids Get Working Class Jobs*. New York: Columbia University Press.

Wilthagen, Ton, and Frank Tros. 2004. "The Concept of Flexicurity: A New Approach to Regulating Employment and Labour Markets." *Transfer: European Review of Labour and Research* 10:166–186.

Wilthagen, Ton, Frank Tros, and Harm van Lieshout. 2003. "Towards 'Flexicurity': Balancing Flexibility and Security in EU Member States." Working Paper Series. Retrieved September 7, 2012 (http://papers.ssrn.com/sol3/papers.cfm?abstract_id=1133940).

Wu, Lawrence, and Elizabeth Thomson. 2001. "Race Differences in Family Experience and Early Sexual Initiation: Dynamic Models of Family Structure and Family Change." *Journal of Marriage and Family* 63:682–696.

Young, Michael, and Peter Willmott. 1962. *Family and Kinship in East London*. Rev. ed. London: Institute of Community Studies.

Zedlewski, Sheila, and Sarahela Loprest. 2011. "What Role Is Welfare Playing In This Period of High Unemployment?" *Unemployment and Recovery Project Fact Sheet 3, Urban Institute*. Retrieved December 17, 2011 (http://www.urban.org/UploadedPDF/412378-Role-of-Welfare-in-this-Period-of-High-Unemployment.pdf).

Zelizer, Viviana. 1985. *Pricing the Priceless Child*. Princeton, NJ: Princeton University Press.

Zimmerman/Volk Associates. 2007. "Housing and Market Analysis." Richmond Downtown Plan. Retrieved January 22, 2013 (http://www.ci.richmond.va.us/planninganddevelopmentreview/documents/PlansDowntown/Rich_Ch6_080,509_lores.pdf.).

INDEX

adaptability, 170, 175, 201, 214,
    217n2
adoption, 109, 116, 121, 149, 235n1
    legal issues, 194–195
advantaged workers, 42–50, 198
    commitment and, 51, 57
    insecurity culture and, 49–50, 52–55,
        60, 62, 153, 171
    intimate relationships among, 42–44,
        51–52, 58–59, 63–64, 152
    job insecurity and, 44–48, 50–52, 67
    language of choice and, 58
    in long-term relationships, 59–63
    pragmatism and, 63–65, 199
    relocators, 13, 15, 171–172, 198,
        201–202, 210, 225n1
    work ethic of, 48–49, 198
    work flexibility and, 156
    See also high-performance, low
        loyalty workers
"aggrieved entitlement," 90, 93
AstroTurf society, 187
authenticity, 221n26
    "bounded authenticity," 228n1

backup plans, 231n9
Bauman, Zygmunt, 12, 221n22
betrayal, 92–94, 108, 132, 178–179
    flexibility as response to, 170
    layoffs and, 28, 88, 231n2
    stable employment and, 142–144
blame, distribution of, 30–33, 41
    self-blame, 8, 33, 154, 224n18
Brines, Florence, 47, 164, 166–167
Burning Man, 52

Cappelli, Peter, 11
career choice tests, 49–50, 226n9

caregiving, 64, 238n4
    caregiver discrimination, 202
    care work ethic, 100–101, 103–107,
        122–123, 127, 159, 165,
        223n12
    cautionary tales and, 76–77
    contrasted with paid work, 69
    devaluation of, 86
    individuals as care givers, 113–114,
        115
    men as caregivers, 104–107
    precariousness of employment and,
        199
    women as caregivers, 12, 21, 66–68,
        69, 124, 153, 220n21, 238n2
care work ethic, 100–101, 103–107,
    122–123, 127, 159, 165,
    223n12
cautionary tales, 9, 37–41, 70, 76
Cherlin, Andrew, 6
child-centered families, 189–190
children, care of, 9, 45, 156–182,
    189–193
    care of difficult children, 116–119,
        121, 128–131, 167–168,
        233n3
    child-centered families, 189–190
    commitment and, 9, 13, 21, 85, 117,
        163, 165, 168, 170–171, 192
    detachment and, 85–86, 158, 169,
        230n20
    duty and, 158–161
    effect of divorce on children, 81, 84,
        98, 116, 160, 164, 187,
        230n19, 237n5
    effect of instability on, 187
    fatherhood, 91, 97–106, 125, 226n13,
        232n15, 232n16, 233n5